LIONEL PRIMARY SCHOOL
LIONEL ROAD
BRENTFORD, TW8 9QT

March 2000 .

The
OXFORD

Junior
THESAURUS

Compiled by
Alan Spooner

OXFORD
UNIVERSITY PRESS

OXFORD
UNIVERSITY PRESS

Great Clarendon Street, Oxford OX2 6DP

Oxford University Press is a department of the University of Oxford.
It furthers the University's objective of excellence in research, scholarship, an
education by publishing worldwide in

Oxford New York

Athens Auckland Bangkok Bogotá Buenos Aires Calcutta
Cape Town Chennai Dar es Salaam Delhi Florence Hong Kong Istanbul
Karachi Kuala Lumpur Madrid Melbourne Mexico City Mumbai
Nairobi Paris São Paulo Singapore Taipei Tokyo Toronto Warsaw

with associated companies in Berlin Ibadan

Oxford is a trade mark of Oxford University Press
© Alan Spooner 1995

First published 1995
New impression 2000
1 3 5 5 9 10 8 6 4 2

ISBN 0 19 910735 1 (Hardback - Educational Edition)
ISBN 0 19 910734 3 (Hardback - Trade Edition)

British Library cataloguing in Publication data available

Typeset by Pentacor PLC, High Wycombe
Printed in Great Britain by Butler and Tanner, Frome

Do you have a query about words, their origin, meaning, use, spelling,
pronunciation, or any other aspect of the English language? Then write to
OWLS at Oxford University Press, Great Clarendon Street, Oxford, OX2 6DP.

All queries will be answered using the full resources of the
Oxford Dictionary Department

PREFACE for teachers and parents

This thesaurus contains two main types of entry.

1 There are entries which give *synonyms* for the common words in a child's vocabulary. Where appropriate, opposites are also given. Example sentences or phrases put each word in a meaningful context.

2 There are *topic entries* which give lists of words which are not synonyms but which are related to the headword. For example, various kinds of animal are listed under **animal**; musical terms are given under **music**; and so on. These entries will be helpful to individual children who just need a jog to the memory to find the word they were looking for; they also provide opportunities for them to explore and discuss the vocabulary of a particular topic.

The arrangement of the thesaurus is simple and user-friendly. Each entry is self-explanatory: there are no abbreviations or cryptic devices. The headwords, which comprise all the words children are likely to look up as starting-points for a word-search, are arranged in simple alphabetical sequence, avoiding the need for a separate index (a common but awkward and confusing feature of some other thesauruses). The more discussable entries – topic entries, and entries for headwords with a particular complex range of senses or usages – are boxed in a blue tint. This will encourage young readers to browse.

The English language is infinitely variable and adaptable. Ultimately, children's awareness of this variety and adaptability will come not from a book like this, but from their experience of language in use. I hope, therefore, that they will be encouraged to see the thesaurus not just as a book to refer to, but as a book which raises questions about vocabulary – and about language in general – which they will want to discuss with teachers, parents, and other experienced users of our language.

The headword list in this thesaurus is derived from that of *The Oxford Junior Dictionary* (Third Edition), to which this book will make an ideal companion volume.

Alan Spooner

Headwords
The words you look up are printed bold in blue, so that they are easy to find.

Examples
Sentences or phrases showing how you might use the word are printed in ordinary type.

Related words
Sometimes we give lists of words which are specially interesting. These entries are in the blue boxes. Many of these are not lists of synonyms, but lists of words related to a topic.

bolt *verb*
1 Remember to bolt the back door.
   OTHER VERBS YOU MIGHT USE ARE   **to bar**   **to fasten**   **to lock**
2 The horse bolted.
   OTHER VERBS ARE   **to escape**   **to run away**
For other words, see run
   OTHER VERBS ARE   **to gobble**   **to gulp**

book *noun*
VARIOUS KINDS OF BOOK ARE
album   **annual**   **atlas**   **diary**   **dictionary**
directory   **encyclopedia**   **hymn book**   **novel**
paperback   **story book**   **thesaurus**

bottom *noun*
1 the bottom of a wall.
   OTHER WORDS YOU MIGHT USE ARE   **base**   **foot**   **foundation**
The opposite is top
2 the bottom of the sea.
   ANOTHER WORD IS **bed**
The opposite is surface

Synonyms
Words which mean the same as the word you look up are the synonyms. These are words you might use instead of the word you look up. They are printed in bold black type.

Numbers
When a word has more than one meaning, or if it is used in more than one way, we number the different uses.

Antonyms
If the word you look up has a useful opposite, it comes after the synonyms.

USING THIS THESAURUS

A thesaurus helps you find words to make your language more interesting, and to help you say exactly what you want to say. It gives you words which have the same meaning as the word you thought of. These are called *synonyms*.

It may give you words which mean the *opposite* of the word you thought of.

It will often give you words which are useful when you are talking or writing about a particular *topic*.

Remember that a thesaurus does not give you explanations or definitions of what words mean. If you want to know what a word means, you need to look it up in a dictionary like *The Oxford Junior Dictionary*.

IN THIS THESAURUS YOU WILL FIND...

Headwords
The words you look up are printed bold in blue, so that they are easy to find.

Examples
Sentences or phrases showing how you might use the word are printed in ordinary type.

Synonyms
Words which mean the same as the word you look up are the *synonyms*. These are words you might use instead of the word you look up. They are printed in bold black type.

Antonyms
If the word you look up has a useful opposite, it comes after the synonyms.

Numbers
When a word has more than one meaning, or if it is used in more than one way, we number the different uses.

Related words
Sometimes we give lists of words which are specially interesting. These entries are in the blue boxes. Many of these are not lists of synonyms, but lists of words related to a topic.

Aa

abandon *verb*
1 It's cruel to abandon a pet.
   OTHER VERBS YOU MIGHT USE ARE **to desert** **to forsake** **to leave**
2 We abandoned the game when it rained.
   OTHER VERBS ARE **to cancel** **to give up** **to postpone**

able *adjective*
1 Are you able to play tomorrow?
   OTHER WORDS YOU MIGHT USE ARE **allowed** **free**
2 Jo is an able tennis player.
   OTHER WORDS ARE **capable** **clever** **skilful** **talented**

abolish *verb*
I wish they would abolish tests.
   OTHER VERBS YOU MIGHT USE ARE **to end** **to get rid of** **to remove**

accept *verb*
1 Please accept this gift.
   OTHER VERBS YOU MIGHT USE ARE **to receive** **to take**
2 I accept that it was my fault.
   OTHER VERBS ARE **to admit** **to agree** **to believe**

accident *noun*
1 OTHER WORDS YOU MIGHT USE ARE **collision** **crash** **mishap**
   WORDS YOU MIGHT USE FOR A VERY SERIOUS ACCIDENT ARE **calamity**
   catastrophe **disaster**
2 We met by accident.
   OTHER WORDS ARE **chance** **coincidence**

accompany *verb*
Dad accompanied us to school.
   A PHRASE YOU MIGHT USE IS **to go with**

account *noun*
Jo wrote an account of the match.
   OTHER WORDS YOU MIGHT USE ARE **description** **report** **story**

accurate *adjective*

1 Is your watch accurate?

OTHER WORDS YOU MIGHT USE ARE   **correct**   **right**

2 Give me an accurate account of what happened.

OTHER WORDS ARE   **exact**   **precise**   **true**

ache *noun* and *verb*

For other words, see **pain**

achievement *noun*

It was a great achievement to win by four goals.

OTHER WORDS YOU MIGHT USE ARE   **accomplishment**   **feat**   **success**

act *verb*

1 She acted quickly to put out the fire.

PHRASES YOU MIGHT USE ARE   **to do something**   **to take action**

2 Jo likes to act in plays.

OTHER VERBS YOU MIGHT USE ARE   **to appear**   **to perform**

To act without using words is **to mime**

3 He was acting like an idiot.

ANOTHER VERB IS **to behave**

action *noun*

1 The film was full of action.

OTHER WORDS YOU MIGHT USE ARE   **activity**   **excitement**

2 It was a kind action to dig Mr Brown's garden.

OTHER WORDS ARE   **act**   **deed**

active *adjective*

1 Our puppy is very active.

OTHER WORDS YOU MIGHT USE ARE   **energetic**   **lively**

2 Mum is active in charity work.

OTHER WORDS ARE   **busy**   **involved**   **working**

activity *noun*

1 What activities do you enjoy?

OTHER WORDS YOU MIGHT USE ARE   **hobby**   **job**   **project**   **task**

2 The shops are full of activity when the sales are on.

OTHER WORDS ARE   **action**   **bustle**   **excitement**

actual *adjective*

Is that the actual tree Robin Hood lived in?

OTHER WORDS YOU MIGHT USE ARE   **genuine**   **real**

add *verb*
1 Add the milk and the sugar.
OTHER VERBS YOU MIGHT USE ARE   **to combine   to mix   to put together**
2 We added the numbers together.
For other words you might use when you do maths, see **mathematics**
The opposite is subtract

additional *adjective*
OTHER WORDS ARE   **extra   more**

admire *verb*
1 We admired the firemen's skill.
OTHER VERBS YOU MIGHT USE ARE   **to praise   to respect   to wonder at**
2 I admired the view.
OTHER VERBS ARE   **to appreciate   to enjoy   to like**

admit *verb*
1 Jo admitted that she was wrong.
OTHER VERBS YOU MIGHT USE ARE   **to accept   to confess   to own up**
2 They only admit you if you have a ticket.
OTHER VERBS ARE   **to allow in   to let in**

adore *verb*
Jo's dog adores her.
OTHER VERBS YOU MIGHT USE ARE   **to idolize   to love   to worship**

adult *noun*
ANOTHER WORD IS **grown-up**

advance *verb*
As the army advanced, the enemy ran away.
OTHER VERBS YOU MIGHT USE ARE   **to approach   to come near
to move forward   to progress**
The opposite is retreat

advantage *noun*
It's an advantage to have the wind behind you when you run.
ANOTHER WORD IS **help**

advertise *verb*
They advertised a new car on TV.
OTHER VERBS YOU MIGHT USE ARE   *(informal)* **to plug   to promote
to publicize**

advertisement *noun*
OTHER WORDS YOU MIGHT USE ARE (*informal*) **ad** or **advert** **commercial**
poster

advice *noun*
My advice is to save your money.
OTHER WORDS YOU MIGHT USE ARE **recommendation** **suggestion**

advise *verb*
What did the doctor advise?
OTHER VERBS YOU MIGHT USE ARE **to recommend** **to suggest**

aeroplane *noun*
For other machines that fly, see **aircraft**

affect *verb*
The weather affects my mood.
OTHER VERBS YOU MIGHT USE ARE **to alter** **to change** **to influence**

afraid *adjective*
The dog is afraid of thunder.
OTHER WORDS YOU MIGHT USE ARE **frightened** **scared** **terrified**

aggressive *adjective*
That dog looks rather aggressive.
OTHER WORDS YOU MIGHT USE ARE **hostile** **rough** **violent**
The opposite is friendly

agree *verb*
1 Mum agreed that I was right.
OTHER VERBS YOU MIGHT USE ARE **to accept** **to admit**
2 We agreed to go shopping.
OTHER VERBS ARE **to arrange** **to consent** **to decide**

aid *verb*
For other verbs, see **help**

aim *verb*
1 Aim the gun at the target.
OTHER VERBS YOU MIGHT USE ARE **to direct** **to point**
2 We aimed to arrive by tea-time.
OTHER VERBS ARE **to intend** **to plan** **to try** **to want**

aircraft *noun*
VARIOUS KINDS OF AIRCRAFT ARE
aeroplane **air-liner** **balloon** **glider** **helicopter** **jet** **jumbo jet** **plane**

alarm *noun*
1 An alarm goes if there is a fire.
OTHER WORDS YOU MIGHT USE ARE **signal** **siren** **warning**
2 The storm was so bad that the animals were filled with alarm.
OTHER WORDS ARE **dismay** **fear** **fright** **panic** **terror**

alarm *verb*
The thunder alarmed the animals.
OTHER VERBS YOU MIGHT USE ARE **to frighten** **to scare** **to upset**

alert *adjective*
A sentry must be alert.
OTHER WORDS YOU MIGHT USE ARE **attentive** **awake** **observant** **watchful**

allow *verb*
You are allowed to drive when you have passed a test.
OTHER VERBS YOU MIGHT USE ARE **to authorize** **to license** **to permit**

ally *noun*
For other words, see **friend**

alter *verb*
For other verbs, see **change**

amaze *verb*
The conjuror's tricks amazed us.
OTHER VERBS YOU MIGHT USE ARE **to astonish** **to astound** **to surprise**

amazing *adjective*
For other words, see **extraordinary**

ambition *noun*
Sam's ambition is to be a pilot.
OTHER WORDS YOU MIGHT USE ARE **aim** **goal** **objective** **wish**

ambush *verb*
The soldiers ambushed the enemy.
> OTHER VERBS YOU MIGHT USE ARE   **to attack**   **to jump out on**
> **to take by surprise**   **to trap**

ammunition *noun*
> KINDS OF AMMUNITION ARE
> **bullet**   **cannonball**   **hand grenade**   **missile**   **shell**
> For other words, see **weapon**

amount *noun*
> OTHER WORDS YOU MIGHT USE ARE   **quantity**   **total**

amuse *verb*
While we waited for the bus I tried to amuse the others.
> OTHER VERBS YOU MIGHT USE ARE   **to cheer up**   **to divert**   **to entertain**

amusing *adjective*
an amusing joke.
> OTHER WORDS YOU MIGHT USE ARE   **comic**   **funny**   **humorous**   **witty**

ancient *adjective*
For other words, see **old**

anger *noun*
He showed his anger by slamming the door.
> OTHER WORDS YOU MIGHT USE ARE   **annoyance**   **fury**   **rage**   **temper**

angry *adjective*
Mum was angry when Jo broke the window.
> OTHER WORDS YOU MIGHT USE ARE   **annoyed**   **cross**   **furious**
> **in a temper**   **infuriated**   **irate**   (*informal*) **mad**   **vexed**
The opposite is pleased

animal *noun*, see opposite page

announce *verb*
1 Jo announced that she was ready.
> OTHER VERBS YOU MIGHT USE ARE   **to declare**   **to report**   **to state**
2 The DJ announced our record.
> ANOTHER VERB IS **to introduce**

animal *noun*

OTHER WORDS YOU MIGHT USE ARE

beast   **creature**

A word you might use for a big animal you don't like is **brute**

DIFFERENT CLASSES OF ANIMAL ARE

amphibian   **bird**   **fish**   **mammal**
reptile

ANIMALS THAT FARMERS KEEP ARE

bull   **cow**   **goat**   **horse**
ox   **pig**   **sheep**

ANIMALS PEOPLE KEEP AS PETS ARE

cat   **dog**   **donkey**   **ferret**
gerbil   **guinea pig**   **hamster**   **horse**
mouse   **rabbit**   **rat**   **tortoise**

WILD ANIMALS YOU MIGHT SEE IN BRITAIN ARE

badger   **bat**   **deer**   **dormouse**
fox   **hare**   **hedgehog**   **mole**
otter   **shrew**   **squirrel**   **stoat**
vole   **weasel**

OTHER WILD ANIMALS ARE

antelope   **ape**   **baboon**   **bear**
beaver   **bison**   **buffalo**   **camel**
cheetah   **chimpanzee** **dromedary** **elephant**
elk   **giraffe**   **gorilla**   **grizzly bear**
hippopotamus **hyena**   **jackal**   **jaguar**
kangaroo   **koala**   **leopard**   **lion**
llama   **mongoose**   **monkey**   **moose**
panda   **panther**   **platypus**   **polar**
bear   **porcupine**   **reindeer**   **rhinoceros**
skunk   **snake**   **tiger**   **wallaby**
wolf   **zebra**

ANIMALS THAT LIVE IN THE SEA ARE

dolphin   **fish**   **octopus**   **porpoise**
seal   **sea lion**   **turtle**   **walrus**
whale

announcement *noun*
The head read some announcements.
> OTHER WORDS YOU MIGHT USE ARE   **notice**   **statement**

annoy *verb*
The wasps were annoying me.
> OTHER VERBS YOU MIGHT USE ARE   **to bother**   **to irritate**
> **to pester**   **to torment**   **to trouble**   **to upset**
> **to worry**

answer *noun*
1 an answer to a question.
> OTHER WORDS YOU MIGHT USE ARE   **reply**   **response**

2 the answer to a problem.
> OTHER WORDS ARE   **explanation**   **solution**

anxious *adjective*
1 Mum gets anxious if I'm late.
> OTHER WORDS YOU MIGHT USE ARE   **concerned**   **nervous**   **worried**

2 We were anxious to start.
> OTHER WORDS ARE   **eager**   **keen**

apologize *verb*
I apologized for being rude.
> A PHRASE IS **to say sorry**

appeal *verb*
The sick man appealed for help.
> OTHER VERBS YOU MIGHT USE ARE   **to ask**   **to beg**   **to plead**

appear *verb*
1 He appeared out of the mist.
> OTHER VERBS YOU MIGHT USE ARE   **to arrive**   **to come out**
> **to turn up**

2 You appear tired.
> OTHER VERBS ARE   **to look**   **to seem**

appetite *noun*
1 an appetite for food.
> OTHER WORDS YOU MIGHT USE ARE   **greed**   **hunger**

2 an appetite for adventure.
> OTHER WORDS ARE   **desire**   **longing**   **passion**   **wish**

appointment *noun*
The head can't see us this afternoon because she has another appointment.
> OTHER WORDS YOU MIGHT USE ARE   **arrangement   engagement   meeting**

approach *verb*
I got nervous when the big dog approached me.
> A PHRASE IS **to come near**

appropriate *adjective*
£10 was an appropriate price.
> OTHER WORDS YOU MIGHT USE ARE   **fitting   proper   right   suitable**

approve *verb*
Did you approve of what I did?
> OTHER VERBS YOU MIGHT USE ARE   **to admire   to like   to praise**

approximately *adverb*
The trip costs approximately £10.
> OTHER WORDS YOU MIGHT USE ARE   **about   nearly   roughly**

area *noun*
1 The playground is a large area.
> OTHER WORDS YOU MIGHT USE ARE   **expanse   surface**
2 Uncle Tom lives in a nice area of London.
> OTHER WORDS ARE   **district   neighbourhood   part   region**

argue *verb*
Jo and Sam are good friends: they don't often argue.
> OTHER VERBS YOU MIGHT USE ARE   **to disagree   to quarrel**

argument *noun*
1 We had an argument about who was going to pay.
> OTHER WORDS YOU MIGHT USE ARE   **disagreement   dispute   quarrel**
2 There has been a lot of argument in the paper about a bypass.
> OTHER WORDS YOU MIGHT USE ARE   **controversy   debate**

arm *noun*
For other parts of the body, see **body**

arrange *verb*
1 Jo arranged the books on the shelf.
OTHER VERBS YOU MIGHT USE ARE   **to set out   to sort   to tidy**
2 We arranged a trip to the sea.
OTHER VERBS ARE   **to decide on   to fix   to organize   to plan**

arrest *verb*
The police arrested the suspect.
OTHER VERBS YOU MIGHT USE ARE   **to capture   to catch   to detain
to take into custody**

arrive *verb*
1 When will Granny arrive?
OTHER VERBS YOU MIGHT USE ARE   **to appear   to come   to turn up**
The opposite is depart
2 We arrived home for dinner.
OTHER VERBS ARE   **to come   to get to   to reach**

art *noun*
KINDS OF ART ARE
**collage   drawing   embroidery   modelling
needlework   painting   photography   pottery
sculpture   sewing   sketching   weaving**

DIFFERENT ARTISTS ARE
painter   photographer   potter   sculptor   weaver

artificial *adjective*
1 Sam wore an artificial beard in the play.
OTHER WORDS YOU MIGHT USE ARE   **false   pretend**
2 This dress is made of artificial material.
OTHER WORDS ARE   **man-made   synthetic**
The opposite is genuine

ask *verb*
1 What did you ask?
OTHER VERBS YOU MIGHT USE ARE   **to enquire   to find out   to inquire**
2 The criminal asked to be given another chance.
OTHER VERBS ARE   **to beg   to implore   to plead   to request**
3 My friends asked me to go out.
ANOTHER VERB IS **to invite**

assist *verb*
For other verbs, see **help**

assistant *noun*
You can't do that job on your own: you need an assistant.
OTHER WORDS YOU MIGHT USE ARE   **helper   partner**
Someone who helps a person with an official job is a **deputy.**
Someone who helps a person commit a crime is an **accomplice.**

assorted *adjective*
For other words, see **various**

astonish *verb*
The player's skill astonished us.
OTHER VERBS YOU MIGHT USE ARE   **to amaze   to astound   to surprise**

athlete *noun*
OTHER WORDS YOU MIGHT USE ARE   **sportsman   sportswoman**
For various sports, see **sport**

attach *verb*
WAYS TO ATTACH THINGS ARE   **to bind   to connect   to fasten   to fix
to glue   to join   to link   to stick   to tie**

attack *verb*
1 The soldiers attacked the enemy.
   DIFFERENT WAYS TO ATTACK ARE   **to ambush   to assault   to bomb
   to bombard   to charge   to raid**
2 Two men attacked him in the street.
   OTHER VERBS YOU MIGHT USE ARE   **to mug   to set on**
The opposite is defend

attempt *verb*
Jo attempted to swim ten lengths.
OTHER VERBS AND PHRASES ARE   **to endeavour   to exert yourself
to make an effort   to try**

attend *verb*
1 We attended the school concert.
   PHRASES YOU MIGHT USE ARE   **to be present at   to go to**
2 Are you attending to me?
   OTHER VERBS YOU MIGHT USE ARE   **to listen   to pay attention**

attract *verb*
The bright lights attracted us.
> OTHER VERBS YOU MIGHT USE ARE   **to appeal to**   **to fascinate**
> **to interest**

attractive *adjective*
1 an attractive person.
> OTHER WORDS YOU MIGHT USE ARE   **beautiful**   **charming**
> **glamorous**   **good-looking**   **handsome**   **likeable**   **pleasant**
> **pretty**
The opposite is ugly
2 an attractive idea.
> OTHER WORDS ARE   **appealing**   **interesting**   **pleasing**   **tempting**
The opposite is boring

audience *noun*
The audience enjoyed the play.
> OTHER WORDS YOU MIGHT USE ARE   **listeners**   **spectators**

author *noun*
> ANOTHER WORD IS **writer**
For other words, see **write**

available *adjective*
Our magazine is now available.
> OTHER WORDS YOU MIGHT USE ARE   **on sale**   **ready**

average *adjective*
It was an average kind of day.
> OTHER WORDS YOU MIGHT USE ARE   **middling**   **normal**   **ordinary**
> **typical**   **usual**
The opposite is extraordinary

avoid *verb*
Sam avoided the washing-up.
> OTHER VERBS YOU MIGHT USE ARE   **to dodge**   **to escape**   **to get out of**
> **to shirk**

awake *adjective*
I was awake all night because of the storm.
> OTHER WORDS YOU MIGHT USE ARE   **alert**   **conscious**
The opposite is asleep

award *noun*
Jo got an award for swimming ten lengths.
OTHER WORDS YOU MIGHT USE ARE **badge   medal   prize
reward   trophy**

aware *adjective*
Jo was aware that Mum would worry if she was late.
ANOTHER WORD IS **conscious**

awful *adjective*
For other words, see **bad**

awkward *adjective*
1 Ducks look awkward when they walk on dry land.
ANOTHER WORD IS **clumsy**
2 Are you trying to be awkward?
OTHER WORDS ARE **difficult   uncooperative**
3 The visitors came at an awkward time.
ANOTHER WORD IS **inconvenient**

Bb

baby *noun*
ANOTHER WORD IS **infant**
A baby just starting to walk is a **toddler.**

back *noun*
I had to wait at the back of the queue.
OTHER WORDS ARE **end   rear   tail end**
The opposite is front

back *verb*
Dad backed the car into the gate.
ANOTHER VERB IS **to reverse**

bad *adjective*

THIS WORD HAS MANY USES. HERE ARE SOME OF THE WAYS YOU CAN USE IT, AND SOME OTHER WORDS YOU COULD CHOOSE

1 a bad deed.
criminal   cruel   evil   immoral   sinful
villainous   wicked   wrong

2 a bad child.
disobedient   mischievous   naughty

3 a bad player.
hopeless   incompetent   rotten   useless

4 a bad accident.
appalling   awful   dreadful   frightful   horrible
serious   severe   shocking   terrible

5 a bad piece of work.
careless   incorrect   poor   shoddy   useless
weak   worthless

6 bad food.
decayed   mouldy   rotten   smelly

7 a bad smell.
nasty   objectionable   offensive   revolting
sickening   unpleasant

8 a bad habit.
dangerous   harmful   nasty   unhealthy

9 I feel bad today.
feeble   ill   poorly   sick   unwell

The opposite is good

badge *noun*
a school badge.
OTHER WORDS YOU MIGHT USE ARE   crest   emblem   sign   symbol

bad-tempered *adjective*
OTHER WORDS YOU MIGHT USE ARE   angry   cross   grumpy   irritable
short-tempered
The opposite is cheerful

bag *noun*
For other words, see **container**

bake *verb*
For other ways to cook things, see **cook**

ball *noun*
THINGS SHAPED LIKE A BALL ARE   **globe**   **sphere**
For other shapes, see **shape**

ban *verb*
They banned smoking on the buses.
OTHER VERBS YOU MIGHT USE ARE   **to forbid**   **to make illegal**
to prohibit

band *noun*
1 Robin Hood lived with a band of outlaws.
ANOTHER WORD IS **gang**
2 Jo plays the guitar in a band.
OTHER WORDS ARE   **group**   **orchestra**
For more words to do with music, see **music**
3 A wooden barrel has bands of metal round it.
OTHER WORDS ARE   **hoop**   **loop**   **ring**

bang *noun*
1 We heard a loud bang.
OTHER WORDS YOU MIGHT USE ARE   **blast**   **boom**   **crash**
explosion
For other sounds, see **sound**
2 I got a nasty bang on the head.
OTHER WORDS ARE   **blow**   **bump**   **hit**   **knock**

banish *verb*
The traitor was banished from his country.
OTHER VERBS ARE   **to exile**   **to expel**   **to send away**

bank *noun*
We sat on a grassy bank.
OTHER WORDS YOU MIGHT USE ARE   **embankment**   **slope**

banner *noun*
The people in the procession waved banners.
OTHER WORDS YOU MIGHT USE ARE   **flag**   **standard**   **streamer**

banquet *noun*
OTHER WORDS ARE   **dinner**   **feast**   (*informal*) **spread**
For other words, see **meal**

bar *noun*
1   a wooden bar.
    OTHER WORDS YOU MIGHT USE ARE   **beam   rail   rod**
2   an iron bar.
    ANOTHER WORD YOU MIGHT USE IS **girder**
3   a bar of chocolate.
    ANOTHER WORD IS **block**

bare *adjective*
    OTHER WORDS YOU MIGHT USE ARE   **naked   nude   unclothed
    uncovered   undressed**

barely *adverb*
Sam was so tired that he could barely keep his eyes open.
    OTHER WORDS YOU MIGHT USE ARE   **hardly   only just   scarcely**

barrel *noun*
For other containers, see **container**

barren *adjective*
The desert was completely barren.
    OTHER WORDS YOU MIGHT USE ARE   **bare   lifeless   sterile**

barrier *noun*
They put up a barrier to keep the crowd off the field.
    OTHER WORDS ARE   **barricade   fence   railings   wall**

base *noun*
1   Dad used cement to make a firm base for the shed.
    ANOTHER WORD IS **foundation**
2   Don't sit near the base of the cliff.
    OTHER WORDS YOU MIGHT USE ARE   **bottom   foot**
3   After a long march, the soldiers returned to their base.
    OTHER WORDS ARE   **depot   headquarters**

bashful *adjective*
The little boy was too bashful to say 'thank you'.
    OTHER WORDS YOU MIGHT USE ARE   **modest   shy   timid**

basic *adjective*
I know the basic facts, but I've still got a lot to learn.
    OTHER WORDS ARE   **chief   essential   important   main   principal**

basin *noun*
>OTHER WORDS ARE   **bowl**   **dish**

basket *noun*
For other kinds of container, see **container**

bat *noun*
The special bat you use in tennis is a **racket**.
The stick you hit the ball with in golf is a **club**.

bath *noun*
>SPECIAL KINDS OF BATH ARE
>**Jacuzzi**   **sauna**   **shower**

battle *noun*
For other words, see **war**

bay *noun*
>OTHER WORDS YOU MIGHT USE ARE   **cove**   **estuary**   **gulf**   **inlet**

beach *noun*
Jo and Sam spent a happy day at the beach.
>OTHER WORDS YOU MIGHT USE ARE   **sands**   **shore**
For other words, see **seaside**

beam *noun*
1 a beam of wood.
>OTHER WORDS YOU MIGHT USE ARE   **bar**   **plank**
2 a beam of light.
>OTHER WORDS ARE   **ray**   **shaft**

beam *verb*
He beamed when he heard my voice.
>OTHER VERBS YOU MIGHT USE ARE   **to grin**   **to laugh**   **to look happy**
>**to smile**

bear *verb*

1 Will this branch bear my weight?
    OTHER VERBS YOU MIGHT USE ARE   **to carry**   **to hold**
       to support
2 She bore the pain bravely.
    OTHER VERBS ARE   **to endure**   **to put up with**   **to stand**
       to suffer

beast *noun*

OTHER WORDS YOU MIGHT USE ARE   **animal**   **creature**
ANIMALS THAT MAKE YOU AFRAID ARE   **brute**   **monster**

beat *verb*

1 We beat our opponents 6-0.
    OTHER VERBS YOU MIGHT USE ARE   **to conquer**   **to defeat**
       to outdo   **to overcome**   (*informal*) **to thrash**
2 It's cruel to beat animals.
   For other verbs, see **hit**
3 Dad beat some eggs to make an omelette.
    OTHER VERBS ARE   **to mix**   **to stir**   **to whisk**
4 When I run my heart beats fast.
    OTHER VERBS ARE   **to knock**   **to pound**   **to throb**

beautiful *adjective*

1 a beautiful bride.
    OTHER WORDS YOU MIGHT USE ARE   **attractive**   **charming**
       elegant   **glamorous**   **good-looking**   **gorgeous**
       handsome   **lovely**   **pretty**
   The opposite is ugly
2 beautiful weather.
    OTHER WORDS ARE   **enjoyable**   **fine**   **good**   **nice**
       pleasant

beckon *verb*

Sam beckoned to me to join him.
    OTHER VERBS YOU MIGHT USE ARE   **to make a sign**   **to signal**

become *verb*

In time the little shoot will become a big tree.
    PHRASES YOU MIGHT USE ARE   **to change into**   **to grow into**
       to turn into

bed *noun*

PARTS OF A BED ARE

base   headboard   mattress

A bed with a base and a mattress is a **divan**.
Two beds one above the other are **bunks**.
A bunk on a ship is a **berth**.
An old-fashioned bed with curtains round is a **four-poster**.

THINGS YOU USE TO MAKE A BED ARE

bedclothes or **bedding**

DIFFERENT KINDS OF BEDCLOTHES ARE

**bed linen   bedspread   blanket   counterpane
coverlet   duvet   eiderdown   pillow   pillowcase
quilt   sheet**

bee *noun*

KINDS OF BEE ARE   **bumble-bee   drone   queen bee**

begin *verb*

When does the film begin?

OTHER VERBS YOU MIGHT USE ARE   **to commence**   (*informal*) **to get going
to start**

The opposite is end

behave *verb*

1 Sam behaved strangely today.

ANOTHER VERB IS **to act**

2 Our teacher told us to behave.

A PHRASE IS **to be good**

behaviour *noun*

Our teacher praised our good behaviour.

OTHER WORDS ARE   **conduct   manners**

belief *noun*

1 It's my belief that ghosts don't exist.

OTHER WORDS YOU MIGHT USE ARE   **opinion   view**

2 We had a special service where people with different religious beliefs said prayers together.

OTHER WORDS ARE   **creed   faith   religion**

believe *verb*
1 You can't believe all he says.
OTHER VERBS YOU MIGHT USE ARE   **to accept   to rely on   to trust**
2 I believe he cheated.
OTHER VERBS ARE   **to consider   to feel sure   to think**

bell *noun*
DIFFERENT WAYS BELLS SOUND ARE
**chime   clang   jangle   jingle   peal   ping   ring
tinkle   toll**

belongings *noun*
Be sure to take your belongings when you get off the train.
OTHER WORDS YOU MIGHT USE ARE   **possessions   property   things**

bench *noun*
1 a bench to sit on.
OTHER WORDS YOU MIGHT USE ARE   **form   seat**
2 a carpenter's bench.
ANOTHER WORD IS **table**

bend *noun*
a bend in the road.
OTHER WORDS YOU MIGHT USE ARE **corner   curve   turn   twist**

bend *verb*
1 The blacksmith bent the metal into fantastic shapes.
OTHER VERBS YOU MIGHT USE ARE   **to coil   to curl   to curve
to distort   to fold   to twist   to wind**
2 He was so tall that he had to bend to go through the door.
OTHER VERBS ARE   **to bow down   to crouch   to duck
to stoop**

bet *verb*
ANOTHER VERB IS **to gamble**
KINDS OF BETTING ARE   **lottery   the pools**

bewildered *adjective*
We were bewildered by all the different traffic signs.
OTHER WORDS YOU MIGHT USE ARE   **confused   muddled   puzzled**

bewitched *adjective*
I was bewitched by the magical music.
> OTHER WORDS ARE   **charmed   enchanted   spellbound**

biased *adjective*
The referee was biased.
> OTHER WORDS YOU MIGHT USE ARE   **one-sided   prejudiced   unfair**

big *adjective*
1 a big person. a big thing.
> OTHER WORDS YOU MIGHT USE ARE   **colossal   enormous   fat   giant   gigantic   great   huge   large   massive   monstrous   tall**
2 a big hall.
> OTHER WORDS ARE   **roomy   spacious   vast**
3 a big event.
> OTHER WORDS ARE   **grand   impressive   spectacular**
4 a big decision.
> OTHER WORDS ARE   **important   serious**
The opposite is small

bill *noun*
Keep the bill to prove how much you paid.
> OTHER WORDS YOU MIGHT USE ARE   **account   receipt**

bind *verb*
They bound the prisoner's hands.
> OTHER VERBS YOU MIGHT USE ARE   **to secure   to tie**

bird *noun*, see next page.

bit *noun*
1 I don't want it all, only a bit of it.
> OTHER WORDS YOU MIGHT USE ARE   **chunk   crumb   dollop   fraction   morsel   part   piece   portion   section**
2 Mum told Jo to sweep up every bit of the broken mug.
> OTHER WORDS ARE   **chip   fragment   speck   splinter**
3 I picked up the bits of paper and put them in the rubbish bin.
> ANOTHER WORD IS **scrap**

bite *verb*
The dog tried to bite me!
> OTHER VERBS YOU MIGHT USE ARE   **to nip   to snap at**
For other words, see **eat**

bird *noun*

A male bird is a **cock**.
A female bird is a **hen**.

WORDS FOR A YOUNG BIRD ARE

chick	fledgling	nestling

SOME BIRDS KEPT AS PETS ARE

budgerigar	canary	cockatoo	macaw
parakeet	parrot		

BIRDS KEPT ON A FARM ARE **poultry**

KINDS OF POULTRY ARE

chicken	duck	goose	turkey

COMMON BRITISH GARDEN BIRDS ARE

blackbird	bullfinch	chaffinch	goldfinch
greenfinch	robin	sparrow	starling
thrush	tit	wren	

SOME BIRDS YOU MIGHT SEE OR HEAR IN THE BRITISH COUNTRYSIDE ARE

crow	cuckoo	curlew	dove
grouse	jackdaw	jay	lapwing
lark	linnet	magpie	martin
nightingale	partridge	peewit	pheasant
pigeon	raven	rook	skylark
swallow	swift	wagtail	warbler
woodpecker	yellowhammer		

SOME BIRDS OF PREY ARE

buzzard	eagle	falcon	hawk
kestrel	kite	osprey	owl
sparrowhawk			

BIRDS THAT LIVE NEAR WATER ARE

coot	duck	flamingo	goose
grebe	heron	kingfisher	moorhen
pelican	swan		

SOME SEA BIRDS ARE

cormorant	puffin	seagull	tern

OTHER BIRDS ARE

ostrich	peacock	penguin	stork
vulture			

bitter *adjective*
1 a bitter taste.
    OTHER WORDS YOU MIGHT USE ARE   **acid   harsh   sharp   sour**
2 a bitter wind.
    OTHER WORDS ARE   **biting   piercing**
For other words, see **cold**
3 a bitter quarrel.
    OTHER WORDS ARE   **angry   resentful   spiteful**

black *adjective*
    OTHER WORDS ARE   **dark   inky   pitch-black   sooty**

blade *noun*
    THINGS WITH A SHARP BLADE ARE
    axe   dagger   knife   razor   scissors   shears   sword

blame *verb*
When she saw the mess, Mum blamed me!
    OTHER VERBS YOU MIGHT USE ARE   **to accuse   to criticise   to scold**

blank *adjective*
1 a blank piece of paper.
    OTHER WORDS YOU MIGHT USE ARE   **clean   unmarked   unused**
2 Fill in the blank spaces.
    ANOTHER WORD IS **empty**

blast *noun*
1 a blast of cold air.
For other words, see **wind**
2 the blast of a bomb.
    OTHER WORDS ARE   **bang   boom   explosion**

blaze *verb*
    OTHER VERBS YOU MIGHT USE ARE   **to burn   to flame   to flare up**
For other words, see **fire**

bleak *adjective*
a bleak hillside.
    OTHER WORDS YOU MIGHT USE ARE   **bare   cold   exposed   miserable**
    windswept   windy

blend *verb*
Dad blended the ingredients to make a cake.
OTHER VERBS YOU MIGHT USE ARE **to beat** **to combine** **to mix** **to stir together** **to whisk**

blessed *adjective*
OTHER WORDS ARE **holy** **sacred**

blind *adjective*
OTHER WORDS YOU MIGHT USE ARE **sightless** **visually handicapped**

block *noun*
a block of concrete.
OTHER WORDS ARE **chunk** **lump** **slab**

block *verb*
1 A flock of sheep blocked the road.
ANOTHER VERB IS **to obstruct**
2 The roads were blocked with traffic.
OTHER VERBS YOU MIGHT USE ARE **to clog** **to jam**

bloom *verb*
Roses bloom in the summer.
OTHER VERBS YOU MIGHT USE ARE **to blossom** **to flower**

blossom *noun*
In spring we have masses of blossom on our apple tree.
OTHER WORDS ARE **blooms** **flowers**

blow *noun*
Sam got a nasty blow on the head.
For other words, see **hit**

blow *verb*
The wolf tried to blow the pigs' house down.
ANOTHER VERB IS **to puff**
to blow up a tyre
ANOTHER VERB IS **to inflate**
to blow up with a loud bang
OTHER VERBS YOU MIGHT USE ARE **to burst** **to explode** **to go off**

blunt *adjective*
The opposite is sharp

blurred *adjective*
a blurred photograph.
OTHER WORDS YOU MIGHT USE ARE **cloudy** **faint** **fuzzy** **hazy** **misty** **unclear** **unfocused**
The opposite is clear

blush *verb*
She blushed when the teacher praised her work.
OTHER VERBS YOU MIGHT USE ARE **to flush** **to go red** **to redden**

boast *verb*
He boasted that he was best at everything.
ANOTHER VERB IS **to brag**

boat *noun*
OTHER WORDS ARE
craft **ship** **vessel**

DIFFERENT KINDS OF BOAT ARE

aircraft carrier	**barge**	**battleship**	**canoe**
cruiser	**destroyer**	**dinghy**	**ferry**
galleon	**house boat**	**junk**	**launch**
lifeboat	**liner**	**motor boat**	**oil tanker**
paddle steamer	**punt**	**raft**	**rowing boat**
sailing boat	**speed-boat**	**steamer**	**submarine**
tanker	**trawler**	**tug**	**warship**
yacht			

body *noun*, see next page

bodyguard *noun*
OTHER WORDS YOU MIGHT USE ARE **guard** (*informal*) **minder** **protector**

bog *noun*
OTHER WORDS ARE **marsh** **quicksands** **swamp**

boil *verb*
1 Is the water boiling?
ANOTHER VERB IS **to bubble**
2 Jo put the potatoes on to boil.
For other ways to cook things, see **cook**

body *noun*

Another word for the body of a dead person is **corpse**.
Another word for the body of a dead animal is **carcass**.
The main part of your body, not including the head, arms, and legs, is the **trunk**.

PARTS OF YOUR TRUNK ARE
abdomen or **tummy**   **back**   **bottom** or **buttocks**   **breast**
chest   **navel** or **tummy button**   **nipples**   **shoulders**

THE INNER ORGANS OF YOUR BODY INCLUDE
bladder   **bowels**   **glands**   **heart**   **intestines**
kidneys   **liver**   **lungs**   **ovaries**   **stomach**   **womb**

Your **arteries** take blood from the heart to other parts of the body, and your **veins** take blood back to the heart.
Your **muscles** are the parts you use when you move.
The **nerves** take messages to and from the brain.
Your **sexual organs** are your **penis** or **vagina**.

PARTS OF YOUR HEAD ARE
brain   **cheeks**   **chin**   **ears**   **eyes**   **forehead**   **gums**
hair   **jaw**   **lips**   **mouth**   **nose**   **nostrils**   **scalp**
teeth   **throat**   **tongue**

Your arms and legs are your **limbs**.

PARTS OF YOUR ARM ARE
elbow   **hand**   **shoulder**   **wrist**

PARTS OF YOUR HAND ARE
fingers   **fingernails**   **knuckles**   **palm**   **thumb**

PARTS OF YOUR LEG ARE
ankle   **calf**   **foot**   **knee**   **shin**   **thigh**

PARTS OF YOUR FOOT ARE
heel   **instep**   **toe**   **toenails**

Your bones are your **skeleton**.

THE MAIN BONES OF YOUR HEAD ARE   **jaw**   **skull**

IMPORTANT BONES IN YOUR BODY ARE
backbone or **spine** or **vertebrae**   **pelvis**   **ribs**

THE MAIN JOINTS IN YOUR BODY ARE
ankle   **elbow**   **hip**   **knee**   **knuckle**   **neck**
shoulder   **vertebra**   **wrist**

bold *adjective*
1 a bold deed.
For other words, see **brave**
2 bold handwriting.
OTHER WORDS YOU MIGHT USE ARE   **big   clear   large**

bolt *verb*
1 Remember to bolt the back door.
OTHER VERBS YOU MIGHT USE ARE   **to bar   to fasten   to lock**
2 The horse bolted.
OTHER VERBS ARE   **to escape   to run away**
For other words, see **run**
3 Don't bolt down your food!
OTHER VERBS ARE   **to gobble   to gulp**

bone *noun*
For other words you might use, see **body**

book *noun*
VARIOUS KINDS OF BOOK ARE
**album   annual   atlas   diary   dictionary
directory   encyclopedia   hymn book   novel
paperback   story book   thesaurus**

boot *noun*
For other things you wear on your feet, see **shoe**

bore *verb*
to bore a hole through something.
OTHER VERBS YOU MIGHT USE ARE   **to drill   to pierce**

boring *adjective*
a boring television programme.
OTHER WORDS YOU MIGHT USE ARE   **dreary   dry   dull   monotonous
tedious   tiresome   uninteresting   wearisome**
The opposite is interesting

borrow *verb*
If someone lets you use something for a time, you borrow it.
If you give something to someone to use, you lend it.

boss *noun*
For other words, see **chief**

bother *verb*
Is the loud music bothering you?

OTHER VERBS YOU MIGHT USE ARE   **to annoy   to disturb   to irritate   to pester   to trouble   to upset   to worry**

bottle *noun*
For other kinds of container, see **container**

bottom *noun*
1 the bottom of a wall.

OTHER WORDS YOU MIGHT USE ARE   **base   foot   foundation**
The opposite is top
2 the bottom of the sea.

ANOTHER WORD IS **bed**
The opposite is surface
3 the bottom that you sit on.

OTHER WORDS ARE   **backside   behind   buttocks**

boulder *noun*
There were some huge boulders on the beach.

OTHER WORDS ARE   **rock   stone**

bounce *verb*
The ball bounced off the wall.

ANOTHER VERB IS **to rebound**

bound *verb*
The dog bounded over the gate.

OTHER VERBS YOU MIGHT USE ARE   **to jump   to leap   to spring**

bound *adjective*
bound to
It's bound to rain if we go out.

PHRASES ARE   **certain to   sure to**
bound for
The rocket is bound for the moon.

PHRASES YOU MIGHT USE ARE   **aimed at   going towards**

boundary *noun*
OTHER WORDS YOU MIGHT USE ARE   **border   edge   frontier   limit**

bouquet *noun*
a bouquet of flowers.
OTHER WORDS YOU MIGHT USE ARE   **bunch**   **posy**   **spray**

bowl *noun*
OTHER WORDS YOU MIGHT USE ARE   **basin**   **dish**   **tureen**

bowl *verb*
For other verbs, see **throw**

box *noun*
OTHER WORDS YOU MIGHT USE ARE   **carton**   **case**   **chest**   **crate**

brains *noun*
Use your brains!
OTHER WORDS YOU MIGHT USE ARE   **intelligence**   **mind**   **reason**
understanding

branch *noun*
a branch of a tree.
OTHER WORDS YOU MIGHT USE ARE   **bough**   **limb**

brand *noun*
Which brand of butter do you buy?
OTHER WORDS YOU MIGHT USE ARE   **kind**   **make**

brave *adjective*
OTHER WORDS YOU MIGHT USE ARE   **bold**   **courageous**   **daring**
fearless   **heroic**   **plucky**
The opposite is cowardly

bravery *noun*
OTHER WORDS YOU MIGHT USE ARE   **courage**   **daring**   **heroism**
valour

bread *noun*
DIFFERENT FORMS IN WHICH YOU BUY BREAD ARE
baguette   **French stick**   **loaf**   **roll**
sliced bread

For different kinds of bread, see **food**

break *noun*

1 a break in a pipe. a break in the fence.
> OTHER WORDS YOU MIGHT USE ARE   crack   cut   gap   hole   leak
> opening   slit   split   tear

2 a break in a game.
> OTHER WORDS ARE   half time   interval   lull   pause   rest

break *verb*

DIFFERENT WAYS THINGS BREAK ARE
> to chip   to collapse   to crack   to crumble   to decay
> to fall apart   to fracture   to shatter   to snap
> to splinter   to split

DIFFERENT WAYS YOU CAN BREAK THINGS ARE
> to crush   to demolish   to destroy   to drop   to smash
> to squash   to wreck

breed *noun*

What breed of dog is that?
> OTHER WORDS YOU MIGHT USE ARE   kind   species   variety

breed *verb*

Most birds breed in the spring.
> OTHER VERBS YOU MIGHT USE ARE   to produce young ones   to reproduce

bridge *noun*

> KINDS OF BRIDGE ARE   fly-over   viaduct

brief *adjective*

> OTHER WORDS YOU MIGHT USE ARE   concise   little   short

The opposite is long

bright *adjective*

1 bright lights.
> OTHER WORDS YOU MIGHT USE ARE   brilliant   colourful   dazzling
> flashing   gleaming   glittering   shining   shiny   sparkling

2 a bright boy.
> OTHER WORDS ARE   brainy   clever   intelligent   quick   smart

3 a bright smile.
> OTHER WORDS ARE   cheerful   happy   radiant

The opposite is dull

brilliant *adjective*
For other words, see **bright**

brim *noun*
My cup was full to the brim.
OTHER WORDS YOU MIGHT USE ARE   **brink**   **edge**   **rim**   **top**

bring *verb*
1 I helped to bring the shopping home.
OTHER VERBS YOU MIGHT USE ARE   **to carry**   **to fetch**   **to take**
2 The captain brought her team onto the field.
OTHER VERBS ARE   **to guide**   **to lead**

brisk *adjective*
We set off at a brisk walk.
OTHER WORDS YOU MIGHT USE ARE   **fast**   **lively**   **quick**   **rapid**

brittle *adjective*
The shell of an egg is brittle.
OTHER WORDS YOU MIGHT USE ARE   **fragile**   **weak**
The opposite is strong

broad *adjective*
a broad area of sand.
OTHER WORDS YOU MIGHT USE ARE   **extensive**   **large**   **wide**
The opposite is narrow

brook *noun*
ANOTHER WORD IS **stream**

brother *noun*
For other members of a family, see **family**

brush *noun*
A brush with a long handle is a **broom**.

bubbles *noun*
OTHER WORDS YOU MIGHT USE ARE   **foam**   **froth**   **lather**   **suds**

bubbly *adjective*
OTHER WORDS YOU MIGHT USE ARE   **boiling**   **effervescent**   **fizzy**
foaming   **sparkling**

buffet *noun*
1 For other places where you can buy and eat food, see **café**
2 For other kinds of meal, see **meal**

build *verb*
OTHER VERBS YOU MIGHT USE ARE **to construct   to erect   to put up**

building *noun*
VARIOUS BUILDINGS ARE

abbey	barn	bungalow	cabin
castle	cathedral	chapel	church
cinema	cottage	factory	farmhouse
flats	garage	hotel	house
inn	lighthouse	mansion	monastery
mosque	museum	pagoda	palace
police-station	post office	power station	prison
pub	restaurant	shop	skyscraper
stable	synagogue	temple	theatre
tower	warehouse	windmill	

PARTS OF BUILDINGS ARE
**balcony   doors   floors   foyer   lobby   passage
porch   rooms   staircase   veranda   walls   windows**

TOP PARTS OF A BUILDING ARE
**ceilings   chimney   dome   eaves   gable   gutters
rafters   roof   spire   steeple   tower   turret**

UNDERGROUND PARTS OF A BUILDING ARE
basement   cellar   crypt   foundations

For various rooms in a house, see **home**

bully *verb*
I was angry with the big girl who bullied the small ones.
OTHER VERBS YOU MIGHT USE ARE **to frighten   to persecute
to threaten   to torment**

bump *noun*
Jo has a nasty bump on the head.
OTHER WORDS YOU MIGHT USE ARE **bulge   hump   lump   swelling**

bump *verb*
For other words, see **hit**

bunch *noun*
1 a bunch of carrots.
   OTHER WORDS YOU MIGHT USE ARE   **clump   cluster**
2 a bunch of flowers.
   OTHER WORDS ARE **bouquet   posy   spray**
3 a bunch of friends.
   OTHER WORDS ARE **crowd   gathering   group   set**

bundle *noun*
a bundle of papers.
   OTHER WORDS YOU MIGHT USE ARE   **pack   package   parcel
   sheaf**

burden *noun*
a heavy burden.
   OTHER WORDS YOU MIGHT USE ARE   **load   weight**

burglar *noun*
   OTHER WORDS YOU MIGHT USE ARE   **intruder   robber   thief**
For other words, see **steal**

burn *verb*
   OTHER VERBS YOU MIGHT USE ARE   **blaze   flame   flare
   smoulder**
   WAYS YOU CAN DAMAGE THINGS BY HEAT ARE   **to char   to scald
   to scorch   to singe**
To burn a dead person's body is **to cremate** it.
For other useful words, see **fire**

burrow *noun*
Rabbits live in a burrow.
   OTHER WORDS YOU MIGHT USE ARE   **hole   tunnel**
A place where rabbits make a lot of burrows is a **warren**.

burst *verb*
1 He burst open the door.
   OTHER VERBS YOU MIGHT USE ARE   **to break   to force open**
2 The balloon burst.
   OTHER VERBS ARE   **to explode   to pop**

bush *noun*
   ANOTHER WORD IS **shrub**

business *noun*

1 Dad's business is selling cars.
OTHER WORDS YOU MIGHT USE ARE   **job**   **occupation**   **trade**   **work**

2 I work for a computer business.
OTHER WORDS ARE   **company**   **firm**   **industry**   **organization**
shop

3 Don't be nosey - it's none of your business!
OTHER WORDS ARE   **affair**   **concern**

busy *adjective*

1 Our teacher is always busy.
OTHER WORDS YOU MIGHT USE ARE   **active**   **doing things**   **occupied**
(*informal*) **on the go**
The opposite is idle

2 The shops are busy during the sales.
OTHER WORDS ARE   **bustling**   **lively**

buy *verb*

I bought my bike for £30.
OTHER VERBS YOU MIGHT USE ARE   **to get**   **to obtain**   **to purchase**

Cc

cable *noun*

1 electric cables.
OTHER WORDS YOU MIGHT USE ARE   **flex**   **lead**   **wire**

2 cables for tying up a ship.
OTHER WORDS ARE   **cord**   **line**   **rope**

café *noun*

We went into a café for a snack.
OTHER PLACES WHERE YOU MIGHT GET THINGS TO EAT ARE
bar   **bistro**   **buffet**   **cafeteria**   **canteen**
fish and chip shop   **restaurant**   **snack bar**
take-away

cage *noun*
OTHER WORDS FOR PLACES TO KEEP ANIMALS IN ARE
an aviary for birds
a coop for chickens
an enclosure for zoo animals
a hutch for rabbits
a kennel for a dog
a pen for sheep

cake *noun*
For kinds of cake, see **food**

call *verb*
1 I heard someone call.
   OTHER VERBS YOU MIGHT USE ARE   **to cry out**   **to exclaim**   **to shout**
   to yell
2 They called the baby Robert.
   ANOTHER VERB IS **to name**
3 Mum called us in for dinner.
   OTHER VERBS ARE   **to send for**   **to summon**
4 I didn't call because the phone wasn't working.
   OTHER VERBS ARE   **to phone**   **to ring**   **to telephone**

calm *adjective*
1 a calm sea.
   OTHER WORDS YOU MIGHT USE ARE   **even**   **flat**   **peaceful**   **smooth**
   still
The opposite is stormy
2 Don't panic - keep calm!
   OTHER WORDS ARE   **cool**   **patient**   **quiet**   **sensible**

camera *noun*
DIFFERENT KINDS OF CAMERA ARE
   camcorder   **cine-camera**   **Polaroid**
PARTS OF A CAMERA ARE
   flash   **focus**   **lens**   **light meter**   **shutter**   **viewfinder**
   zoom lens

cancel *verb*
They cancelled the game because of the snow.
OTHER VERBS YOU MIGHT USE ARE   **to abandon**   **to give up**   **to postpone**

cap *noun*
For things you wear on your head, see **hat**

capacity *noun*
What is the capacity of this kettle?
OTHER WORDS YOU MIGHT USE ARE   **size**   **volume**

captain *noun*
the captain of a team.
For words for people in charge, see **chief**

captive *noun*
The captives were locked in a dungeon.
OTHER WORDS YOU MIGHT USE ARE   **hostage**   **prisoner**

capture *verb*
Did they capture the thief?
OTHER VERBS YOU MIGHT USE ARE   **to arrest**   **to catch**   **to seize**

car *noun*
VARIOUS KINDS OF CAR ARE
estate   **hatchback**   **racing car**   **saloon**   **taxi**
For other things you ride in, see **travel**

card *noun*
1 CARDS YOU CAN SEND TO PEOPLE ARE
birthday card   **Christmas card**   **get-well card**
invitation   **postcard**   **Valentine**

2 IN CARD GAMES, THE SUITS ARE
clubs   **diamonds**   **hearts**   **spades**
THE CARDS WITH PICTURES ON ARE
Jack   **Joker**   **King**   **Queen**

care *noun*

1 He hasn't a care in the world!
   OTHER WORDS YOU MIGHT USE ARE   **trouble**   **worry**
2 Mum drives with great care.
   OTHER WORDS ARE   **attention**   **caution**
to take care
Take care when you cross the road.
   VERBS YOU MIGHT USE ARE   **to be careful**   **to look out**
to take care of
I took care of Jo's money while she went swimming.
   PHRASES YOU MIGHT USE ARE   **to keep something safe**
   to look after something

care *verb*

He doesn't care who wins.
   ANOTHER VERB IS **to mind**
to care for
1 We care for our pets.
   OTHER VERBS ARE   **to look after**   **to protect**   **to take care of**
2 You send a Valentine card to show that you care for someone.
For other words, see **love**

careful *adjective*

1 Mum is a careful driver.
   OTHER WORDS YOU MIGHT USE ARE   **alert**   **attentive**   **cautious**
2 Jo's work is always careful.
   OTHER WORDS ARE   **neat**   **orderly**   **organized**   **thorough**
The opposite is careless

careless *adjective*

1 careless driving.
   OTHER WORDS YOU MIGHT USE ARE   **negligent**   **reckless**   **thoughtless**
2 careless work.
   OTHER WORDS ARE   **disorganized**   **hasty**   **messy**   **untidy**
The opposite is careful

cargo *noun*

The ship unloaded its cargo at the docks.
   OTHER WORDS YOU MIGHT USE ARE   **freight**   **goods**

carnival *noun*

   OTHER WORDS YOU MIGHT USE ARE   **fair**   **festival**   **fête**   **gala**   **show**

carriage *noun*
For other things you can ride in, see **travel**

carry *verb*
1 Sam carried the food into the dining room.
OTHER VERBS YOU MIGHT USE ARE   **to bring   to lift   to move   to take to transfer**
2 Trains can carry a lot of passengers.
OTHER VERBS ARE   **to convey   to transport**

cart *noun*
OTHER WORDS YOU MIGHT USE ARE   **barrow   wagon   wheelbarrow**

carve *verb*
For ways to cut things, see **cut**

case *noun*
For other words, see **box**

castle *noun*
OTHER WORDS YOU MIGHT USE ARE
fort   fortress
PARTS OF A CASTLE ARE
**battlements   courtyard   drawbridge   dungeon
keep   moat   parapet   portcullis   tower   turret**

cat *noun*
INFORMAL WORDS ARE
moggy   pussy   pussycat
A young cat is a **kitten**.
A male cat is a **tomcat**.
KINDS OF CAT ARE
Manx   marmalade cat   Persian   Siamese   tabby

For other pets, see **pet**
'BIG CATS' OR WILD ANIMALS RELATED TO CATS ARE
**cheetah   jaguar   leopard   lion   lynx   panther
puma   tiger   wildcat**

catalogue *noun*
1 a shopping catalogue.
> ANOTHER WORD IS **brochure**
2 a catalogue of books in the library.
> OTHER WORDS FOR A LIST OF NAMES OR THINGS YOU MIGHT WANT TO LOOK UP ARE
> **directory**   **index**   **register**

catch *verb*
1 to catch a ball.
> OTHER VERBS YOU MIGHT USE ARE   **to grasp**   **to hold**   **to seize**
> **to take hold of**

The opposite is miss
2 to catch a thief.
> OTHER VERBS ARE   **to arrest**   **to capture**   **to stop**
3 to catch fish.
> OTHER VERBS ARE   **to hook**   **to net**
4 to catch an animal.
> OTHER VERBS ARE   **to snare**   **to trap**
5 to catch a bus.
> ANOTHER VERB IS **to get**

catching *adjective*
I hope your cold isn't catching.
> ANOTHER WORD IS **infectious**

cattle *noun*
> ANIMALS THAT FARMERS KEEP AS CATTLE ARE
> **bull**   **bullock**   **cow**   **ox**
> Young cattle are called **calves**.

cause *verb*
The storm caused terrible floods.
> PHRASES YOU MIGHT USE ARE   **to bring about**   **to lead to**
> **to result in**

cautious *adjective*
For other words, see **careful**

cave *noun*
> OTHER WORDS YOU MIGHT USE ARE   **cavern**   **grotto**   **pothole**

cease *verb*
Cease work!
> OTHER VERBS YOU MIGHT USE ARE   **to break off**   **to end**   **to finish**
> **to stop**

cellar *noun*
> OTHER UNDERGROUND PARTS OF BUILDINGS ARE   **basement**   **crypt**   **vault**

cemetery *noun*
> ANOTHER WORD IS **graveyard**
A graveyard round a church is a **churchyard**.

centre *noun*
the centre of the earth.
> OTHER WORDS YOU MIGHT USE ARE   **core**   **heart**   **middle**
The centre of a wheel is the **hub**.

cereal *noun*
> OTHER WORDS ARE   **corn**   **grain**
> 1 KINDS OF CEREAL FARMERS GROW ARE
> **barley**   **maize** or **sweet corn**   **oats**   **rice**   **rye**   **wheat**
>
> 2 KINDS OF BREAKFAST CEREAL ARE
> **bran**   **cornflakes**   **muesli**   **porridge**

certain *adjective*
Are you certain it will rain?
> OTHER WORDS YOU MIGHT USE ARE   **confident**   **definite**   **positive**
> **sure**

chair *noun*
For things to sit on, see **seat**

champion *noun*
> OTHER WORDS YOU MIGHT USE ARE   **hero**   **winner**   **victor**

chance *noun*
1 This is your last chance.
> ANOTHER WORD IS **opportunity**

2 I met him by chance.
OTHER WORDS ARE **accident**   **coincidence**
3 There's a chance of rain.
OTHER WORDS ARE **danger**   **possibility**   **risk**

change *noun*
I need some change to pay for the bus.
OTHER WORDS YOU MIGHT USE ARE **cash**   **coins**

change *verb*
1 I changed the end of my story.
OTHER VERBS YOU MIGHT USE ARE **to adjust**   **to alter**
to make different   **to revise**   **to transform**
2 I want to change this apple for an orange.
OTHER VERBS YOU MIGHT USE ARE **to exchange**   **to substitute**
to switch   (*informal*) **to swap**
3 Tadpoles change into frogs.
OTHER VERBS YOU MIGHT USE ARE **to become**   **to develop into**
to turn into

channel *noun*
1 a channel to take water away.
OTHER WORDS YOU MIGHT USE ARE **canal**   **ditch**   **gutter**
2 a TV channel.
ANOTHER WORD IS **station**

chaos *noun*
There was chaos when the lights went out.
OTHER WORDS YOU MIGHT USE ARE **confusion**   **a mix-up**

character *noun*
1 My favourite character in the pantomime was Cinderella.
OTHER WORDS YOU MIGHT USE ARE **part**   **role**
2 Granny has a kind character.
OTHER WORDS ARE **manner**   **nature**   **personality**
3 Who is that character at the bus stop?
OTHER WORDS ARE **individual**   **person**

charge *noun*
Mum left me in charge of the washing-up.
OTHER WORDS YOU MIGHT USE ARE **command**   **control**

charge *verb*

1 They charge £1 for an ice cream.
   PHRASES YOU MIGHT USE ARE   **to ask   to make you pay**
2 The soldiers charged the enemy.
   OTHER VERBS ARE   **to attack   to rush at**

charm *verb*

He charmed us with his music.
   OTHER VERBS ARE   **to bewitch   to enchant   to fascinate**

charming *adjective*

   OTHER WORDS YOU MIGHT USE ARE   **attractive   pretty**
For other words, see **beautiful**

chart *noun*

   OTHER WORDS YOU MIGHT USE ARE   **diagram   graph   map   plan**

chase *verb*

The dog chased the hare for miles.
   OTHER VERBS YOU MIGHT USE ARE   **to follow   to hunt   to pursue
   to tail   to track   to trail**

chat, chatter *verbs*

For other verbs, see **talk**

cheap *adjective*

Jo bought a cheap coat in a sale.
   OTHER WORDS YOU MIGHT USE ARE   **cut-price   inexpensive
   reasonable**
The opposite is expensive

cheat *verb*

He cheated us by keeping all the money for himself.
   OTHER VERBS YOU MIGHT USE ARE   **to deceive   to fool   to swindle
   to trick**

check *verb*

1 Mum always checks the car before we go on a journey.
   OTHER VERBS YOU MIGHT USE ARE   **to examine   to look over   to test**
2 A traffic jam checked our progress.
   OTHER VERBS YOU MIGHT USE ARE   **to halt   to hold up   to prevent
   to slow down   to stop**

cheeky *adjective*
My teacher hates cheeky behaviour.
OTHER WORDS YOU MIGHT USE ARE **bold   impertinent   impolite   impudent   insolent   rude**
The opposite is polite

cheer *verb*
The audience cheered.
ANOTHER VERB IS **to applaud**
to cheer someone up
OTHER VERBS YOU MIGHT USE ARE **to comfort   to encourage**

cheerful *adjective*
OTHER WORDS YOU MIGHT USE ARE **bright   happy   jolly   laughing   light-hearted   lively   merry   pleased**
The opposite is gloomy

chest *noun*
a chest full of treasure.
OTHER WORDS YOU MIGHT USE ARE **box   case   crate**
For other words, see **container**

chew *verb*
For other verbs, see **eat**

chief *adjective*
We learned the chief spelling rules.
OTHER WORDS YOU MIGHT USE ARE
basic   essential   important   main   major   principal

chief *noun*
WORDS FOR PEOPLE IN CHARGE OF VARIOUS THINGS ARE
boss   captain   commander   director   employer   governor   head   leader   manager   president   principal   ruler

child *noun*
OTHER WORDS ARE **baby   boy   girl   infant   (*informal*) kid   (*informal*) toddler   (*informal*) youngster**

china *noun*

When you wash up, make sure you don't chip the china.

OTHER WORDS YOU MIGHT USE ARE

crockery   porcelain   pots   pottery

THINGS MADE OF CHINA ARE

bowl   cup   dish   jug   plate   saucer   teapot

chip *noun*

OTHER WORDS FOR A SMALL PIECE BROKEN OFF SOMETHING ARE   **flake   fragment splinter**

chip *verb*

I chipped one of the best plates.
For other words, see **break**

choke *verb*

This collar is choking me.

OTHER VERBS YOU MIGHT USE ARE   **to stifle   to strangle   to suffocate**

choose *verb*

We chose Jo as captain.

OTHER VERBS YOU MIGHT USE ARE   **to decide on   to elect   to name to pick   to select   to settle on   to vote for**

chop *verb*

For ways to cut things, see **cut**

chunk *noun*

a chunk of cheese.

OTHER WORDS YOU MIGHT USE ARE   **block   hunk   lump   piece   slab**

church *noun*

For places where people worship, see **religion**

cinema *noun*

OTHER WORDS ARE   **the pictures   the movies**

circle *noun*

OTHER WORDS YOU MIGHT USE ARE   **disc   hoop   ring**
For other shapes, see **shape**

circus *noun*
PEOPLE WHO PERFORM IN A CIRCUS ARE
**acrobat   clown   juggler   lion-tamer   ringmaster
trapeze artist**

citizen *noun*
the citizens of a town.
OTHER WORDS YOU MIGHT USE ARE   **inhabitant   resident**

claim *verb*
Jo claimed her lost property.
OTHER VERBS YOU MIGHT USE ARE   **to ask for   to demand   to request**

clap *verb*
We clapped at the end of the play.
ANOTHER VERB IS **to applaud**

class *noun*
Which class are you in?
OTHER WORDS YOU MIGHT USE ARE   **form   group   set**

clean *adjective*
1 clean clothes.
   ANOTHER WORD IS **spotless**
2 clean water.
   OTHER WORDS YOU MIGHT USE ARE   **clear   fresh   pure**
3 a clean sheet of paper.
   OTHER WORDS ARE   **blank   unmarked   unused**
The opposite is dirty

clean *verb*
Sam cleaned the floor while Jo was cleaning the car.
WAYS TO CLEAN THINGS ARE
**to brush   to dust   to hoover   to mop up   to rinse
to scrub   to shampoo   to sponge down   to sweep out
to swill   to vacuum   to wash   to wipe**

clear *adjective*

THIS WORD HAS MANY USES. HERE ARE SOME OF THE WAYS YOU CAN USE IT, AND SOME OTHER WORDS YOU COULD CHOOSE

1 clear water.
   clean   colourless   pure
2 a clear sky.
   blue   bright   cloudless   starlit   sunny
3 clear plastic.
   transparent
4 a clear photograph.
   focused   sharp   well-defined
5 a clear voice.
   audible   distinct
6 a clear space.
   empty   free   open
7 a clear case of cheating.
   obvious
8 a clear explanation.
   plain   simple   understandable

clear *verb*

1 We cleared a space to play in.
   OTHER VERBS YOU MIGHT USE ARE   **to empty   to free**
2 Please clear the dishes.
   OTHER VERBS ARE   **to carry away   to move   to remove   to take away**
3 The fog cleared.
   OTHER VERBS ARE   **to disappear   to melt away   to vanish**

clever *adjective*

1 a clever pupil.
   OTHER WORDS YOU MIGHT USE ARE   (*informal*) **brainy   bright   brilliant   intelligent   quick   sharp   talented   wise**
2 clever with your hands.
   OTHER WORDS ARE   **expert   handy   skilful**
3 a clever trick.
   OTHER WORDS ARE   **crafty   cunning**
The opposite is stupid

cliff *noun*

ANOTHER WORD IS **precipice**

climb *verb*
Take care when you climb the ladder.
OTHER VERBS YOU MIGHT USE ARE   **to ascend   to go up   to mount**

cling *verb*
1 The ivy clings to the wall.
ANOTHER VERB IS **to stick**
2 The baby clung to her mother.
OTHER VERBS YOU MIGHT USE ARE   **to hold on   to grasp   to hug**

clock *noun*
THINGS WHICH TELL THE TIME ARE
**alarm clock   digital clock   grandfather clock
hourglass   sundial   watch**

clog *verb*
The leaves clogged up the drain.
OTHER VERBS YOU MIGHT USE ARE   **to block**   (*informal*) **to bung up**

close (rhymes with dose) *adjective*
1 Our house is close to the park.
ANOTHER WORD IS **near**
2 Mum took a close look at the cut on Jo's hand.
OTHER WORDS YOU MIGHT USE ARE   **careful   thorough**

close (rhymes with doze) *verb*
1 Please close the door.
OTHER VERBS YOU MIGHT USE ARE   **to fasten   to lock   to shut**
2 We closed the concert with some songs.
OTHER VERBS ARE   **to conclude   to end   to finish**
The opposite is open

cloth *noun*
OTHER WORDS YOU MIGHT USE ARE   **fabric   material   textiles**
DIFFERENT KINDS OF CLOTH ARE
**canvas   corduroy   .cotton   denim   felt   flannel
lace   linen   muslin   nylon   polyester   satin   silk
tartan   tweed   velvet   viscose   wool**

clothes, clothing *nouns,* see opposite page

cloudy *adjective*
1 a cloudy sky.
    OTHER WORDS YOU MIGHT USE ARE   **dull**   **grey**   **overcast**
2 cloudy water.
    OTHER WORDS ARE   **milky**   **murky**
3 a cloudy atmosphere.
    OTHER WORDS ARE   **misty**   **steamy**
The opposite is clear

club *noun*
1 a football club. a chess club.
    OTHER WORDS YOU MIGHT USE ARE   **association**   **group**   **league**
    organization   **society**
2 The intruder tried to hit me with a club.
    OTHER WORDS ARE   **baton**   **cudgel**   **stick**   **truncheon**

clue *noun*
Give me a clue about what we are having for dinner.
    OTHER WORDS YOU MIGHT USE ARE   **hint**   **indication**   **sign**
    suggestion

clumsy *adjective*
She's clumsy and keeps dropping things.
    OTHER WORDS YOU MIGHT USE ARE   **awkward**   **blundering**

clutch *verb*
I clutched the rope to stop myself from falling.
    OTHER VERBS YOU MIGHT USE ARE   **to cling to**   **to grab**   **to grasp**
    to grip   **to hold on to**   **to seize**   **to snatch**

coach *noun*
1 We went to the seaside by coach.
For other things you travel in, see **travel**
2 Our team has got a new coach.
    ANOTHER WORD IS **trainer**

coarse *adjective*
The coarse cloth tickled my skin.
    OTHER WORDS YOU MIGHT USE ARE   **hairy**   **rough**   **scratchy**
The opposite is smooth

clothes, clothing *nouns*

OTHER WORDS YOU MIGHT USE ARE

costume   dress   garments

DIFFERENT THINGS YOU WEAR ARE

belt	**blazer**	**blouse**	**braces**
cardigan	**coat**	**dress**	**frock**
jacket	**jeans**	**jersey**	**jumper**
kilt	**leotard**	**miniskirt**	**pullover**
rompers	**sari**	**shawl**	**shorts**
skirt	**socks**	**stockings**	**suit**
sweater	**sweatshirt**	**tie**	**trousers**
t-shirt	**tunic**	**waistcoat**	

THINGS YOU WEAR TO KEEP CLEAN ARE

**apron   bib   dungarees   overalls
pinafore**

CLOTHES YOU WEAR WHEN YOU GO OUT ARE

anorak	**cagoule**	**cloak**	**duffle coat**
gloves	(*informal*) **mac** or **mack**		**mackintosh**
mittens	**muffler**	**overcoat**	**raincoat**
scarf			

CLOTHES YOU USE AT NIGHT ARE

dressing gown   night-dress   nightie   pyjamas

UNDERCLOTHES ARE

bra	**knickers**	**panties**	**pants**
pantyhose	**petticoat**	**slip**	**tights**
underpants	**vest**		

THINGS YOU WEAR WHEN YOU GO SWIMMING ARE

bikini   swimming costume   swimsuit   trunks

For things you wear on your head, see **hat**
For things you wear on your feet, see **shoe**

coat *noun*
For things we wear, see **clothes**

coil *verb*
The snake coiled round a branch.

OTHER VERBS YOU MIGHT USE ARE   **to curl   to entwine   to loop
to twist   to wind**

cold *adjective*

1 cold weather.

OTHER WORDS YOU MIGHT USE ARE   **Arctic   bitter   chilly   cool freezing   fresh   frosty   icy** (*informal*) **nippy   wintry**

2 I feel cold.

OTHER WORDS ARE   **chilled   frozen   shivery**

The opposite is hot

collapse *verb*

1 The shed collapsed in the storm.

PHRASES YOU MIGHT USE ARE   (*informal*) **to cave in   to fall down to tumble down**

2 People collapsed because it was so hot.

ANOTHER VERB IS **to faint**

collect *verb*

1 A crowd collected to watch the fire.

OTHER VERBS YOU MIGHT USE ARE   **to assemble   to gather**

2 We collected all the litter.

OTHER VERBS ARE   **to accumulate   to gather together   to heap up to pile up**

3 Mum collected Jo from school.

OTHER VERBS ARE   **to bring   to fetch   to pick up**

collection *noun*

Jo has a collection of toys.

OTHER WORDS YOU MIGHT USE ARE   **assortment   gathering   hoard pile   set   stack**

For other words, see **group**

college *noun*

For other words, see **educate**

collide *verb*

The car collided with a van.

OTHER PHRASES YOU MIGHT USE ARE   **to bump into   to crash into to run into**

For other words, see **hit**

collision *noun*

OTHER WORDS YOU MIGHT USE ARE   **accident   bump   crash   smash**

colour *noun*
We admired the lovely colours of the sunset.
OTHER WORDS YOU MIGHT USE ARE

hue   shade   tint

DIFFERENT COLOURS ARE

amber	black	blue	bronze
brown	cream	crimson	fawn
gold	green	grey	ivory
jet-black	khaki	maroon	mauve
navy blue	orange	pink	purple
red	rosy	scarlet	tan
turquoise	vermilion	violet	white
yellow			

colour *verb*
OTHER VERBS YOU MIGHT USE ARE

to dye   to paint   to stain   to tinge   to tint

colourful *adjective*
1 colourful flowers.
OTHER WORDS YOU MIGHT USE ARE   **bright   brilliant   flashy   gaudy showy**
2 a colourful description.
OTHER WORDS ARE   **lively   interesting   vivid**
The opposite is dull

column *noun*
The palace had stone columns in front of the door.
OTHER WORDS YOU MIGHT USE ARE   **pillar   pole   post   shaft support**

combine *verb*
1 Our class combined with Jo's class to put on a play.
OTHER VERBS YOU MIGHT USE ARE   **to come together   to join   to merge to unite**
2 I combined the cake ingredients in a big bowl.
OTHER VERBS ARE   **to add together   to blend   to mix to put together**

come *verb*
1 Some dark clouds are coming.
OTHER VERBS YOU MIGHT USE ARE   **to advance   to approach   to draw near**
2 Our visitors have come.
OTHER VERBS ARE   **to appear   to arrive   to turn up**
The opposite is go

comfort *verb*
Jo comforts baby when he cries.
OTHER VERBS YOU MIGHT USE ARE   **to calm   to reassure   to soothe**

comfortable *adjective*
a comfortable chair.
OTHER WORDS YOU MIGHT USE ARE   **cosy   luxurious   relaxing   snug   soft**

comic *adjective*
We laughed at his comic remarks.
OTHER WORDS YOU MIGHT USE ARE   **amusing   comical   funny   humorous   laughable   witty**
The opposite is serious

command *verb*
1 The general commanded that the fighting must stop.
OTHER VERBS YOU MIGHT USE ARE   **to instruct   to order**
2 The captain commands the ship.
OTHER VERBS ARE   **to be in charge of   to control   to govern   to manage   to supervise   to take over**

comment *noun*
The teacher asked for our comments.
OTHER WORDS YOU MIGHT USE ARE   **opinion   remark**

commercial *noun*
a TV commercial.
OTHER WORDS YOU MIGHT USE ARE   *(informal)* **advert   advertisement**

commit *verb*
to commit a crime.
OTHER VERBS YOU MIGHT USE ARE   **to be guilty of   to carry out**

common *adjective*
1 It's common for people to go to the seaside for a holiday.
    OTHER WORDS YOU MIGHT USE ARE   **customary   normal   ordinary
    usual**
2 Colds are common in winter.
    OTHER WORDS ARE   **frequent   widespread**
3 'Too many cooks spoil the broth' is a common saying.
    ANOTHER WORD IS **well known**
The opposite is rare

communication *noun*
    Mum got a communication from school about the parents'
    evening.
    OTHER WORDS ARE   **message   note**
    DIFFERENT WAYS TO COMMUNICATE ARE
    **computer network   letter   newspaper   magazine
    radar   radio   satellite   telephone   television**

compact *adjective*
1 a compact set of instructions.
    OTHER WORDS YOU MIGHT USE ARE   **brief   concise   short**
2 a compact typewriter.
    OTHER WORDS ARE   **neat   portable   small**

company *noun*
We enjoy the company of other people.
    OTHER WORDS YOU MIGHT USE ARE   **companionship   friendship**
For other words, see **crowd**

compare *verb*
Compare your answers with your neighbour's.
    OTHER VERBS YOU MIGHT USE ARE   **to check   to contrast**

compartment *noun*
The box has separate compartments for knives, forks, and spoons.
    OTHER WORDS YOU MIGHT USE ARE   **division   section   space**

compel *verb*
You can't compel me to go swimming in this weather!
    OTHER VERBS YOU MIGHT USE ARE   **to force   to order**

competition *noun*

1 a sports competition.

> OTHER WORDS YOU MIGHT USE ARE   **championship   contest   game   match   tournament**

2 There was fierce competition between the two teams.

> ANOTHER WORD IS **rivalry**

complain *verb*

We complained about the bad food.

> OTHER VERBS YOU MIGHT USE ARE   **to grumble   to object   to protest**

complete *adjective*

1 Did he tell you the complete story?

> OTHER WORDS YOU MIGHT USE ARE   **entire   full   whole**

2 He was talking complete rubbish.

> OTHER WORDS ARE   **absolute   pure   total   utter**

complete *verb*

Can I go out when I've completed my homework?

> OTHER VERBS YOU MIGHT USE ARE   **to carry out   to end   to finish**

complicated *adjective*

The instructions were too complicated for me to understand.

> OTHER WORDS YOU MIGHT USE ARE   **complex   difficult   involved**

The opposite is simple

computer *noun*

WORDS TO DO WITH COMPUTING ARE

**cursor   data   disk drive   floppy disk   hard disk
hardware   interface   joystick   keyboard
micro-chip   micro-computer   micro-processor
monitor   mouse   PC   printer   print-out   program
screen   software   terminal   VDU   word processor**

conceal *verb*

1 The bird concealed its nest.

> OTHER VERBS YOU MIGHT USE ARE   **to camouflage   to disguise   to hide**

2 He tried to conceal the truth.

> PHRASES ARE   **to cover up   to keep quiet about**

The opposite is show

conceited *adjective*
There's no need to be conceited just because you got a prize.
OTHER WORDS YOU MIGHT USE ARE   **boastful**   (*informal*) **cocky**
proud
The opposite is modest

concentrate *verb*
Concentrate on your work.
PHRASES YOU MIGHT USE ARE   **to attend to**   **to think about**

concern *verb*
Road safety concerns all of us.
OTHER VERBS YOU MIGHT USE ARE   **to affect**   **to be important to**
to involve   **to matter to**

concerned *adjective*
Dad is concerned about Jo's cough.
OTHER WORDS YOU MIGHT USE ARE   **anxious**   **bothered**
worried

conclude *verb*
1 We concluded the concert with a song.
OTHER VERBS YOU MIGHT USE ARE   **to close**   **to end**   **to finish**
to round off
2 After waiting 15 minutes, I concluded that I'd missed the bus.
OTHER VERBS ARE   **to decide**   **to reach a conclusion**

condemn *verb*
1 The head condemned the vandals who broke the window.
OTHER VERBS YOU MIGHT USE ARE   **to blame**   **to criticise**
2 The judge condemned the thief to spend a year in prison.
OTHER VERBS ARE   **to convict**   **to punish**   **to sentence**

condition *noun*
1 Is your bike in good condition?
ANOTHER WORD IS **order**
2 Is your dog in good condition?
ANOTHER WORD IS **health**

confess *verb*
Jo confessed that she lost her gloves.
OTHER VERBS YOU MIGHT USE ARE   **to admit**   **to own up**

confident *adjective*
1 Sam is a confident swimmer.
    OTHER WORDS YOU MIGHT USE ARE   **bold**   **fearless**
    The opposite is nervous
2 Jo was confident that she knew the answer.
    OTHER WORDS ARE   **certain**   **definite**   **positive**
       sure
    The opposite is doubtful

confuse *verb*
1 Complicated sums confuse me.
    OTHER VERBS YOU MIGHT USE ARE   **to bewilder**   **to puzzle**
2 I always confuse the names of the twins.
    OTHER VERBS ARE   **to mix up**   **to muddle**

congratulate *verb*
We congratulated Sam when he won.
    OTHER VERBS YOU MIGHT USE ARE   **to compliment**   **to praise**

connect *verb*
Dad connected a loudspeaker to the TV set.
    OTHER VERBS YOU MIGHT USE ARE   **to attach**   **to join**   **to link**

conquer *verb*
We easily conquered the opposition.
    OTHER VERBS YOU MIGHT USE ARE   **to beat**   **to defeat**   **to overcome**
    (*informal*) **to thrash**   **to win against**

conscious *adjective*
In spite of the knock on the head, he remained conscious.
    OTHER WORDS YOU MIGHT USE ARE   **alert**   **awake**
    The opposite is unconscious

consent *verb*
We can go on the trip if Mum and Dad consent.
    OTHER VERBS YOU MIGHT USE ARE   **to agree**   **to allow it**   **to approve**
       to permit it

consider *verb*
We considered the problem.
    OTHER VERBS YOU MIGHT USE ARE   **to study**   **to think about**

considerate *adjective*
It was considerate of you to lend me your umbrella.
OTHER WORDS YOU MIGHT USE ARE   **friendly   helpful   kind
thoughtful   unselfish**
The opposite is selfish

construct *verb*
We constructed a model aeroplane.
OTHER VERBS YOU MIGHT USE ARE   **to assemble   to build   to make
to put together**

consume *verb*
The hungry dog consumed the food.
For other words, see **eat**

contain *verb*
1 What does this box contain?
ANOTHER VERB IS **to hold**
2 What does this stew contain?
A PHRASE IS **to consist of**

container *noun*
THINGS THAT CONTAIN WATER OR LIQUID ARE
**barrel   basin   bath   bin   bottle   bucket   can
cask   casserole   cauldron   churn   cup   dish
flask   glass   goblet   jar   jug   kettle   mug   pail
pan   pot   saucepan   tank   teapot   tub   tumbler
vase   watering can**

CONTAINERS FOR OTHER THINGS ARE
**bag   basket   box   carton   case   casket   chest
dustbin   envelope   handbag   haversack   holdall
knapsack   money box   pouch   purse   rucksack
sack   satchel   suitcase   tin   trunk   wallet**

contented *adjective*
The cat looks very contented.
OTHER WORDS YOU MIGHT USE ARE   **happy   relaxed   satisfied**

contest *noun*
For other words, see **competition** or **fight**

continent *noun*
THE SEVEN CONTINENTS ARE
**Africa   Antarctica   Asia   Australasia   Europe
North America   South America**

continual *adjective*
Continual chatter annoys the teacher.
OTHER WORDS YOU MIGHT USE ARE   **ceaseless   constant   continuous
endless   everlasting   incessant   non-stop   persistent
repeated   unending**

continue *verb*
1 How long will this rain continue?
OTHER VERBS YOU MIGHT USE ARE   **to go on   to keep on   to last
to persist**
2 Please continue with your work.
OTHER VERBS ARE   **to carry on   to keep going   to persevere**

continuous *adjective*
For other words, see **continual**

contrast *noun*
OTHER WORDS YOU MIGHT USE ARE   **comparison   difference**

contribute *verb*
I contributed £1 to the collection.
OTHER VERBS YOU MIGHT USE ARE   **to donate   to give**

control *verb*
She couldn't control the horse.
OTHER VERBS YOU MIGHT USE ARE   **to command   to deal with
to handle   to manage   to restrain**

convenient *adjective*
1 There's a convenient shop just round the corner.
OTHER WORDS YOU MIGHT USE ARE   **handy   useful**
2 It isn't convenient for Granny to visit us today.
OTHER WORDS ARE   **appropriate   easy   suitable**
The opposite is inconvenient

conversation *noun*
Jo and Sam had a long conversation about their holiday.
OTHER WORDS ARE   (*informal*) **chat   discussion   talk**

cook *noun*
The chief cook in a big restaurant or hotel is the **chef.**

cook *verb*
WAYS TO COOK THINGS ARE
**to bake   to barbecue   to boil   to fry   to grill
to poach   to roast   to steam   to stew   to toast**

cool *adjective*
1 a cool wind.
OTHER WORDS YOU MIGHT USE ARE   **chilly   cold**
The opposite is warm
2 Don't panic – keep cool!
ANOTHER WORD IS **calm**

copy *noun*
The painting was not genuine: it was a copy.
OTHER WORDS YOU MIGHT USE ARE   **counterfeit   fake   forgery**

copy *verb*
1 The budgie copies Jo's voice.
OTHER VERBS YOU MIGHT USE ARE   **to imitate   to impersonate**
2 Our teacher copied our poems so that everyone could read them.
OTHER VERBS ARE   **to duplicate   to photocopy   to reproduce**

corn *noun*
ANOTHER WORD IS **cereal**
KINDS OF CORN ARE   **barley   maize** or **sweet corn   oats   rye
wheat**

corner *noun*
1 a corner between two walls.
ANOTHER WORD IS **angle**
2 the corner of the road.
OTHER WORDS ARE   **bend   crossroads   junction**

correct *adjective*
Is that the correct time?
OTHER WORDS YOU MIGHT USE ARE **accurate** **exact** **precise** **right** **true**
The opposite is wrong

corridor *noun*
ANOTHER WORD IS **passage**

costly *adjective*
costly jewels.
OTHER WORDS YOU MIGHT USE ARE **expensive** **precious** **valuable**
The opposite is cheap

costume *noun*
costumes for a play.
OTHER WORDS YOU MIGHT USE ARE **clothes** **clothing** **disguise** **fancy dress**

cosy *adjective*
For other words, see **comfortable**

council *noun*
GROUPS OF PEOPLE WHO DISCUSS THINGS AND MAKE DECISIONS ARE
assembly **committee** **conference** **parliament**

count *verb*
Jo counted her pocket money.
OTHER VERBS YOU MIGHT USE ARE **to add up** **to calculate** **to total** **to work out**

country *noun*
1 I like to visit other countries.
OTHER WORDS YOU MIGHT USE ARE **land** **nation** **state**
2 There's some lovely country near here.
OTHER WORDS ARE **countryside** **landscape** **scenery**

courage *noun*
The firemen showed great courage.
OTHER WORDS ARE **bravery** **daring** **heroism**

cover *noun*

DIFFERENT KINDS OF COVER ARE

cap　coat　covering　envelope　folder　hat　lid
roof　top　wrapper

cover *verb*

DIFFERENT WAYS TO COVER THINGS ARE

to bury　to camouflage　to clothe　to conceal
to hide　to mask　to screen

crack *noun*
a crack in the wall.

OTHER WORDS YOU MIGHT USE ARE　break　crevice　gap　opening
split

crafty *adjective*
People say that the fox is a crafty animal.

OTHER WORDS YOU MIGHT USE ARE　clever　cunning　sly　wily

crash *noun*
1 a crash on the motorway.

OTHER WORDS YOU MIGHT USE ARE　accident　collision
For other words, see **hit**
2 There was a loud crash when Sam dropped the plates.
For other words, see **sound**

crazy *adjective*
1 The poor dog went crazy when she was stung by a wasp.

OTHER WORDS YOU MIGHT USE ARE　berserk　frantic　wild
2 It was a crazy idea to go for a walk in the rain.

OTHER WORDS ARE　absurd　mad　ridiculous　silly
stupid
The opposite is sensible

crease *verb*
Don't crease the paper.

OTHER VERBS YOU MIGHT USE ARE　to crumple　to fold　to wrinkle

create *verb*
Mum created a new kind of cake.
> OTHER VERBS YOU MIGHT USE ARE **to invent   to make   to produce
to think up**
For other words, see **make**

creator *noun*
> ANOTHER WORD IS **maker**
The creator of a new way to do something is an **inventor**.
The creator of a book is an **author** or **poet** or **writer**.
The creator of a piece of music is a **composer**.
The creator of a painting or a statue is an **artist**.

creature *noun*
For names of different creatures, see **animal** and **bird**

creep *verb*
For other ways to move, see **move**

crime *noun*
> OTHER WORDS YOU MIGHT USE ARE
> **dishonesty   offence   wrongdoing**
>
> SOME CRIMES ARE
> **arson   blackmail   burglary   forgery   hijacking
joy-riding   kidnapping   manslaughter   murder
poaching   robbery   shoplifting   smuggling   stealing**

criminal *noun*
> OTHER WORDS YOU MIGHT USE ARE
> (*informal*) **crook   culprit   delinquent   offender
wrongdoer**
>
> DIFFERENT KINDS OF CRIMINAL ARE
> **blackmailer   burglar   gangster   hijacker
kidnapper   mugger   murderer   poacher   robber
shoplifter   smuggler   terrorist   vandal**

crippled *adjective*
She has been crippled since her road accident.
OTHER WORDS YOU MIGHT USE ARE   **disabled   handicapped   lame**

crisp *adjective*
I like biscuits if they are crisp.
OTHER WORDS TO DESCRIBE THINGS WHICH BREAK EASILY ARE   **brittle   crackly
fragile**
The opposite is soft

crooked *adjective*
a crooked path.
OTHER WORDS YOU MIGHT USE ARE   **bent   twisting   winding   zigzag**
The opposite is straight

cross *adjective*
For other words, see **angry**

cross *verb*
Take care when you cross the road.
A PHRASE YOU MIGHT USE IS **to go across**
to cross something out
OTHER VERBS ARE   **to cancel   to delete   to erase**

crossroads *noun*
OTHER WORDS ARE   **intersection   junction**

crouch *verb*
We had to crouch to go through the small opening.
OTHER VERBS YOU MIGHT USE ARE   **to bend   to stoop**

crowd *noun*
a crowd of people.
OTHER WORDS YOU MIGHT USE ARE   **company   group   horde**
A noisy, violent crowd is a **mob**.
Another word for the crowd at a football match is **spectators**.
For other words, see **group**

cruel *adjective*
I think it's cruel to hunt foxes.
OTHER WORDS YOU MIGHT USE ARE   **bloodthirsty   brutal   cold-hearted
heartless   merciless   pitiless   ruthless   unkind   vicious**
The opposite is kind

crumb *noun*
a crumb of bread.

OTHER WORDS YOU MIGHT USE ARE   **bit   fragment   scrap**

crumple *verb*
Don't crumple the clothes I've just ironed!

OTHER VERBS YOU MIGHT USE ARE   **to crease   to crush   to fold
to wrinkle**

crush *verb*
I crushed my finger in the door.

OTHER VERBS YOU MIGHT USE ARE   **to smash   to squash   to squeeze**

cry *verb*
Baby cries when she's tired.

OTHER VERBS YOU MIGHT USE ARE   **to grizzle   to shed tears   to sob
to wail   to weep**

to cry out

OTHER VERBS ARE   **to call   to shout   to yell**

cuddle *verb*
Sam loves to cuddle the baby.

OTHER VERBS YOU MIGHT USE ARE   **to embrace   to hug**

cunning *adjective*
We had a cunning plan to trick our friends.

OTHER WORDS YOU MIGHT USE ARE   **clever   crafty   ingenious   skilful
sly   wily**

cup *noun*
THINGS YOU CAN DRINK FROM ARE
beaker   glass   goblet   mug   tumbler

cure *noun*
Have you got a cure for a cold?

OTHER WORDS YOU MIGHT USE ARE   **medicine   remedy   treatment**

cure *verb*
Will this medicine cure me?

ANOTHER VERB IS **to heal**

curious *adjective*
1 Jo is curious about what she will get for Christmas.
   OTHER WORDS YOU MIGHT USE ARE   **inquisitive   interested**
2 Sam thought there was a curious smell in the pantry.
   OTHER WORDS ARE   **funny   odd   peculiar   queer   strange
   unusual**

curl *verb*
I curl my hair round my fingers.
   OTHER VERBS YOU MIGHT USE ARE   **to bend   to coil   to loop   to twist
   to wind**

curse *verb*
He cursed when he hit his finger with the hammer.
   ANOTHER VERB IS **to swear**

curtain *noun*
   OTHER WORDS YOU MIGHT USE ARE   **blind   drape   screen**

curve *noun*
The driver slowed down as she approached the curve in the road.
   OTHER WORDS YOU MIGHT USE ARE   **bend   turn   twist**
   THINGS THAT MAKE THE SHAPE OF A CURVE ARE   **arch   bow   curl
   hook   horse shoe   loop   rainbow   semi-circle
   wave**

curved *adjective*
   OTHER WORDS YOU MIGHT USE ARE   **arched   bent   bowed
   concave   convex   crescent-shaped   curled   rounded
   twisted**

custom *noun*
It's a custom to give presents on a person's birthday.
   OTHER WORDS YOU MIGHT USE ARE   **convention   habit   tradition**

cut *noun*
a cut on your finger.
   OTHER WORDS ARE   **gash   injury   nick   wound**

cut *verb*

There are a lot of verbs which mean 'to cut'.
You **carve** meat, or an artist can **carve** a statue.
You can **chisel** wood.
You **chop** things with an axe.
You **clip** the hedge with shears.
You **mince** meat into tiny pieces.
You **mow** the lawn.
You can **prune** branches off a tree.
You **saw** wood.
You **shave** with a razor.
You **slice** bread with a breadknife.
You can **slit** open an envelope.
You **snip** things with scissors.
You **stab** with a dagger.
You **trim** your hair to make it tidy.
To **cut** prices is to lower or reduce them.

cutlery *noun*

ITEMS OF CUTLERY ARE

breadknife	**carving knife**	**dessertspoon**	**fork**
knife	**spoon**	**tablespoon**	**teaspoon**

cycle *noun*

A cycle with two wheels is a **bicycle** or **bike**.
A cycle with three wheels is a **tricycle**.
A cycle with an engine is a **moped** or **motorbike**.

Dd

damage *noun*
The storm caused a lot of damage.
OTHER WORDS YOU MIGHT USE ARE   **destruction**   **havoc**

damage *verb*
OTHER VERBS YOU MIGHT USE ARE   **to harm**   **to hurt**   **to injure**
to spoil
WAYS YOU CAN DAMAGE THINGS ARE   **to break**   **to chip**   **to dent**
to scratch   **to smash**   **to wound**

damp *adjective*
Don't sit on the damp grass.
OTHER WORDS YOU MIGHT USE ARE   **moist**   **rather wet**
The opposite is dry

dance *noun*
Sam and Jo went to a dance on St Valentine's Day.
A very formal dance is a **ball**.
A dance where music is played on records is a **disco**.
A dance you see in a theatre or on TV which tells a story is
a **ballet**.

dance *verb*
OTHER VERBS YOU MIGHT USE ARE   **to jump about**   **to leap about**
to prance   **to skip**

danger *noun*
1 The rocks are a danger to ships.
ANOTHER WORD IS **peril**
2 In summer there's a danger of getting sunburnt.
OTHER WORDS YOU MIGHT USE ARE   **chance**   **possibility**   **risk**
threat

dangerous *adjective*
1 a dangerous adventure.
   OTHER WORDS YOU MIGHT USE ARE **hazardous   perilous   risky   unsafe**
2 a dangerous criminal.
   OTHER WORDS ARE **desperate   treacherous   violent**
3 a dangerous poison.
   OTHER WORDS ARE **deadly   harmful   lethal**
   The opposite is safe

daring *adjective*
Sam thought Jo was very daring to climb up the big rock.
   OTHER WORDS YOU MIGHT USE ARE **adventurous   bold   brave   fearless**
   The opposite is cowardly

dark *adjective*
1 a dark night.
   OTHER WORDS YOU MIGHT USE ARE **black   starless**
2 a dark place.
   OTHER WORDS YOU MIGHT USE ARE **gloomy   shadowy   shady   sunless   unlit**
   The opposite is bright

darling *noun*
   OTHER WORDS YOU MIGHT USE ARE **beloved   dear   love   sweetheart**

dawdle *verb*
Don't dawdle: we're late!
   OTHER VERBS YOU MIGHT USE ARE **to be slow   to hang about   to linger**
   The opposite is hurry

day *noun*
THE DAYS OF THE WEEK ARE
   Monday   Tuesday   Wednesday   Thursday   Friday   Saturday   Sunday
For times of the day and special days of the year, see **time**

dead *adjective*
   OTHER WORDS YOU MIGHT USE ARE **deceased   killed   lifeless**
   The opposite is alive

deal *verb*
I dealt the cards.
> OTHER VERBS YOU MIGHT USE ARE   **to distribute**   **to give out**
> **to share out**

to deal with
Jo can deal with the problem.
> OTHER VERBS ARE   **to attend to**   **to handle**   **to manage**
> **to sort out**

dear *adjective*
1 a dear friend.
> OTHER WORDS YOU MIGHT USE ARE   **beloved**   **loved**   **precious**
2 Mum didn't buy any shoes because they were too dear.
> OTHER WORDS ARE   **costly**   **expensive**   (*informal*) **pricey**

decay *verb*
Meat smells nasty when it decays.
> OTHER VERBS YOU MIGHT USE ARE   **to decompose**   **to go bad**   **to rot**

deceitful *adjective*
We knew he was often deceitful, so we didn't believe him.
> OTHER WORDS YOU MIGHT USE ARE   **dishonest**   **insincere**   **lying**
> **untrustworthy**
The opposite is honest

deceive *verb*
He tried to deceive us, but we discovered the truth.
> OTHER VERBS YOU MIGHT USE ARE   **to cheat**   **to mislead**   **to swindle**
> **to trick**

decorate *verb*
1 I decorated the room with flowers.
> ANOTHER VERB YOU MIGHT USE IS **to adorn**
2 Dad decorated Sam's bedroom.
> OTHER VERBS ARE   **to paint**   **to paper**

decrease *verb*
1 They decreased my pocket money!
> OTHER VERBS YOU MIGHT USE ARE   **to cut**   **to reduce**
2 The number of children in Jo's class decreased this term.
> OTHER VERBS ARE   **to get smaller**   **to go down**   **to lessen**
The opposite is increase

deep *adjective*
deep water. a deep hole.
The opposite is shallow

defeat *verb*
Our team defeated them 8–0.
OTHER VERBS YOU MIGHT USE ARE   **to beat   to conquer**
(*informal*) **to thrash**

defend *verb*
The mother bird defended her babies.
OTHER VERBS YOU MIGHT USE ARE   **to guard   to keep safe
to protect**
The opposite is attack

definite *adjective*
1 Is it definite that I can go?
OTHER WORDS YOU MIGHT USE ARE   **certain   positive   settled**
2 He gave a definite signal.
OTHER WORDS ARE   **clear   noticeable   obvious   sure**
The opposite is vague

delay *verb*
1 A traffic jam delayed us.
OTHER VERBS YOU MIGHT USE ARE   **to hinder   to hold up   to slow down**
2 They had to delay the start of the match.
OTHER VERBS ARE   **to postpone   to put off**
3 Don't delay - do it now!
OTHER VERBS ARE   **to hang about   to hesitate   to wait**

deliberate *adjective*
a deliberate mistake.
OTHER WORDS YOU MIGHT USE ARE   **intentional   planned**
The opposite is accidental

delicate *adjective*
1 delicate material.
OTHER WORDS YOU MIGHT USE ARE   **dainty   fine   flimsy   fragile
soft**
2 a delicate child.
OTHER WORDS ARE   **sickly   unhealthy   weak**
The opposite is strong

delicious *adjective*
a delicious dinner.
OTHER WORDS YOU MIGHT USE ARE   **appetizing   tasty**
For other words, see **taste**

delighted *adjective*
I was delighted with your gift.
ANOTHER WORD IS **pleased**
For other words, see **happy**

deliver *verb*
The postman delivers letters.
PHRASES YOU MIGHT USE ARE   **to hand over   to take round**

demand *verb*
When the new TV didn't work, Mum demanded to have her money back.
OTHER VERBS YOU MIGHT USE ARE   **to ask   to beg   to request**

demolish *verb*
They had to demolish some houses when they built the new road.
OTHER VERBS YOU MIGHT USE ARE   **to destroy   to dismantle
to knock down**

demonstration *noun*
1 We gave a PE demonstration.
OTHER WORDS YOU MIGHT USE ARE   **display   exhibition   show**
2 There was a big demonstration against the new motorway.
OTHER WORDS YOU MIGHT USE ARE   *(informal)* **demo   march   protest**

dense *adjective*
1 dense fog. a dense crowd.
ANOTHER WORD IS **thick**
2 a dense pupil.
For other words, see **stupid**

deny *verb*
He denied that he had cheated.
PHRASES YOU MIGHT USE ARE   **to refuse to agree   to reject the idea**

depart *verb*
She departed without saying where she was going.
OTHER VERBS YOU MIGHT USE ARE   **to go away   to go out   to leave
to set off   to set out**

depend *verb*
We can depend on Jo to do her best.
> OTHER VERBS YOU MIGHT USE ARE   **to count on**   **to rely on**   **to trust**

depress *verb*
His dog's death depressed him.
> OTHER VERBS YOU MIGHT USE ARE   **to sadden**   **to upset**

depressed, depressing *adjectives*, see **sad**

describe *verb*
Can you describe what happened?
> OTHER VERBS YOU MIGHT USE ARE   **to explain**   **to tell**

deserted *adjective*
a deserted house.
> OTHER WORDS YOU MIGHT USE ARE   **abandoned**   **empty**   **forsaken**

design *verb*
When we moved into our new house, we helped Mum design the garden.
> OTHER VERBS YOU MIGHT USE ARE   **to draw**   **to plan**   **to sketch**

desire *verb*
The fairy promised he could have what he desired.
> OTHER VERBS YOU MIGHT USE ARE   **to fancy**   **to long for**   **to want**
> **to wish for**

desperate *adjective*
The situation was desperate.
> OTHER WORDS YOU MIGHT USE ARE   **hopeless**   **serious**

destroy *verb*
1   The explosion destroyed the building.
> OTHER VERBS YOU MIGHT USE ARE   **to demolish**   **to knock down**   **to ruin**
> **to wreck**

2   Dad used a special powder to destroy the ants in the garden.
> OTHER VERBS YOU MIGHT USE ARE   **to exterminate**   (*informal*) **to finish off**
> **to kill**   **to wipe out**

detest *verb*
Jo detests the smell of onions.
> OTHER VERBS YOU MIGHT USE ARE   **to dislike**   **to hate**   **to loathe**

The opposite is love

develop *verb*
1 Jo's swimming is developing.
OTHER VERBS YOU MIGHT USE ARE   **to get better   to improve to progress**
2 You must water plants if you want them to develop.
OTHER VERBS YOU MIGHT USE ARE   **to get bigger   to grow**

device *noun*
Our new tin-opener is a clever device.
OTHER WORDS YOU MIGHT USE ARE   **contraption   gadget   implement instrument   tool**

diagram *noun*
We drew a diagram to show how the machine worked.
OTHER WORDS YOU MIGHT USE ARE   **chart   graph   plan   sketch**

die *verb*
OTHER VERBS YOU MIGHT USE ARE   **to pass away   to perish**

difference *noun*
1 Will it make any difference to our plans if it rains?
OTHER WORDS YOU MIGHT USE ARE   **alteration   change**
2 Can you see any difference between these two colours?
OTHER WORDS YOU MIGHT USE ARE   **contrast   distinction**

different *adjective*
1 The sweets are different flavours.
OTHER WORDS YOU MIGHT USE ARE   **assorted   mixed   various**
2 Jo and Sam often have different ideas about things.
OTHER WORDS YOU MIGHT USE ARE   **contradictory   contrasting dissimilar   opposite**
The opposite is the same

difficult *adjective*
a difficult problem.
OTHER WORDS YOU MIGHT USE ARE   **complex   complicated   hard tough**   (*informal*) **tricky**
The opposite is easy

difficulty *noun*
The explorers met many difficulties before they reached home.
OTHER WORDS YOU MIGHT USE ARE   **complication   hardship   obstacle problem   snag   trouble**

dig *verb*
OTHER VERBS ARE **to burrow** **to excavate** **to hollow out** **to scoop** **to tunnel**

dignified *adjective*
Please behave in a dignified way.
OTHER WORDS YOU MIGHT USE ARE **calm** **formal** **proper** **serious** **sober** **solemn** **stately**

dilute *verb*
You dilute squash with water.
PHRASES YOU MIGHT USE ARE **to make weaker** **to water down**

dim *adjective*
We saw a dim outline in the mist.
OTHER WORDS YOU MIGHT USE ARE **dark** **faint** **gloomy** **indistinct** **shadowy**
The opposite is clear

din *noun*
OTHER WORDS YOU MIGHT USE ARE **noise** (*informal*) **racket** (*informal*) **row** **uproar**
For other words, see **sound**

direct *verb*
1 Please direct me to the bus stop.
   OTHER VERBS YOU MIGHT USE ARE **to guide** **to point** **to show**
2 The officer directed the soldiers to stand in a line.
   OTHER VERBS YOU MIGHT USE ARE **to command** **to instruct** **to order** **to tell**

dirt *noun*
OTHER WORDS YOU MIGHT USE ARE **dust** **filth** **grime** **muck** **mud** **pollution**

dirty *adjective*
OTHER WORDS YOU MIGHT USE ARE **dusty** **filthy** **foul** **grimy** **grubby** **mucky** **muddy** **polluted** **soiled** **stained**
The opposite is clean

disagree *verb*
OTHER VERBS YOU MIGHT USE ARE **to argue** **to differ** **to quarrel**
The opposite is agree

disappear *verb*
OTHER VERBS YOU MIGHT USE ARE   **to fade**   **to melt away**   **to vanish**
The opposite is appear

disapprove *verb*
We disapprove of cruelty to pets.
OTHER VERBS YOU MIGHT USE ARE   **to condemn**   **to criticize**
to dislike

disaster *noun*
Many people died in the disaster.
OTHER WORDS YOU MIGHT USE ARE   **accident**   **calamity**
catastrophe

discipline *noun*
Our teacher likes to have discipline in the classroom.
OTHER WORDS YOU MIGHT USE ARE   **control**   **obedience**   **order**

discover *verb*
1 I discovered a lot about dinosaurs in the library.
OTHER VERBS YOU MIGHT USE ARE   **to find**   **to learn**   **to research**
to track down
2 Dad discovered an old coin in the garden.
OTHER VERBS YOU MIGHT USE ARE   **to come across**   **to uncover**
to unearth
The opposite is hide

discuss *verb*
Let's discuss the problem.
OTHER VERBS YOU MIGHT USE ARE   **to argue about**   **to consider**
to talk about

disease *noun*
OTHER WORDS YOU MIGHT USE ARE   **ailment**   **illness**
sickness
For other words, see **health**

disguise *verb*
1 Dad disguised himself as Father Christmas.
PHRASES ARE   **to dress up as**   **to pretend to be**
2 We disguised our hiding-place.
OTHER VERBS ARE   **to camouflage**   **to conceal**   **to cover up**
to hide

disgust *verb*
The dirty kitchen disgusted us.
OTHER VERBS YOU MIGHT USE ARE   **to offend   to revolt   to sicken**
disgusting *adjective*, see **nasty**

dishonest *adjective*
1 It is dishonest to tell lies.
OTHER WORDS YOU MIGHT USE ARE   **deceitful   insincere**
2 It is dishonest to steal.
OTHER WORDS YOU MIGHT USE ARE   **cheating   criminal   unfair**
The opposite is honest

dislike *verb*
OTHER VERBS YOU MIGHT USE ARE   **to detest   to loathe   to hate**
The opposite is like

dismiss *verb*
1 The teacher dismissed the class.
OTHER VERBS YOU MIGHT USE ARE   **to let go   to release   to send away**
2 The boss dismissed her from her job.
OTHER VERBS ARE   **to fire   to sack**

disorder *noun*
Jo and Sam cleared up the disorder after the party.
OTHER WORDS YOU MIGHT USE ARE   **chaos   confusion   mess   muddle**

display *noun*
We put up a display of our work.
OTHER WORDS YOU MIGHT USE ARE   **exhibition   presentation   show**

display *verb*
We display our work when parents come to school.
OTHER VERBS YOU MIGHT USE ARE   **to exhibit   to present   to show**

distance *noun*
What's the distance between the goal posts?
OTHER WORDS YOU MIGHT USE ARE   **gap   space**
For more words, see **measurement**

distant *adjective*
distant places.
OTHER WORDS YOU MIGHT USE ARE   **far-away   remote**
The opposite is near

distinct *adjective*
1 I heard a distinct echo.
   OTHER WORDS YOU MIGHT USE ARE   **audible   clear**
2 The footprints in the mud were quite distinct.
   OTHER WORDS ARE   **definite   obvious   plain   visible**
3 The twins wear distinct colours.
   OTHER WORDS ARE   **contrasting   different**

distressed *adjective*
The mother blackbird was very distressed when she saw the cat.
   OTHER WORDS YOU MIGHT USE ARE   **anxious   frightened   upset
   worried**

distribute *verb*
Jo distributed the pencils and paper.
   OTHER VERBS YOU MIGHT USE ARE   **to deal out   to give out   to hand out
   to share out**

district *noun*
We live in a hilly district.
   OTHER WORDS YOU MIGHT USE ARE   **area   locality   region   zone**

disturb *verb*
1 Don't disturb me while I'm working.
   OTHER VERBS YOU MIGHT USE ARE   **to bother   to interrupt   to trouble
   to worry**
2 A fox disturbed the chickens.
   OTHER VERBS ARE   **to alarm   to excite   to frighten   to upset**

dive *verb*
We watched the sea birds diving into the water.
   OTHER VERBS YOU MIGHT USE ARE   **to drop   to plunge   to swoop**

divide *verb*
1 Divide the sweets between you.
   OTHER VERBS YOU MIGHT USE ARE   **to deal out   to distribute   to share**
2 At the next junction the road divides.
   OTHER VERBS YOU MIGHT USE ARE   **to branch   to fork   to separate
   to split**

dizzy *adjective*
I feel dizzy if I stand up quickly.
   OTHER WORDS YOU MIGHT USE ARE   **faint   giddy   unsteady**

do *verb*

THIS VERB HAS MANY USES. HERE ARE SOME OF THE WAYS YOU CAN USE IT, AND
SOME OTHER VERBS YOU COULD CHOOSE.

1 I have done my work.
   to carry out   to complete   to finish   to perform
2 Sam is going to do the dinner.
   **to attend to   to deal with   to handle   to make
   to manage   to prepare**
3 Will four big potatoes do?
   to be enough   to be sufficient   to be suitable

doctor *noun*

For other people who look after our health, see **health**

dog *noun*

A female dog is a **bitch**.
A young dog is a **pup** or **puppy**.
VARIOUS BREEDS OF DOG ARE

Alsatian	**bloodhound**	**bulldog**	**collie**
dachshund	**Dalmatian**	**greyhound**	**Labrador**
Pekingese	**poodle**	**retriever**	**Rotweiller**
sheepdog	**spaniel**	**terrier**	**whippet**

A dog of mixed breed is a **mongrel**.

dot *noun*

OTHER WORDS YOU MIGHT USE ARE   **mark   point   speck   spot**

doubt *noun*

There's some doubt about whether Sam is well enough to play.
OTHER WORDS YOU MIGHT USE ARE   **anxiety   hesitation   question
uncertainty   worry**

doubtful *adjective*

The rain made us doubtful about our picnic.
OTHER WORDS YOU MIGHT USE ARE   **uncertain   unsure
worried**
The opposite is certain

drag *verb*
The tractor was dragging a load of logs.
OTHER VERBS YOU MIGHT USE ARE   **to draw   to haul   to pull   to tow
to tug**

drama *noun*
1 Drama is one of Sam's favourite lessons.
OTHER WORDS YOU MIGHT USE ARE   **acting   improvisation   plays**
2 We had some drama today when the fire engines came.
ANOTHER WORD IS **excitement**

draw *verb*
1 Jo drew a picture with a pencil.
ANOTHER VERB IS **to sketch**
2 The pony was drawing a cart.
OTHER VERBS YOU MIGHT USE ARE   **to haul   to pull   to tow**
3 The match drew a large crowd.
OTHER VERBS ARE   **to attract   to bring in   to pull in**
4 We drew 1–1 on Saturday.
OTHER VERBS ARE   **to be equal   to tie**

dreadful *adjective*
a dreadful storm.
OTHER WORDS YOU MIGHT USE ARE   **alarming   awful   fearful
frightening   horrifying   terrible**
The opposite is wonderful

dream *noun*
A nasty dream is a **nightmare**.
SOMETHING LIKE A DREAM WHICH YOU HAVE WHILE YOU ARE AWAKE IS A
daydream   fantasy   illusion   vision

dream *verb*
OTHER VERBS YOU MIGHT USE ARE   **to fancy   to imagine**

dress *noun*
A DRESS FOR A SPECIAL OCCASION IS   **evening dress   gown
party dress**
For things you wear, see **clothes**

dribble *verb*

When I cut my knee, blood dribbled down my leg.

OTHER VERBS YOU MIGHT USE ARE **to drip**   **to flow**   **to ooze**   **to run**
to trickle

drink *verb*

To drink greedily is **to gulp** or **to guzzle** or **to swig**.
To drink a tiny bit at a time is **to sip**.
To drink with your tongue like a cat is **to lap**.

DIFFERENT COLD DRINKS ARE
juice   **lemonade**   **milk**   **mineral water**   **orangeade**
squash   **water**

SOME ALCOHOLIC DRINKS ARE
beer   **champagne**   **cider**   **lager**   **whisky**   **wine**

SOME HOT DRINKS ARE
cocoa   **coffee**   **tea**

drip *verb*

Don't let paint drip on to the carpet!

OTHER VERBS YOU MIGHT USE ARE **to dribble**   **to drop**   **to leak**
to trickle

drive *verb*

1 Is it easy to drive a car?

OTHER VERBS YOU MIGHT USE ARE **to control**   **to steer**

2 I drove the cow into the field.

OTHER VERBS ARE **to force**   **to push**   **to urge**

droop *verb*

The weather was so dry that the flowers began to droop.

OTHER VERBS YOU MIGHT USE ARE **to flop**   **to go limp**   **to sag**
to wilt

drop *noun*

drops of water.

OTHER WORDS YOU MIGHT USE ARE **bead**   **drip**   **tear**

drop *verb*

1 A lorry dropped its load on the motorway.

OTHER VERBS YOU MIGHT USE ARE **to dump**   **to shed**

2 The waterfall drops from a high cliff.
OTHER VERBS ARE   **to cascade**   **to fall**   **to plunge**
3 The temperature drops at night.
OTHER VERBS ARE   **to decrease**   **to fall**   **to go down**

dry *adjective*
1 Is the washing dry?
The opposite is wet
2 I feel dry: can I have a drink?
OTHER WORDS YOU MIGHT USE ARE   **parched**   **thirsty**

duck *noun*
A male duck is a **drake**.
A young duck is a **duckling**.

dull *adjective*
1 dull colours.
OTHER WORDS YOU MIGHT USE ARE   **dingy**   **drab**   **gloomy**
2 a dull day.
OTHER WORDS ARE   **cloudy**   **grey**   **overcast**
3 a dull pupil.
OTHER WORDS ARE   **dim**   **slow**   **stupid**
The opposite is bright
4 a dull film.
OTHER WORDS ARE   **boring**   **uninteresting**
The opposite is interesting

dumb *adjective*
She was dumb with amazement.
OTHER WORDS YOU MIGHT USE ARE   **mute**   **silent**   **speechless**

dump *verb*
1 I hate people who dump rubbish by the side of the road.
OTHER VERBS YOU MIGHT USE ARE   **to abandon**   **to discard**
   to throw away
2 I dumped my things on the table.
OTHER VERBS ARE   **to drop**   **to leave**   **to unload**

duty *noun*
1 If you see a crime, it's your duty to tell the police.
ANOTHER WORD IS **responsibility**
2 We can go to play when we've finished our duties.
OTHER WORDS ARE   **job**   **task**

Ee

eager *adjective*
We were eager to start the game.
>OTHER WORDS YOU MIGHT USE ARE **enthusiastic   impatient   keen**

earn *verb*
How much does Sam earn when he washes the car?
>OTHER VERBS YOU MIGHT USE ARE **to deserve   to get   to make**

earth *noun*
1 We live on the planet Earth.
>OTHER WORDS YOU MIGHT USE ARE **the globe   the world**
2 Plants grow in the earth.
>OTHER WORDS ARE **ground   land   soil**

easy *adjective*
1 Jo finished her work quickly because the sums were easy.
>OTHER WORDS YOU MIGHT USE ARE **simple   straightforward uncomplicated**
The opposite is **difficult**
2 The cat has an easy life.
>OTHER WORDS ARE **carefree   comfortable   relaxing   restful**

eat *verb*
The dog ate our dinner!
>OTHER VERBS YOU MIGHT USE ARE
>**to consume   to feed on   to swallow   to tuck into**
>DIFFERENT WAYS TO EAT THINGS ARE
>**to bite   to chew   to munch**
>IF YOU EAT FOOD GREEDILY, OTHER VERBS ARE
>**to bolt   to devour   to gobble   to gulp   to guzzle**

If you eat a tiny bit at a time, you **nibble**.
A cow **grazes** on grass.
A chicken **pecks** at its food.
A dog will **gnaw** at a bone.

edge *noun*

THIS WORD HAS MANY USES. HERE ARE SOME OF THE WAYS YOU CAN USE IT, AND SOME OTHER WORDS YOU CAN CHOOSE

1 The edge of a picture.
   border   **frame**
2 The edge of a cricket field.
   boundary   **perimeter**
3 The edge of the road.
   side   **verge**
4 The edge of a curtain.
   frill   **fringe**   **hem**
5 The edge of a cup.
   brim   **rim**
6 The edge of a circle.
   circumference

The space down the edge of a piece of paper you have written on is the **margin**.

educate *verb*

Our parents and teachers educate us.

OTHER VERBS YOU MIGHT USE ARE
   to bring up   **to instruct**   **to teach**   **to train**

PLACES WHERE PEOPLE GO TO BE EDUCATED ARE
   college   **playgroup**   **school**   **university**

DIFFERENT KINDS OF SCHOOL ARE
   boarding school   **comprehensive school**   **infant school**
   junior school   **kindergarten**   **nursery school**
   playgroup   **primary school**   **secondary school**

effort *noun*

1 You deserve a rest after all that effort.
   OTHER WORDS YOU MIGHT USE ARE   **labour**   **toil**   **trouble**   **work**
2 I made an effort to be good.
   OTHER WORDS ARE   **attempt**   **try**

elect *verb*

We elected Jo as captain of the rounders team.

OTHER VERBS YOU MIGHT USE ARE   **to choose   to pick   to select
to vote for**

election *noun*

We had an election to choose the captain of the team.

OTHER WORDS YOU MIGHT USE ARE   **ballot   vote**

embarrassed *adjective*

1 Jo was embarrassed when she forgot her words in the play.

OTHER WORDS YOU MIGHT USE ARE   **ashamed   upset**

2 He was too embarrassed to ask for a second helping.

ANOTHER WORD IS **shy**

emergency *noun*

We knew there was an emergency when we heard the fire engine.

ANOTHER WORD IS **crisis**

empty *adjective*

1 an empty cup.

ANOTHER WORD IS **unfilled**

The opposite is full

2 an empty space.

ANOTHER WORD IS **hollow**

The opposite is solid

3 an empty house.

OTHER WORDS YOU MIGHT USE ARE   **deserted   uninhabited
unoccupied   vacant**

The opposite is occupied

encourage *verb*

We shouted to encourage our team.

OTHER VERBS YOU MIGHT USE ARE   **to support . to urge on**

end *noun*

1 We didn't stay for the end of the film.

OTHER WORDS YOU MIGHT USE ARE   **conclusion   ending   finish**

2 We walked to the end of the train.

OTHER WORDS ARE   **back   rear   tail**

3 He poked me with the end of a stick.

OTHER WORDS ARE   **point   tip**

end *verb*
1 We waited for the storm to end.
OTHER VERBS YOU MIGHT USE ARE   **to cease   to finish   to stop**
The opposite is begin
2 It would be wonderful if we could end all wars.
ANOTHER VERB IS **to abolish**

enemy *noun*
OTHER WORDS YOU MIGHT USE ARE   **attacker   foe   opponent**
Opposites are ally friend

energetic *adjective*
Mum says that we are so energetic that she can't keep up with us.
OTHER WORDS YOU MIGHT USE ARE   **active   enthusiastic   lively
vigorous**
The opposite is lazy

energy *noun*
You use up a lot of energy playing rounders.
OTHER WORDS YOU MIGHT USE ARE   **power   strength**

engine *noun*
Cars, ships, and aeroplanes have engines to keep them going.
DIFFERENT KINDS OF ENGINE ARE
**diesel engine   electric motor   jet engine
petrol engine   steam engine**
A railway engine is a **locomotive.**

enjoy *verb*
The things Jo enjoys most are ice-skating and reading.
OTHER VERBS YOU MIGHT USE ARE   **to appreciate   to like   to love**
The opposite is dislike

enough *adjective*
Have you had enough food?
OTHER WORDS YOU MIGHT USE ARE   **adequate   sufficient**

enter *verb*
Don't enter the classroom until the teacher tells you to.
PHRASES YOU MIGHT USE ARE   **to come in   to go in**

entertain *verb*

A conjuror entertained us at Jo's party.

ANOTHER VERB IS **to amuse**

entertainment *noun*

OTHER WORDS YOU MIGHT USE ARE

amusement   enjoyment   fun

ENTERTAINMENTS YOU GO OUT TO ENJOY INCLUDE

**ballet   cinema   circus   concert   dance   disco
drama   fair   opera   pantomime   play   waxworks
zoo**

ENTERTAINMENTS YOU ENJOY AT HOME INCLUDE

computer games   music   radio   television   video

PEOPLE WHO ENTERTAIN US IN THE THEATRE OR ON RADIO AND TV ARE

**actor   actress   broadcaster   comedian   comic
conjuror   dancer   DJ   magician   musician   singer
ventriloquist**

PEOPLE WHO ENTERTAIN US IN A CIRCUS ARE

acrobat   clown   juggler   lion tamer   trapeze artist

enthusiastic *adjective*

Sam is an enthusiastic member of the football team.

OTHER WORDS YOU MIGHT USE ARE   **eager   interested   keen**

entrance *noun*

Pay your money at the entrance.

OTHER WORDS YOU MIGHT USE ARE   **door   entry   way in**

The opposite is exit

envious *adjective*

Jo was a bit envious when she saw what Sam got for his birthday.

ANOTHER WORD IS **jealous**

equal *adjective*

At half time the scores were equal.

OTHER WORDS YOU MIGHT USE ARE   **even   identical   level   the same**

The opposite is different

equipment *noun*
We keep the games equipment in a shed in the playground.
OTHER WORDS YOU MIGHT USE ARE   **apparatus**   (*informal*) **gear**   **tackle**

error *noun*
Our teacher corrects the errors in our work.
OTHER WORDS YOU MIGHT USE ARE   **fault**   **mistake**   (*informal*) **slip**

escape *verb*
The cat chased the mouse, but it escaped.
PHRASES YOU MIGHT USE ARE   **to get away**   **to run away**

essential *adjective*
It's essential to start early if you want to avoid traffic jams.
OTHER WORDS YOU MIGHT USE ARE   **important**   **necessary**   **vital**
The opposite is unnecessary

estimate *verb*
Jo estimated how many sandwiches everyone would eat at her party.
OTHER VERBS YOU MIGHT USE ARE   **to calculate**   **to guess**   **to work out**

even *adjective*
1 You need an even field for playing rounders.
OTHER WORDS ARE   **flat**   **level**   **smooth**
The opposite is bumpy
2 At half time the scores were even.
OTHER WORDS YOU MIGHT USE ARE   **equal**   **level**   **the same**
The opposite is different
3 Even numbers are numbers you can divide by two, such as 2, 8, 20.
The opposite is odd

evening *noun*
VARIOUS TIMES OF THE EVENING ARE   **dusk**   **sunset**   **twilight**

event *noun*
The fathers' sack race was the funniest event on sports day.
OTHER WORDS YOU MIGHT USE ARE   **happening**   **incident**   **occasion**

evidence *noun*
The police had evidence that he was guilty.
OTHER WORDS YOU MIGHT USE ARE   **information**   **proof**

·evil *adjective*
Murder is an evil thing.
OTHER WORDS YOU MIGHT USE ARE   **hateful   immoral   sinful   wicked
wrong**
The opposite is good

exact *adjective*
Have you got the exact time?
OTHER WORDS YOU MIGHT USE ARE   **accurate   correct   precise   right
true**

examination *noun*
1 Sam had a music examination at the end of term.
OTHER WORDS YOU MIGHT USE ARE   (*informal*) **exam   test**
2 When I was ill, I went to the doctor's for an examination.
ANOTHER WORD IS (*informal*) **check-up**

examine *verb*
1 We examined the strange insect carefully.
OTHER VERBS YOU MIGHT USE ARE   **to inspect   to study**
2 The police examined the suspect.
OTHER VERBS ARE   **to interrogate   to question**

example *noun*
When the parents come to school, we display examples of our work.
OTHER WORDS YOU MIGHT USE ARE   **sample   specimen**

excellent *adjective*
OTHER WORDS YOU MIGHT USE ARE   (*informal*) **brilliant**
(*informal*) **fantastic   marvellous   outstanding**
(*informal*) **tremendous   wonderful**
For other words, see good

exchange *verb*
Sam exchanged his old bike for some roller skates.
OTHER VERBS YOU MIGHT USE ARE   **to substitute**   (*informal*) **to swop
to trade in**

excite *verb*
The amazing goal excited the crowd.
OTHER VERBS YOU MIGHT USE ARE   **to arouse   to provoke   to rouse
to stimulate   to stir up   to thrill**

excited *adjective*
We were excited on the morning before we had the party.
OTHER WORDS YOU MIGHT USE ARE   **boisterous   lively   worked up**

excitement *noun*
The game was full of excitement.
OTHER WORDS YOU MIGHT USE ARE   **action   drama   suspense
thrills**

exclaim *verb*
OTHER VERBS YOU MIGHT USE ARE   **to call out   to shout   to yell**

excuse *verb*
1 Please excuse our dog's bad behaviour.
OTHER VERBS YOU MIGHT USE ARE   **to forgive   to overlook   to pardon**
2 I was excused from swimming because I had a cold.
A PHRASE IS **to let off**

exhausted *adjective*
I was exhausted after my long walk.
OTHER WORDS YOU MIGHT USE ARE   **tired   weary   worn out**

exhibition *noun*
We had an exhibition of our work.
OTHER WORDS YOU MIGHT USE ARE   **display   show**

exist *verb*
Plants can't exist without water.
OTHER VERBS YOU MIGHT USE ARE   **to keep going   to live   to survive**

exit *noun*
OTHER WORDS YOU MIGHT USE ARE   **door   way out**
The opposite is entrance

expect *verb*
I expect it will rain later.
ANOTHER VERB IS **to   forecast**

expedition *noun*
On Saturday, Mum and Jo went on an expedition to the shops.
OTHER WORDS YOU MIGHT USE ARE   **journey   outing   trip**

expel *verb*
The dog was expelled from the shop because he was a nuisance.
OTHER VERBS YOU MIGHT USE ARE   (*informal*) **to kick out   to throw out**
TO EXPEL SOMEONE FROM A COUNTRY   **to banish   to deport   to exile**
TO EXPEL SOMEONE FROM THEIR HOME **to evict**

expensive *adjective*
Mum didn't buy me any new jeans because they were too expensive.
OTHER WORDS YOU MIGHT USE ARE   **costly   dear**   (*informal*) **pricey**
The opposite is cheap

explain *verb*
Mum explained how computers work.
OTHER VERBS YOU MIGHT USE ARE   **to make clear   to show**

explode *verb*
The firework exploded.
OTHER VERBS YOU MIGHT USE ARE   **to blow up   to burst   to go off**

explore *verb*
Sam went off with his friends to explore the caves.
OTHER VERBS YOU MIGHT USE ARE   **to investigate   to look round**

expression *noun*
I noticed Jo's unhappy expression.
OTHER WORDS YOU MIGHT USE ARE   **face   look**
DIFFERENT EXPRESSIONS YOU SEE ON PEOPLE'S FACES ARE
**frown   glare   grin   laugh   scowl   smile   sneer
yawn**

extra *adjective*
Do you want some extra milk in your tea?
OTHER WORDS YOU MIGHT USE ARE   **additional   more**

extraordinary *adjective*
I didn't believe his extraordinary story about a space ship.
OTHER WORDS YOU MIGHT USE ARE   **amazing   incredible   odd
peculiar   queer   remarkable   strange   unbelievable
uncommon   unusual**
The opposite is ordinary

extravagant *adjective*
Mum says it's extravagant to cook more food than you can eat.
OTHER WORDS YOU MIGHT USE ARE   **expensive   wasteful**

extreme *adjective*
1 extreme cold.
OTHER WORDS YOU MIGHT USE ARE   **exceptional   great   intense
severe**
2 the extreme corner of the playground.
OTHER WORDS ARE   **farthest   furthest**

Ff

face *noun*
1 He made a funny face.
For other words, see **expression**
2 Each face of a dice has a different number of dots.
OTHER WORDS YOU MIGHT USE ARE   **side   surface**

facts *noun*
You find lots of facts in an encyclopaedia.
OTHER WORDS YOU MIGHT USE ARE   **data   evidence   information**

fade *verb*
1 The sun faded the curtains.
OTHER VERBS YOU MIGHT USE ARE   **to bleach   to discolour   to whiten**
2 In the evening, the light fades and the stars begin to shine.
OTHER VERBS ARE   **to disappear   to dwindle   to melt away**

fail *verb*
1 He failed to stop at the red light.
OTHER VERBS YOU MIGHT USE ARE   **to neglect   to omit**
2 He failed his driving test.
A PHRASE IS **to be unsuccessful**
The opposite is pass

faint *adjective*

1 I saw a faint shape in the mist.

> OTHER WORDS YOU MIGHT USE ARE **blurred   dim   hazy   misty   pale   unclear**

The opposite is clear

2 We heard faint cries for help.

> OTHER WORDS ARE **distant   low   muffled   weak**

The opposite is loud

3 Sam felt faint because he stood up too quickly.

> OTHER WORDS ARE **dizzy   giddy   unsteady**

faint *verb*

It was so hot that he fainted.

> OTHER VERBS ARE **to become unconscious   to collapse**

fair *adjective*

1 fair hair.

> OTHER WORDS YOU MIGHT USE ARE **blond   light   pale**

The opposite is dark

2 It's not fair if she gets more than me.

> OTHER WORDS ARE **just   proper   right**

The opposite is unfair

3 Was the referee fair?

> OTHER WORDS YOU MIGHT USE ARE **honest   unbiased**

The opposite is biased

4 I had a fair chance of winning.

> OTHER WORDS ARE **moderate   reasonable**

faithful *adjective*

The dog is his faithful companion.

> OTHER WORDS YOU MIGHT USE ARE **devoted   loyal   reliable   trustworthy**

The opposite is treacherous

fall *verb*

1 The dog was so excited that he fell in the river.

> OTHER VERBS YOU MIGHT USE ARE **to drop   to plunge   to slip   to topple   to tumble**

2 The burning tower fell to the ground.

> OTHER VERBS YOU MIGHT USE ARE **to collapse   to crash**

3 The temperature falls at night.

> OTHER VERBS ARE **to decrease   to go down**

The opposite is rise

false *adjective*
1 He gave us false information.
   OTHER WORDS YOU MIGHT USE ARE   **inaccurate**   **incorrect**   **made-up**
   misleading   **wrong**
The opposite is correct
2 Father Christmas wore a false beard.
   OTHER WORDS ARE   **artificial**   **fake**   **imitation**
The opposite is real

familiar *adjective*
I like to be back in my familiar surroundings after a holiday.
   OTHER WORDS YOU MIGHT USE ARE   **normal**   **regular**   **usual**
   well-known
The opposite is strange

family *noun*
The members of your family are your **relations** or **relatives**.
   MEMBERS OF YOUR IMMEDIATE FAMILY ARE
   brother   **daughter**   **father**   **husband**   **mother**
   sister   **son**   **stepfather**   **stepmother**   **wife**

   OTHER RELATIONS YOU MIGHT HAVE ARE
   aunt   **cousins**   **grandfather**   **grandmother**   **nephew**
   niece   **uncle**

Members of your family who lived in the past are your **ancestors**.

famous *adjective*
a famous TV actor.
   ANOTHER WORD IS **well-known**

fan *noun*
Sam is a fan of our football team.
   OTHER WORDS YOU MIGHT USE ARE   **admirer**   **follower**   **supporter**

fancy *verb*
1 What do you fancy to eat?
   OTHER VERBS YOU MIGHT USE ARE   **to feel like**   **to long for**   **to want**
   to wish for
2 I fancied I saw a ghost.
   OTHER VERBS ARE   **to dream**   **to imagine**   **to think**

fantastic *adjective*

1 We heard a fantastic story about dragons and wizards.
OTHER WORDS YOU MIGHT USE ARE **amazing extraordinary incredible strange weird**
2 (*informal*) We had a fantastic time at the party.
For other words, see **good**

farm *noun*

Another word for a small farm is **smallholding**.
A word for a small farm in Scotland is a **croft**.
A word for a cattle farm in North America is a **ranch**.

BUILDINGS YOU SEE ON A FARM ARE
barn cow-shed farmhouse granary pigsty stable

MACHINES AND EQUIPMENT YOU SEE ON A FARM ARE
combine harvester cultivator drill harrow milking-machine mower plough tractor wagon

OTHER THINGS YOU MIGHT SEE ON A FARM ARE
battery cages farmyard hayrick or **haystack silo**

Farmers grow various crops.
KINDS OF CORN OR CEREALS ARE
barley maize or **sweetcorn oats rye wheat**

OTHER CROPS ARE
potatoes sugarbeet vegetables

ANIMALS THAT FARMERS KEEP ARE
bull calf cow goat horse lamb pig sheep
Bulls and cows are called **cattle**.

BIRDS THAT YOU SEE ON A FARM ARE
chicken duck goose hen turkey
These birds are called **poultry**.

fashion *noun*

Sam knows about the latest fashion in music.
OTHER WORDS YOU MIGHT USE ARE **craze style trend**

fast *adjective*
1 We started off at a fast pace.
> OTHER WORDS YOU MIGHT USE ARE **brisk   hurried   quick   rapid   smart   speedy   swift**
2 Granny caught a fast train to London.
> OTHER WORDS ARE **express   high-speed**
The opposite is slow

fat *adjective*
1 a fat person.
> OTHER WORDS YOU MIGHT USE ARE **chubby   overweight   plump** (*informal*) **podgy   stout** (*informal*) **tubby**
2 a fat book.
> ANOTHER WORD IS **thick**
The opposite is thin

fat *noun*
> KINDS OF FAT YOU MIGHT EAT OR USE IN COOKING ARE **butter   cooking oil   dripping   lard   margarine   suet**

fault *noun*
The teacher pointed out the faults in my work.
> OTHER WORDS YOU MIGHT USE ARE **error   flaw   mistake** (*informal*) **slip   weakness**

favour *noun*
She did me a favour and lent me her umbrella.
> OTHER WORDS YOU MIGHT USE ARE **good deed   kindness**

fear *noun*
Fear spread through the town when the earthquake started.
> OTHER WORDS YOU MIGHT USE ARE **alarm   dread   fright   horror   panic   terror**

feeble *adjective*
I felt feeble after I was ill.
> OTHER WORDS YOU MIGHT USE ARE **delicate   frail   weak**
The opposite is strong

feel *verb*
1   Feel the cat's soft fur.
>   OTHER VERBS YOU MIGHT USE ARE   **to finger**   **to stroke**   **to touch**
2   Granny feels the cold more than I do.
>   OTHER VERBS YOU MIGHT USE ARE   **to notice**   **to suffer from**

feeling *noun*
My feeling is that it will be fine tomorrow.
>   OTHER WORDS YOU MIGHT USE ARE   **guess**   **instinct**   **intuition**
>   **opinion**

feelings
1   When you are very sad, it's hard not to show your feelings.
>   ANOTHER WORD IS **emotions**
2   Vegetarians often have strong feelings about killing animals.
>   OTHER WORDS ARE   **beliefs**   **opinions**

female *noun*
>   OTHER WORDS YOU MIGHT USE

A female human being is a **woman**.
A female dog is a **bitch**.
A female deer or rabbit is a **doe**.
A female sheep is a **ewe**.
A female bird is a **hen**.
A female lion is a **lioness**.
A female horse is a **mare**.
A female goat is a **nanny goat**.
A female pig is a **sow**.
A female fox is a **vixen**.

fence *noun*
>   OTHER THINGS USED TO MARK THE EDGE OF A PIECE OF LAND ARE   **barrier**   **hedge**
>   **railings**   **wall**

fetch *verb*
Jo's dog fetched the newspaper.
>   OTHER VERBS YOU MIGHT USE ARE   **to bring**   **to carry**   **to collect**
>   **to get**

fidget *verb*
Please don't fidget!
>   OTHER VERBS YOU MIGHT USE ARE   **to be restless**   **to fiddle**

field *noun*

OTHER WORDS YOU MIGHT USE ARE
a field of grass: **meadow   pasture**
a small field for horses: **paddock**

fierce *adjective*
a fierce dog.

OTHER WORDS YOU MIGHT USE ARE   **ferocious   savage   vicious**
The opposite is gentle

fight *noun*

OTHER WORDS YOU MIGHT USE ARE
combat   conflict   contest   quarrel   (*informal*) **row**

WORDS FOR DIFFERENT KINDS OF FIGHTING ARE
a fight between armies
battle   war

a fight betwen two people
duel

a fight between two families or gangs
feud

a fight in the street
brawl   riot   scuffle

a fight to entertain people
bout   boxing match   wrestling match

a fight between knights in old times
joust

a friendly or unimportant fight
(*informal*) **scrap   squabble   tussle**

WORDS FOR FIGHTER ARE
soldier   warrior

An archer used to fight with a **bow** and **arrow**.
A boxer fights with **fists**.
A gladiator used to fight to **entertain** people.
A gunman fights with **guns**.
Knights used to fight on **horses**.
A wrestler fights with **hands** and **arms**.

For other words, see **soldier**

figure *noun*

1   Jo added up the figures.
    OTHER WORDS YOU MIGHT USE ARE   **digit   number**
2   Sam has a slim figure.
    ANOTHER WORD IS **shape**

file *noun*

We lined up in a single file.
    OTHER WORDS YOU MIGHT USE ARE   **column   line   queue   row**

fill *verb*

I filled the box with sweets.
    OTHER VERBS YOU MIGHT USE ARE   **to cram   to load   to pack**

film *noun*

I watched a good film on TV.
    ANOTHER WORD IS **movie**
    DIFFERENT KINDS OF FILM ARE
    **adventure   cartoon   comedy   documentary   horror
    science fiction   western**

filthy *adjective*

Put those filthy jeans in the washing machine!
    OTHER WORDS YOU MIGHT USE ARE   **dirty   foul**   (*informal*) **grubby
    messy**   (*informal*) **mucky   muddy**
The opposite is clean

final *adjective*

They scored in the final moments of the game.
    OTHER WORDS YOU MIGHT USE ARE   **closing   concluding   last**
The opposite is first

find *verb*

1   Did you find the money you lost?
    OTHER VERBS YOU MIGHT USE ARE   **to come across   to discover
    to get back   to recover**
    The opposite is lose
2   Did the police find the thief?
    OTHER VERBS ARE   **to trace   to track down**
3   I found the information I need.
    ANOTHER VERB IS **to discover**

fine *adjective*

1 fine thread.
    OTHER WORDS YOU MIGHT USE ARE   **slender**   **thin**
The opposite is thick
2 fine sand.
    ANOTHER WORD IS **powdery**
The opposite is coarse
3 fine weather.
    OTHER WORDS ARE   **bright**   **dry**   **sunny**
The opposite is wet
4 a fine piece of work.
    OTHER WORDS ARE   **good**   **great**   **excellent**
The opposite is bad

finish *verb*

1 Finish your work now.
    OTHER VERBS YOU MIGHT USE ARE   **to complete**   **to round off**
    to stop
2 The film finished with an exciting car chase.
    OTHER VERBS ARE   **to conclude**   **to end**
3 Did you finish those sweets?
    OTHER WORDS ARE   **to consume**   **to use up**
The opposite is start

fire *noun*

We watched the firemen put out the fire.
    OTHER WORDS YOU MIGHT USE ARE
    blaze   **flames**   **inferno**

    FIRES USED FOR HEAT OR COOKING ARE
    barbecue   **boiler**   **camp fire**   **central heating**
    coal fire   **electric fire**   **furnace**   **gas fire**   **gas ring**
    grill   **hot plate**   **immersion heater**   **oven**   **stove**

    FIRES WHICH BURN THINGS WE DON'T WANT ARE
    bonfire   **incinerator**

fire *verb*

to fire a gun.
    OTHER VERBS YOU MIGHT USE ARE   **to let off**   **to shoot**

firm *adjective*
1 Make sure the rock is firm before you step on it.
   OTHER WORDS YOU MIGHT USE ARE   **fixed   secure   steady**
2 Mum whisked the cream until it was firm.
   OTHER WORDS ARE   **set   solid   stiff**

first *adjective*
1 Jo was the first to arrive at the party.
   OTHER WORDS YOU MIGHT USE ARE   **earliest   soonest**
2 Who was the first man in space?
   ANOTHER WORD IS **original**
The opposite is **last**

fish *noun*
SOME DIFFERENT KINDS OF FISH ARE
**carp   cod   eel   goldfish   haddock   herring
jellyfish   mackerel   minnow   octopus   perch
pike   pilchard   plaice   salmon   sardine   shark
sole   stickleback   trout**

ANIMALS WHICH LIVE IN WATER BUT ARE NOT REAL FISH ARE
dolphin   octopus   porpoise   whale

fisherman *noun*
A person who fishes with a rod is an **angler**.
A person who goes to sea in a boat to catch fish is a **trawlerman**.

fit *adjective*
1 You have to be fit to play football.
   OTHER WORDS YOU MIGHT USE ARE   **healthy   strong   well**
2 Is the old house fit to live in?
   ANOTHER WORD IS **suitable**

fit *verb*
Jo helped Sam fit the pieces of his model aeroplane together.
   OTHER VERBS YOU MIGHT USE ARE   **to assemble   to put together**

fix *verb*
Dad fixed a shelf to the wall.
   OTHER VERBS YOU MIGHT USE ARE   **to attach   to secure**
For other verbs, see **fasten**

fizzy *adjective*
fizzy drinks.
OTHER WORDS YOU MIGHT USE ARE **bubbly   effervescent   sparkling**

flame *noun*
For other words, see **fire**

flap *verb*
The flags flapped in the wind.
OTHER VERBS YOU MIGHT USE ARE **to flutter   to wave**

flat *adjective*
A games field must be flat.
OTHER WORDS YOU MIGHT USE ARE **even   level   smooth**

flavour *noun*
I like the flavour of this drink.
ANOTHER WORD IS **taste**

fling *verb*
I flung a pebble into the water.
OTHER VERBS YOU MIGHT USE ARE *(informal)* **to chuck   to throw   to toss**

float *verb*
1 Will this toy boat float?
A PHRASE IS **to stay up**
The opposite is sink
2 The smoke from the bonfire floated in the air.
OTHER VERBS YOU MIGHT USE ARE **to drift   to hover**

flock *noun*
For other words, see **group**

floor *noun*
THINGS USED TO COVER A FLOOR ARE
carpet   lino   mat   rug   tiles

flow *verb*

Water flowed from the broken pipe.

OTHER VERBS YOU MIGHT USE ARE

to flow fast   **to gush   to pour   to run   to spurt   to squirt   to stream**

to flow slowly   **to dribble   to drip   to leak   to ooze   to trickle**

to flow over the edge   **to overflow   to spill**

flower *noun*

OTHER WORDS YOU MIGHT USE ARE

bloom   blossom

WORDS FOR A BUNCH OF FLOWERS ARE

arrangement   bouquet   posy

FLOWERS YOU SEE IN GARDENS ARE

carnation   chrysanthemum   crocus   daffodil   daisy   forget-me-not   geranium   hollyhock   hyacinth   lily   lupin   marigold   pansy   rose   snowdrop   sunflower   tulip   wallflower

FLOWERS THAT OFTEN GROW WILD ARE

bluebell   buttercup   dandelion   foxglove   poppy   primrose   violet

fluffy *adjective*

OTHER WORDS YOU MIGHT USE ARE   **feathery   furry   soft   woolly**

fly *verb*

Birds, bats, and aeroplanes fly.

OTHER VERBS YOU MIGHT USE ARE   **to glide   to hover   to rise   to soar   to swoop**

fog *noun*

I couldn't see because of the fog.

OTHER WORDS YOU MIGHT USE ARE   **haze   mist**

fold *verb*

The paper will go in the envelope if you fold it.

OTHER VERBS YOU MIGHT USE ARE   **to bend over   to crease   to double over**

follow *verb*
1 A dog followed me.
   OTHER VERBS YOU MIGHT USE ARE   **to chase**   **to come after**   **to pursue**
   to tail   **to track**
2 Follow this road.
   OTHER VERBS ARE   **to go along**   **to take**
3 Did you follow what she said?
   ANOTHER VERB IS **to understand**

food *noun*, see next page

foolish *adjective*
It's foolish to run across the main road.
   OTHER WORDS YOU MIGHT USE ARE   (*informal*) **daft**   **idiotic**   **mad**   **silly**
   stupid   **unwise**
The opposite is sensible

foot *noun*
An animal's foot is a **hoof** or **paw**.
A bird has **toes** or **claws**.
For other parts of the body, see **body**

forbid *verb*
The head forbids eating in class.
   OTHER VERBS YOU MIGHT USE ARE   **to ban**   **to prohibit**
The opposite is allow

force *noun*
We had to use force to open the door.
   OTHER WORDS YOU MIGHT USE ARE   **might**   **power**   **strength**   **violence**

force *verb*
They can't force me to play.
   OTHER VERBS YOU MIGHT USE ARE   **to compel**   **to make**   **to order**

forest *noun*
Don't get lost in the forest!
   OTHER WORDS YOU MIGHT USE ARE   **jungle**   **wood**

forgery *noun*
The shopkeeper checked to see if the £10 note was a forgery.
   OTHER WORDS YOU MIGHT USE ARE   **copy**   **fake**   **imitation**

food *noun*

OTHER WORDS YOU MIGHT USE ARE

diet　nourishment　provisions　refreshments

Food for farm animals is **fodder**.

BASIC INGREDIENTS OF FOOD ARE

carbohydrate　fat　fibre　protein　starch　vitamins

CEREALS ARE

barley　maize or sweetcorn　oats　rice　rye　wheat

FOOD MADE FROM CEREALS:

bran · 　　　cornflakes　cornflour　flour
muesli　　　oatmeal　　porridge

KINDS OF BREAD:

bagel　brown bread　chapatti　crusty bread
French bread　nan　rye bread　white bread
wholemeal bread

OTHER FOODS MADE FROM FLOUR:

biscuits　　cake　　　dumplings　noodles
pasta　　　pastry　　pizza

SOME KINDS OF CAKE ARE

bun　　　　doughnut or donut　flan
fruitcake　gingerbread　meringue　muffin
scone　　　shortbread　spongecake　tart

KINDS OF PASTA:

lasagne　　macaroni　spaghetti

THINGS MADE WITH PASTRY:

pasty　pie　mince pies　quiche　sausage rolls

FOOD MADE WITH MILK:

blancmange　butter　　cheese　　cream
custard　　milk pudding yogurt

KINDS OF MEAT ARE

bacon　　beef　　chicken　ham
lamb　　pork　　turkey　veal
venison

FOOD USUALLY MADE WITH MEAT:

burgers　chop suey　curry　fritters
goulash　hash　hot-pot　meat pie
mince　paté　rissole　sausage
stew

Food which doesn't contain any meat is **vegetarian** food.

FOOD MADE WITH EGGS:

omelette   pancakes   soufflé

FISH WHICH PEOPLE EAT ARE

cod	haddock	herring	kipper
mackerel	pilchard	plaice	salmon
sardine	scampi	shellfish	sole
trout	tuna		

A mixture of fish and shellfish is **seafood**.
Caviare is a very expensive food from a fish called **sturgeon**.

FRUIT WHICH YOU CAN EAT ARE

apple	apricot	banana	blackberry
blackcurrant	cherry	coconut	damson
date	fig	gooseberry	grape
grapefruit	kiwi fruit	lemon	lime
melon	orange	peach	pear
pineapple	plum	raspberry	strawberry
tangerine	tomato		

VEGETABLES PEOPLE EAT INCLUDE

asparagus	beans	Brussels sprouts	
cabbage	carrot	cauliflower	greens
leek	marrow	nuts	onion
parsnip	pea	potato	pumpkin
spinach	swede	turnip	

VEGETABLES WE EAT IN SALAD ARE

beetroot	celery	cress	cucumber
lettuce	mustard and cress		onion
potato	radish	tomato	watercress

SOME SWEET FOODS:

honey	ice cream	icing	jam
jelly	marmalade	mousse	pudding
syrup	tart	treacle	trifle

THINGS USED TO ADD FLAVOUR TO FOOD

chutney	dressing	garlic	gravy
herbs	ketchup	mayonnaise	mustard
pepper	pickle	salt	sauce
seasoning	spice	sugar	vanilla
vinegar			

forget *verb*
I forgot my money.
OTHER VERBS YOU MIGHT USE ARE **to leave behind** **to overlook**
The opposite is remember

forgetful *adjective*
He was so forgetful that he left his money behind.
OTHER WORDS YOU MIGHT USE ARE **absent-minded** **careless**
scatterbrained **thoughtless**

forgive *verb*
Sam forgave Jo for forgetting his birthday.
OTHER VERBS YOU MIGHT USE ARE **to excuse** **to pardon**

form *noun*
The wizard could change his form.
OTHER WORDS YOU MIGHT USE ARE **appearance** **shape**

fortunate *adjective*
It's fortunate that it didn't rain.
ANOTHER WORD IS **lucky**
The opposite is unlucky

foul *adjective*
foul slime. foul weather.
OTHER WORDS YOU MIGHT USE ARE **dirty** **disgusting** **filthy** **horrible**
nasty **revolting**
The opposite is nice

fragile *adjective*
Take care with the best china because it is fragile.
OTHER WORDS YOU MIGHT USE ARE **brittle** **delicate** **thin**
The opposite is strong

fragment *noun*
When Jo broke the tea-pot, Mum made her sweep up the fragments.
OTHER WORDS YOU MIGHT USE ARE **bit** **chip** **piece** **scrap**

frail *adjective*
I felt frail after my illness.
OTHER WORDS YOU MIGHT USE ARE **delicate** **feeble** **weak**
The opposite is strong

free *adjective*
1 The cat is free to wander about.
   A PHRASE YOU MIGHT USE IS **at liberty**
2 Is the bathroom free?
   OTHER WORDS ARE   **available**   **unoccupied**   **vacant**

free *verb*
The prisoner asked the guards when they were going to free him.
   OTHER VERBS YOU MIGHT USE ARE   **to let out**   **to liberate**   **to release**
The opposite is capture

frequent *adjective*
Our picnic was spoiled by frequent showers.
   OTHER WORDS YOU MIGHT USE ARE   **many**   **numerous**   **repeated**

fresh *adjective*
1 fresh bread.
   ANOTHER WORD IS **new**
The opposite is stale
2 fresh air.
   OTHER WORDS YOU MIGHT USE ARE   **clean**   **cool**   **pure**
3 fresh after a rest.
   OTHER WORDS ARE   **lively**   **rested**
4 a fresh page.
   OTHER WORDS ARE   **different**   **new**   **unused**

friend *noun*
An informal word is **mate**.
A friend who fights on your side is an **ally**.
A friend who works with you is a **partner**.
Someone you don't know very well is an **acquaintance**.
The opposite is enemy

friendly *adjective*
a friendly smile.   **affectionate**   **kind**   **loving**
The opposite is unfriendly

frighten *verb*
Don't frighten the animals.
   OTHER VERBS YOU MIGHT USE ARE   **to alarm**   **to scare**   **to startle**
   to terrify
frightened *adjective*, see **afraid**
frightening *adjective*, see **terrible**

froth *noun*
The soap leaves froth in the bowl.
OTHER WORDS YOU MIGHT USE ARE　**bubbles　foam　lather　scum**

frown *verb*
Dad frowns when he is angry.
OTHER VERBS YOU MIGHT USE ARE　**to look stern　to scowl**

fruit *noun*
For fruit you can eat, see **food**

fuel *noun*
THINGS WE USE AS FUEL ARE
coal　electricity　gas　oil　petrol　wood

full *adjective*
1 The bus was full.
OTHER WORDS YOU MIGHT USE ARE　**crowded　jammed　packed**
2 My cup is full.
ANOTHER WORD IS **overflowing**
The opposite is empty

fun *noun*
We had lots of fun at Jo's party.
OTHER WORDS YOU MIGHT USE ARE　**amusement　enjoyment　games
jokes　laughing　pleasure**

funeral *noun*
KINDS OF FUNERAL ARE　**burial　cremation**

funny *adjective*
1 funny jokes.
OTHER WORDS YOU MIGHT USE ARE　**amusing　comic　comical
humorous　laughable　ridiculous　witty**
The opposite is serious
2 The ice cream has a funny taste.
For other words, see **peculiar**

furious *adjective*
For other words, see **angry**

furniture *noun*

KINDS OF FURNITURE YOU PUT THINGS IN OR ON ARE

**bookcase   bureau   cabinet   chest of drawers
coffee table   cupboard   desk   dresser   sideboard
table   wardrobe**

KINDS OF FURNITURE YOU SIT ON ARE

**armchair   chair   pouffe   rocking chair   settee
sofa   stool**

KINDS OF FURNITURE YOU CAN SLEEP ON ARE

bed   cot   couch   divan

furry *adjective*
furry animals.

OTHER WORDS YOU MIGHT USE ARE   **fluffy   hairy   woolly**

fuss *noun*
There was a lot of fuss when a lion escaped from the zoo.

OTHER WORDS YOU MIGHT USE ARE   **bother   commotion   excitement
trouble   uproar**

fussy *adjective*
Our cat is fussy about her food.

OTHER WORDS YOU MIGHT USE ARE   **choosy   particular**

Gg

gain *verb*
Sam gained first prize for swimming.

OTHER VERBS YOU MIGHT USE ARE   **to earn   to get   to obtain
to receive   to win**

game *noun*

1 What's your favourite game?
OTHER WORDS YOU MIGHT USE ARE
amusement   entertainment   pastime   sport
2 Let's have a game of chess.
OTHER WORDS ARE   **competition   match   tournament**
VARIOUS GAMES ARE
**bingo   cards   charades   chess   darts   dominoes
draughts   hide-and-seek   hopscotch   ludo   marbles
skittles   snooker   table tennis   tiddlywinks**

For other games, see **sport**

gang *noun*
For other words, see **group**

gaol *noun*
Some people spell this word as 'jail'
OTHER WORDS ARE   **dungeon   prison**

gap *noun*
1 a gap in the fence.
OTHER WORDS YOU MIGHT USE ARE   **break   hole   space**
2 a gap between lessons.
OTHER WORDS ARE   **break   interval   pause   rest**

garden *noun*

THINGS YOU GROW IN A GARDEN ARE
flowers   fruit   shrubs   trees   vegetables

PARTS OF A GARDEN ARE
**border   compost heap   flower bed   greenhouse
hedge   lawn   orchard   path   patio   pond
rockery   shed   shrubbery**

TOOLS YOU USE IN THE GARDEN ARE
**broom   fork   hoe   lawn-mower   rake   shears
spade   trowel   watering can**

OTHER THINGS YOU USE IN THE GARDEN ARE
compost   fertilizer   manure   peat   weedkiller

garment *noun*
For other words, see **clothes**

gasp *verb*
The smoke made us gasp.
OTHER VERBS YOU MIGHT USE ARE   **to choke**   **to pant**   **to puff**
to wheeze

gather *verb*
1 People gathered to watch the fire.
OTHER VERBS YOU MIGHT USE ARE   **to assemble**   **to crowd round**
to meet
2 We gathered information for our project.
OTHER VERBS ARE   **to collect**   **to put together**

general *adjective*
1 The general opinion is that our team is the best.
OTHER WORDS YOU MIGHT USE ARE   **common**   **usual**   **widespread**
2 He only gave us a general idea of what he wanted.
OTHER WORDS ARE   **broad**   **vague**

generous *adjective*
1 It was generous of Jo to share her sweets.
OTHER WORDS YOU MIGHT USE ARE   **kind**   **unselfish**
The opposite is mean
2 Mum gave us generous helpings of pudding.
OTHER WORDS ARE   **big**   **large**   **sizeable**
The opposite is small

gentle *adjective*
1 a gentle kiss.
OTHER WORDS YOU MIGHT USE ARE   **kind**   **soft-hearted**   **tender**
2 a gentle breeze.
OTHER WORDS ARE   **pleasant**   **slight**
The opposite is rough
3 gentle music.
OTHER WORDS ARE   **quiet**   **relaxing**   **restful**   **soft**
The opposite is noisy

genuine *adjective*
genuine gold.
ANOTHER WORD IS **real**
The opposite is false

get *verb*

THIS WORD HAS MANY USES. HERE ARE SOME OF THE WAYS YOU CAN USE IT, AND SOME OTHER WORDS YOU COULD CHOOSE

1 What did you get at the shop?
  to buy   to obtain   to purchase
2 Sam got a nice present from Jo.
  to be given   to receive
3 Jo got first prize for swimming.
  to earn   to win
4 Did the thief get anything valuable?
  to steal   to take
5 Tell the dog to get the ball.
  to bring   to fetch   to retrieve
6 I got cold waiting for the bus.
  to become   to grow   to turn

ghost *noun*

Sam doesn't believe in ghosts.
OTHER WORDS YOU MIGHT USE ARE **phantom   spectre   spirit** (*informal*) **spook**

gift *noun*

1 a birthday gift.
  ANOTHER WORD IS **present**
2 a gift to charity.
  OTHER WORDS YOU MIGHT USE ARE **contribution   donation   offering**

girl *noun*

OLD-FASHIONED WORDS ARE **damsel   maid   maiden   virgin**

give *verb*

1 I gave some sweets to Sam.
  OTHER VERBS YOU MIGHT USE ARE **to hand over   to offer   to pass   to present**
2 Dad gives money to charity.
  OTHER VERBS ARE **to contribute   to donate**
3 Our teacher gave us pencils to write with.
  OTHER VERBS ARE **to provide with   to supply with**
4 Jo gave out the books.
  OTHER VERBS ARE **to deal out   to distribute   to hand out**

glad *adjective*
For other words, see **happy**

glass *noun*
A sheet of glass in a window is a **pane**.
A glass you drink out of is a **tumbler**.
Glasses you wear to help you see better are **spectacles**.
GLASSES YOU LOOK THROUGH TO MAKE DISTANT OBJECTS SEEM NEARER ARE
binoculars   field glasses

gloomy *adjective*
1 a gloomy room.
OTHER WORDS YOU MIGHT USE ARE   cheerless   dark   depressing
dismal
2 a gloomy face.
OTHER WORDS ARE   **depressed   glum   miserable   sad
unhappy**
The opposite is cheerful

glow *verb*
The ashes of the bonfire glowed in the dark.
OTHER VERBS YOU MIGHT USE ARE   **to gleam   to shine**

glue *noun*
OTHER SUBSTANCES YOU STICK THINGS WITH ARE   **adhesive   cement   gum
paste**

go *verb*
1 Jo has gone to the shops.
OTHER VERBS YOU MIGHT USE ARE   **to travel   to walk**
For more verbs, see **move**
2 What time does the train go?
OTHER VERBS ARE   **to depart   to leave   to set out
to start**
3 This road goes into the town.
OTHER VERBS ARE   **to continue   to lead**
4 My watch doesn't go.
OTHER VERBS ARE   **to function   to operate   to work**
5 She went quiet when she heard the bad news.
OTHER VERBS ARE   **to become   to grow   to turn**

good *adjective*

SOME WORDS WHICH MEAN GOOD IN A GENERAL WAY ARE
lovely   marvellous   nice   wonderful

SOME INFORMAL WORDS ARE
brilliant   fabulous   great

THESE ARE SOME PARTICULAR WAYS WE USE THE WORD, AND SOME OF THE OTHER
WORDS YOU MIGHT USE

1 good work.
   correct   faultless   perfect   thorough
2 a good friend.
   **caring   considerate   faithful   generous   helpful
   honest   kind   loving   loyal   reliable   thoughtful
   true**
3 a good dog.
   obedient   well-behaved
4 a good footballer.
   clever   skilful   skilled   talented
5 a good film.
   entertaining   exciting   interesting

The opposite is **bad**

govern *verb*

At election time, we choose people to govern the country.
   OTHER VERBS YOU MIGHT USE ARE   **to be in charge of   to control
   to look after   to manage   to rule   to run**

government *noun*

The person in charge of the government is the **prime minister.**
The people who help the prime minister run the government are
the **cabinet.**
Decisions about how to govern the country are discussed in
parliament.

grab *verb*

For other verbs, see **seize**

graceful *adjective*
graceful movements.
OTHER WORDS YOU MIGHT USE ARE　**attractive**　**elegant**　**flowing**
The opposite is clumsy

gradual *adjective*
There was a gradual improvement in the weather.
OTHER WORDS YOU MIGHT USE ARE　**slow**　**steady**
The opposite is sudden

grand *adjective*
The wedding was a grand occasion.
For other words, see **great**

grant *verb*
The fairy granted Cinderella what she wanted.
OTHER VERBS YOU MIGHT USE ARE　**to allow**　**to give**

grass *noun*
An area of grass in a garden is a **lawn**.
An area of grass on a farm is a **field** or **meadow** or **pasture**.
An area of grass in a village is a **green**.
A large area of grass in North America is a **prairie**.
A large area of grass in South Africa is **veld** or **veldt**.

grateful *adjective*
I was grateful for her help.
OTHER WORDS YOU MIGHT USE ARE　**appreciative**　**thankful**
The opposite is ungrateful

grave *adjective*
Mum looked grave when she heard the bad news.
OTHER WORDS YOU MIGHT USE ARE　**gloomy**　**serious**　**solemn**
thoughtful
The opposite is cheerful

greasy *adjective*
I don't like greasy chips.
OTHER WORDS YOU MIGHT USE ARE　**fatty**　**oily**

great *adjective*
1 a great storm.
   OTHER WORDS YOU MIGHT USE ARE   **huge   tremendous**
   For more words, see **big**
2 a great occasion.
   OTHER WORDS ARE   **grand   important   impressive   magnificent
   spectacular   splendid**
3 a great piece of music.
   OTHER WORDS ARE   **classic   famous   well-known**
4 We had a great time.
   OTHER WORDS ARE   **excellent   marvellous   wonderful**
   For more words, see **good**

greedy *adjective*
It was greedy to eat all the cake.
   OTHER WORDS YOU MIGHT USE ARE   (*informal*) **piggish   selfish**

greet *verb*
I greeted our guests at the door.
   ANOTHER VERB IS **to welcome**

grief *noun*
I sympathized with Jo's grief when the dog died.
   OTHER WORDS YOU MIGHT USE ARE   **misery   sadness   sorrow
   unhappiness**

grim *adjective*
a grim look on someone's face.
   OTHER WORDS YOU MIGHT USE ARE   **bad-tempered   gloomy   serious
   severe   stern   unfriendly**
   The opposite is **happy**

grin *verb*
For other verbs, see **laugh**

groan *verb*
The injured man groaned because of the pain.
   OTHER VERBS YOU MIGHT USE ARE   **to moan   to wail**

grope *verb*
I groped about to find the light switch.
   OTHER VERBS YOU MIGHT USE ARE   **to feel   to fumble**

ground *noun*

1 Potatoes grow in the ground.
OTHER WORDS YOU MIGHT USE ARE
earth   soil

2 We play football on a piece of ground behind the school.
ANOTHER WORD IS **land**
PLACES WHERE YOU CAN PLAY GAMES ARE
playground   playing field   pitch   recreation ground   stadium

Ground where you build something is a **plot** or **site**.
A big area of ground owned by one person or used for a special purpose is an **estate**.
The grounds of a big school or college are called a **campus**.

group *noun,* see next page

grow *verb*

1 Jo grows flowers in the garden.
OTHER VERBS YOU MIGHT USE ARE   **to cultivate   to plant   to raise**

2 The seeds only grow when the weather is warm.
OTHER VERBS ARE   **to germinate   to spring up   to sprout**

3 Jo looks to see how much her vegetables have grown.
OTHER VERBS ARE   **to develop   to fill out   to get bigger   to get taller   to increase**

grown-up *adjective*

OTHER WORDS YOU MIGHT USE ARE   **adult   mature**

gruesome *adjective*

I didn't like the gruesome picture of the accident.
OTHER WORDS YOU MIGHT USE ARE   **disgusting   gory   horrible   nasty   sickening**

gruff *adjective*

a gruff voice.
OTHER WORDS YOU MIGHT USE ARE   **deep   harsh   hoarse   rough**

grumble *verb*

Mum doesn't like it when Sam grumbles about the food.
OTHER VERBS YOU MIGHT USE ARE   **to complain**   (*informal*) **to moan**

group *noun*

OTHER WORDS YOU MIGHT USE ARE

a group of things:
assortment   collection   set

a group of people:
assembly   company   crowd   gang   gathering   mob   throng

an organized group of people:
alliance   army   association   club   force   society   team

a group of musicians:
band   choir   chorus   orchestra

OTHER GROUPS ARE:

An **army** of ants.
A **brood** of chicks.
A **bunch** of flowers.
A **class** of children.
A **clump** of trees.
A **clutch** of eggs.
A **colony** of ants.
A **congregation** in church.
A **constellation** or **galaxy** of stars.
A **convoy** or **fleet** of ships.
A **covey** of partridges.
A **crew** of sailors.
A **flock** of birds.
A **flock** of sheep.
A **gaggle** of geese.
A **gang** of robbers.
A **herd** of cows.
A **herd** of elephants.
A **leap** of leopards.
A **litter** of puppies.
A **pack** of wolves.
A **pride** of lions.
A **school** of whales.
A **shoal** of fish.
A **swarm** of bees.
A **troop** of soldiers.

guard *verb*
The farmer's dog guards the sheep.
OTHER VERBS YOU MIGHT USE ARE   **to care for   to defend   to look after   to protect   to shield   to tend   to watch over**

guess *verb*
1 I guess you are hungry.
OTHER VERBS YOU MIGHT USE ARE   **to assume   to suppose**
2 Jo tried to guess how many sweets there were in the jar.
ANOTHER VERB IS **to estimate**

guide *verb*
I wish someone would guide us out of this maze!
OTHER VERBS YOU MIGHT USE ARE   **to direct   to escort   to lead   to steer**

guilty *adjective*
He was guilty of stealing.
The opposite is innocent

gun *noun*
KINDS OF GUN ARE
airgun   cannon   machine-gun   pistol   revolver   rifle   shotgun

Hh

habit *noun*
1 It's our habit to send people a card when they have a birthday.
OTHER WORDS YOU MIGHT USE ARE   **custom   practice   tradition**
2 Smoking is a bad habit.
ANOTHER WORD IS **addiction**

hair *noun*

DIFFERENT WAYS PEOPLE DO THEIR HAIR ARE

**in curls   with a fringe   permed   in a pigtail
in plaits   in a ponytail**

WORDS TO DESCRIBE THE COLOUR OF PEOPLE'S HAIR ARE

**auburn   black   blond   brown   fair   ginger   grey
red   silver   white**

WORDS FOR HAIR ON AN ANIMAL ARE

bristles   fur

hairy *adjective*

OTHER WORDS YOU MIGHT USE ARE   **bristly   furry   fuzzy   shaggy
woolly**

halt *verb*

You must halt if the light is red.

OTHER VERBS YOU MIGHT USE ARE   **to draw up   to pull up
to stop**

hand *noun*

For other parts of the body, see **body**

handicap *noun*

When you run for the bus, it's a handicap to have lots of shopping.

OTHER WORDS YOU MIGHT USE ARE

disadvantage   drawback   hindrance   inconvenience

handicapped *adjective*

It's hard for you to do some things if you are handicapped.

WAYS YOU CAN BE HANDICAPPED ARE

**blind   deaf   disabled   dumb   lame   limbless
paralysed**

handle *verb*
1 Handle the kittens carefully.
OTHER VERBS YOU MIGHT USE ARE
to feel   to stroke   to touch
2 The rider handled the frightened horse well.
OTHER VERBS ARE
to control   to deal with   to look after   to manage

handsome *adjective*
a handsome man.
OTHER WORDS YOU MIGHT USE ARE   **attractive   good-looking**
The opposite is **ugly**

hang *verb*
to hang on to something
Hang on to the rope!
OTHER VERBS YOU MIGHT USE ARE   **to cling on to   to grasp   to hold
to seize**
to hang about
Don't hang about after school.
OTHER VERBS ARE   **to be slow   to dawdle   to delay   to loiter**

happen *verb*
Did anything interesting happen?
OTHER VERBS YOU MIGHT USE ARE   **to occur   to take place**

happy *adjective*
Jo is happy when the sun shines.
OTHER WORDS YOU MIGHT USE ARE   **cheerful   contented   delighted
glad   good-humoured   joyful   light-hearted   merry
pleased**
The opposite is **sad**

harbour *noun*
PLACES WHERE SHIPS UNLOAD GOODS ARE
docks   port

A place where you see lots of **pleasure boats** is a **marina**.
PLACES WHERE SHIPS TIE UP ARE
jetty   landing stage   mooring   pier   quay   wharf

hard *adjective*
1 hard concrete.
OTHER WORDS YOU MIGHT USE ARE   **firm   rigid   solid**
The opposite is soft
2 hard work.
OTHER WORDS ARE   **exhausting   tiring   tough**
The opposite is easy
3 a hard problem.
OTHER WORDS ARE   **complex   complicated   difficult   puzzling**
The opposite is simple
4 a hard punishment.
OTHER WORDS ARE   **cruel   harsh   merciless   severe**
The opposite is merciful

hardly *adverb*
I'm so tired I can hardly walk.
OTHER WORDS YOU MIGHT USE ARE   **barely   only just   scarcely**

harm *verb*
1 Jo would never harm an animal.
OTHER VERBS YOU MIGHT USE ARE   **to hurt   to injure   to wound**
2 Did the accident harm the car?
OTHER VERBS ARE   **to damage   to spoil**

harmful *adjective*
It can be harmful to take too much medicine.
OTHER WORDS YOU MIGHT USE ARE   **bad   damaging   dangerous**

harsh *adjective*
1 The teacher's harsh voice showed that she was angry.
OTHER WORDS YOU MIGHT USE ARE   **grating   rough   shrill**
2 We blinked in the harsh light.
OTHER WORDS ARE   **brilliant   dazzling   glaring**
3 We thought the decision to send the player off was harsh.
OTHER WORDS ARE   **cruel   hard   merciless   severe**
The opposite is gentle

hasty *adjective*
The teacher said we were too hasty doing our work.
OTHER WORDS YOU MIGHT USE ARE   **careless   hurried   impetuous
quick   (*informal*) slapdash   thoughtless**

hat *noun*
DIFFERENT THINGS PEOPLE WEAR ON THEIR HEADS ARE
beret   bonnet   cap   crash helmet   crown   helmet
hood   turban

hate *verb*
Sam can't understand why some people hate cabbage.
OTHER VERBS YOU MIGHT USE ARE   **to detest   to dislike   to loathe**
The opposite is like

haul *verb*
We hauled our sledge to the top of the hill.
OTHER VERBS YOU MIGHT USE ARE   **to drag   to draw   to pull   to tow**
    to tug

have *verb*
THIS VERB HAS MANY USES. HERE ARE SOME OF THE WAYS YOU CAN USE IT, AND
SOME OTHER VERBS YOU COULD CHOOSE.
1 Jo has a new kitten.
  to own   to possess
2 Jo's class has thirty pupils.
  to consist of   to contain   to include
3 I was having a good time, but Sam had a cold.
  to enjoy   to experience   to suffer
4 I had some nice presents on my birthday.
  to be given   to get   to obtain   to receive

hazy *adjective*
The view from the top of the hill was hazy.
OTHER WORDS YOU MIGHT USE ARE   **blurred   foggy   misty**
The opposite is clear

head *noun*
For other parts of your body, see **body**

heal *verb*
The ointment helps to heal spots.
OTHER VERBS YOU MIGHT USE ARE   **to cure   to make better   to remedy**

health *noun*, see opposite page

healthy *adjective*
We all want to be healthy.
OTHER WORDS YOU MIGHT USE ARE   fit   sound   strong   well
The opposite is ill

heap *noun*
Sam left his clothes in a heap.
OTHER WORDS ARE   mound   pile   stack

hear *verb*
Did you hear the weather forecast?
ANOTHER VERB IS **to listen to**

heart *noun*
The explorers were lost in the heart of the jungle.
OTHER WORDS YOU MIGHT USE ARE   centre   core   middle

heat *noun*
The cat loves the heat from the fire.
OTHER WORDS YOU MIGHT USE ARE   glow   warmth

heat *verb*
VARIOUS WAYS TO HEAT THINGS ARE   **to boil   to burn   to melt   to scald
to scorch**
For other verbs, see **cook**

heater *noun*
VARIOUS KINDS OF HEATER ARE
**central heating   coal fire   convector
electric fire   gas fire   immersion heater
radiator   stove**

heavy *adjective*
a heavy load.
ANOTHER WORD IS **weighty**
The opposite is light

health *noun*

We all want to have good health.

OTHER WORDS YOU MIGHT USE ARE

fitness   strength

PEOPLE WHO LOOK AFTER OUR HEALTH ARE

doctor   health visitor   nurse

A **paediatrician** is a specialist in children's health.

A **midwife** helps to deliver babies.

A **surgeon** does operations.

A **dentist** looks after your teeth.

An **optician** looks at your eyes.

A **physiotherapist** helps people recover from injuries.

A **pharmacist** makes up medicines.

A person who looks after the health of animals is a **vet** or **veterinary surgeon**.

PLACES WHERE WE CAN GET HELP WITH OUR HEALTH ARE

clinic   health centre   hospital   nursing home surgery

We can get medicines at a chemist's or a pharmacy.

OTHER WORDS FOR MEDICINE ARE

cure   remedy   treatment

Medicine you get with a note from the doctor is a **prescription**.

SOME MEDICINES YOU MIGHT TAKE ARE

antibiotic   aspirin   capsule   drug   gargle   linctus lotion   ointment   pill   tablet   tonic

ILLNESSES PEOPLE CAN HAVE ARE

allergy	appendicitis	arthritis	asthma
bilious attack	bronchitis	cancer	catarrh
chickenpox	chill	cholera	cold
constipation	cough	diabetes	diarrhoea
diphtheria	dysentery	earache	epilepsy
fever	flu	hay fever	headache
indigestion	influenza	jaundice	leprosy
leukaemia	malaria	measles	migraine
mumps	paralysis	plague	pneumonia
polio	rabies	rheumatism	scarlet fever
seasickness	smallpox	spina bifida	stroke
sunstroke	tonsillitis	toothache	tuberculosis
typhoid	typhus	whooping cough	

COMPLAINTS YOU CAN GET ON YOUR SKIN ARE

abscess	blister	boil	chilblains
corns	dermatitis	sty	ulcer
verruca	wart		

help *noun*
The policeman radioed for help.
OTHER WORDS YOU MIGHT USE ARE **assistance backing back-up support**

help *verb*
1 I help Dad with the washing up.
OTHER VERBS YOU MIGHT USE ARE **to assist to support**
2 I couldn't help laughing.
ANOTHER VERB IS **to stop**

helpful *adjective*
1 Our neighbours are very helpful.
OTHER WORDS YOU MIGHT USE ARE **considerate kind willing**
2 She gave me some helpful advice.
OTHER WORDS ARE **useful valuable**

helping *noun*
I had a big helping of pudding.
OTHER WORDS YOU MIGHT USE ARE **portion serving**

herd *noun*
a herd of cows.
For other words, see **group**

hesitate *verb*
Jo hesitated before diving in.
OTHER VERBS YOU MIGHT USE ARE **to delay to pause to wait to waver**

hide *verb*
He hid his money under the carpet.
OTHER VERBS YOU MIGHT USE ARE **to conceal to cover to put away**

high *adjective*
1 a high building.
OTHER WORDS YOU MIGHT USE ARE **lofty tall**
2 high prices.
ANOTHER WORD IS **expensive**
The opposite is low

hill *noun*

1 We climbed a hill to see the view.
OTHER WORDS YOU MIGHT USE ARE **mountain   peak**
2 It's hard cycling up that hill.
OTHER WORDS ARE **incline   rise   slope**

hinder *verb*

The firemen were angry because the people watching the fire hindered them.
OTHER VERBS YOU MIGHT USE ARE **to check   to delay
to get in the way of   to hamper**

hint *noun*

1 I can't guess the answer - give me a hint.
ANOTHER WORD IS **clue**
2 The expert gave us some hints on playing chess.
OTHER WORDS ARE **suggestion   tip**

hit *verb*

VARIOUS WAYS TO HIT THINGS ARE
to bang *(informal)* **to bash   to batter   to beat
to bump into   to collide with   to hammer   to knock
to rap   to smash   to strike   to tap   to thump**
(informal) **to wallop** *(informal)* **to whack   to whip**

A goat may **butt** you with horns.
Teachers used to **cane** pupils as a punishment.
You can **flog** someone with a whip.
You **jog** someone with your elbow.
You **kick** with your foot.
You **lash** or **thrash** someone with a whip.
You **poke** or **prod** with a stick.
You **punch** with your fist.
You can **ram** a vehicle into something.
You **slap** or **smack** or **spank** someone with your hand.
You **stub** your toe on something.
You **swat** a fly.

hoarse *adjective*

Dad's voice was hoarse because he had a cold.
OTHER WORDS YOU MIGHT USE ARE **croaking   deep   husky   rough**

hobby *noun*
My hobbies are skating and chess.
OTHER WORDS YOU MIGHT USE ARE   **interest**   **pastime**

hold *verb*
1   I held the ladder while Dad climbed up.
OTHER VERBS YOU MIGHT USE ARE   **to grasp**   **to grip**   **to hang on to**   **to seize**   **to support**
2   Sam held the baby carefully.
OTHER VERBS ARE   **to carry**   **to embrace**   **to hug**
3   The box holds all Jo's toys.
ANOTHER VERB IS **to contain**

hole *noun*
1   a hole in the ground.
OTHER WORDS YOU MIGHT USE ARE   **burrow**   **cave**   **crater**   **pit**   **pothole**   **tunnel**
2   a hole in the fence.
OTHER WORDS ARE   **break**   **chink**   **crack**   **gap**   **opening**
3   a hole in your jacket.
OTHER WORDS ARE   **slit**   **split**   **tear**
4   a hole in a tyre.
OTHER WORDS ARE   **leak**   **puncture**

holiday *noun*
VARIOUS KINDS OF HOLIDAY ARE
adventure holiday   **activity holiday**   **camping holiday**
cruise   **honeymoon**   **package holiday**   **safari**
seaside holiday   **touring holiday**

PLACES PEOPLE STAY ON HOLIDAY ARE
bed and breakfast   **camp site**   **guest house**   **hotel**
motel   **self-catering accommodation**   **youth hostel**

hollow *noun*
a hollow in the ground.
OTHER WORDS YOU MIGHT USE ARE   **depression**   **dip**   **hole**   **valley**

holy *adjective*
The temple is a holy place.
OTHER WORDS YOU MIGHT USE ARE   **religious**   **sacred**

home *noun*

PLACES WHERE PEOPLE LIVE ARE

apartment   bungalow   caravan   chalet   cottage
council house   detached house   farmhouse   flat
maisonette   manor house   mansion   mobile home
semi-detached house   terrace house   thatched cottage

DIFFERENT ROOMS IN A HOME ARE

attic   bathroom   bedroom   cellar   cloakroom
conservatory   dining room   drawing room   hall
kitchen   landing   larder   lavatory   living room
loft   lounge   pantry   parlour   passage   porch
scullery   sitting room   study   toilet   WC

honest *adjective*

Mum believed Sam because he is always honest.
OTHER WORDS YOU MIGHT USE ARE   sincere   trustworthy   truthful
The opposite is dishonest

hop *verb*

Dad hopped up and down when he dropped the hammer on his foot.
OTHER VERBS YOU MIGHT USE ARE   to jump   to leap   to spring

hopeful *adjective*

I'm hopeful that my cold will be better tomorrow.
OTHER WORDS YOU MIGHT USE ARE   confident   optimistic

hopeless *adjective*

Sam's friend is hopeless at games.
OTHER WORDS YOU MIGHT USE ARE   no good   useless

horizontal *adjective*

A snooker table must be perfectly horizontal.
OTHER WORDS YOU MIGHT USE ARE   flat   level
The opposite is vertical

horrible *adjective*

1 a horrible taste.
OTHER WORDS YOU MIGHT USE ARE   horrid   nasty   unpleasant
2 a horrible shock.
OTHER WORDS ARE   dreadful   frightening   terrible

horror *noun*
We were filled with horror when the huge beast ran towards us.
OTHER WORDS YOU MIGHT USE ARE   **dread**   **fear**   **terror**

horse *noun*
VARIOUS WORDS FOR HORSE ARE
carthorse   **nag**   **piebald**   **pony**   **racehorse**
shire-horse   **steed**

A female horse is a **mare**.
A male horse is a **stallion**.
A young horse is a **colt** or **foal**.

hospital *noun*
For other places where you can go if you are ill, see **health**

hostile *adjective*
I didn't like the opposing team's hostile comments.
OTHER WORDS YOU MIGHT USE ARE   **aggressive**   **threatening**
unfriendly
The opposite is friendly

hot *adjective*
1 a hot fire.
OTHER WORDS YOU MIGHT USE ARE   **blazing**   **glowing**   **red-hot**
roasting   **scorching**   **sizzling**
2 hot weather.
ANOTHER WORD IS **sweltering**
3 hot water.
OTHER WORDS ARE   **boiling**   **scalding**
For other words, see **warm**
The opposite is cold
4 hot-tasting food.
OTHER WORDS ARE   **peppery**   **spicy**

hotel *noun*
For other places where people stay, see **holiday**

house *noun*
For places where people live, see **home**

hug *verb*
Granny hugged us and said goodbye.
OTHER VERBS YOU MIGHT USE ARE   **to cuddle**   **to embrace**   **to hold**

huge *adjective*
For other words, see **big**

human *noun*
For other words, see **person**

humble *adjective*
Sam was humble about winning a prize.
ANOTHER WORD IS **modest**
The opposite is proud

humorous *adjective*
We laughed at her humorous remark.
OTHER WORDS YOU MIGHT USE ARE   **amusing**   **comic**   **funny**   **witty**
The opposite is serious

hump *noun*
They put humps in the road to make cars go slower.
OTHER WORDS YOU MIGHT USE ARE   **bulge**   **bump**   **lump**

hunger *noun*
1   Will a sandwich satisfy your hunger?
ANOTHER WORD IS **appetite**
2   In some countries many people die of hunger.
OTHER WORDS ARE   **famine**   **starvation**

hungry *adjective*
I was hungry after my long walk.
OTHER WORDS YOU MIGHT USE ARE   **famished**   (*informal*) **peckish**
ravenous   **starved**   **starving**
If you eat more food than you need you are greedy.

hunt *verb*
1   I think it's cruel to hunt foxes.
OTHER VERBS YOU MIGHT USE ARE   **to chase**   **to pursue**   **to stalk**
to track down
2   We hunted for Mum's lost purse.
OTHER VERBS ARE   **to look for**   **to search for**   **to seek**

hurry *verb*
I hurried home from school.

> OTHER VERBS YOU MIGHT USE ARE **to dash**   **to hasten**   **to hurtle**
> **to race**   **to run**   **to rush**   **to speed**

The opposite is dawdle

hurt *verb*
1 The cut on my hand hurts.

> OTHER VERBS YOU MIGHT USE ARE **to ache**   **to be painful**   **to smart**
> **to sting**   **to throb**

2 Don't hurt the kittens!

> OTHER VERBS ARE **to damage**   **to harm**   **to injure**   **to torment**
> **to wound**

Ii

ice *noun*
A river of ice is a **glacier**.
A large lump of ice floating in the sea is an **iceberg**.
A finger of ice hanging down is an **icicle**.
Dangerous ice on the road is **black ice**.

idea *noun*
1 I've got an idea!

> OTHER WORDS YOU MIGHT USE ARE   *(informal)* **brainwave**   **plan**
> **suggestion**   **thought**

2 I have an idea that you are tired.

> OTHER WORDS ARE **belief**   **feeling**   **impression**   **opinion**

ideal *adjective*
The weather was ideal for a picnic.

> OTHER WORDS YOU MIGHT USE ARE **excellent**   **just right**   **perfect**
> **suitable**

idle *adjective*
Jo is never idle, even in the holidays.
OTHER WORDS YOU MIGHT USE ARE   **doing nothing**   **inactive**   **lazy**
unemployed   **unoccupied**
The opposite is busy

ignorant *adjective*
1 ignorant of the truth.
ANOTHER WORD IS **unaware**
The opposite is aware
2 an ignorant fool.
OTHER WORDS ARE   **foolish**   **stupid**   **unintelligent**
The opposite is clever

ignore *verb*
You get into trouble if you ignore what the teacher says.
OTHER VERBS YOU MIGHT USE ARE   **to disobey**   **to disregard**   **to neglect**
to overlook   **to take no notice of**

ill *adjective*
Sam stayed away from school because he was ill.
OTHER WORDS YOU MIGHT USE ARE   **indisposed**   **in poor health**
(*informal*) **poorly**   **sick**   **unwell**
The opposite is healthy
For other words, see **health**

illegal *adjective*
Stealing is illegal.
OTHER WORDS YOU MIGHT USE ARE   **banned**   **criminal**   **forbidden**
unlawful
The opposite is legal

illness *noun*
OTHER WORDS YOU MIGHT USE ARE   **ailment**   (*informal*) **bug**   **complaint**
disease   **infection**   **malady**   **sickness**
For other words, see **health**

imaginary *adjective*
Unicorns are imaginary animals.
OTHER WORDS YOU MIGHT USE ARE   **fictitious**   **invented**   **made-up**
non-existent   **unreal**
The opposite is real

imagine *verb*
You didn't really see a ghost: you only imagined it.
OTHER VERBS YOU MIGHT USE ARE　**to dream**　**to invent**　**to make up**
to picture　**to think**

imitate *verb*
The budgie can imitate Jo's voice.
OTHER VERBS YOU MIGHT USE ARE　**to copy**　**to impersonate**
to reproduce

imitation *noun*
It isn't real – it's an imitation.
OTHER WORDS YOU MIGHT USE ARE　**copy**　**counterfeit**　**fake**　**forgery**
likeness　**reproduction**

immediate *adjective*
Granny wants an immediate answer to her invitation.
OTHER WORDS YOU MIGHT USE ARE　**instant**　**prompt**
For more words, see **quick**

impatient *adjective*
We were impatient to begin.
OTHER WORDS YOU MIGHT USE ARE　**anxious**　**eager**
The opposite is patient

impertinent *adjective*
Teachers don't like impertinent comments from the children.
OTHER WORDS YOU MIGHT USE ARE　**cheeky**　**impolite**　**improper**
impudent　**insolent**　**rude**
The opposite is polite

important *adjective*
1　The important thing in swimming is to breathe properly.
OTHER WORDS YOU MIGHT USE ARE　**basic**　**chief**　**essential**　**main**
necessary
2　an important person.
OTHER WORDS ARE　**famous**　**great**　**notable**　**powerful**　**respected**
well-known
3　an important message.
OTHER WORDS ARE　**serious**　**urgent**
4　an important event.
OTHER WORDS ARE　**big**　**major**　**significant**　**special**
The opposite is unimportant

impression *noun*
I have the impression that you are bored.
OTHER WORDS YOU MIGHT USE ARE   **feeling   idea   opinion**

impressive *adjective*
an impressive occasion.
OTHER WORDS YOU MIGHT USE ARE   **grand   great   magnificent
memorable   spectacular   splendid   wonderful**

improve *verb*
1 Jo's swimming has improved.
OTHER VERBS YOU MIGHT USE ARE   **to develop   to get better   to progress**
2 Go over your work and try to improve it.
OTHER VERBS ARE   **to make better   to revise**

improvise *verb*
We improvised some music.
OTHER VERBS YOU MIGHT USE ARE   **to invent   to make up**

include *verb*
The packet includes everything you need to make a cake.
OTHER VERBS YOU MIGHT USE ARE   **to consist of   to contain**

inconvenient *adjective*
It is inconvenient to visit auntie today.
OTHER WORDS YOU MIGHT USE ARE   **awkward   troublesome**
The opposite is convenient

incorrect *adjective*
an incorrect answer.
OTHER WORDS YOU MIGHT USE ARE   **false   inaccurate   mistaken
untrue   wrong**
The opposite is correct

increase *verb*
1 They increased the number of children in our class.
OTHER VERBS YOU MIGHT USE ARE   **to add to   to make bigger   to raise**
2 The noise increased as the train got nearer.
OTHER VERBS ARE   **to get louder   to rise**
to increase in size
OTHER VERBS YOU MIGHT USE ARE   **to get bigger   to expand   to swell**
The opposite is decrease

incredible *adjective*
His story about dinosaurs was incredible.
OTHER WORDS YOU MIGHT USE ARE   **far-fetched   unbelievable
unconvincing   unlikely**

infant *noun*
For other words, see **child**

infectious *adjective*
an infectious disease.
ANOTHER WORD IS **catching**

inflate *verb*
to inflate a tyre.
OTHER VERBS YOU MIGHT USE ARE   **to blow up   to pump up**

influence *verb*
1 Does the weather influence the way you behave?
ANOTHER VERB IS **to affect**
2 Don't try to influence the referee!
OTHER VERBS YOU MIGHT USE ARE   **to bribe   to persuade**

inform *verb*
The teacher informed my mother that I was ill.
OTHER VERBS YOU MIGHT USE ARE   **to notify   to tell**

informal *adjective*
1 informal clothes.
OTHER WORDS YOU MIGHT USE ARE   **casual   comfortable**
2 an informal party.
OTHER WORDS ARE   **easygoing   friendly   relaxed**
The opposite is formal

information *noun*
1 We rang up to get some information about the accident.
OTHER WORDS YOU MIGHT USE ARE   **facts   knowledge   news**
2 We put the information into the computer.
ANOTHER WORD IS **data**

injure *verb*
Did you injure yourself when you fell over?
OTHER VERBS YOU MIGHT USE ARE   **to damage   to harm   to hurt**

injury *noun*
For other words, see **wound**

innocent *adjective*
The judge declared that the accused man was innocent.
OTHER WORDS YOU MIGHT USE ARE **blameless   guiltless**
The opposite is guilty

inquisitive *adjective*
It's rude to be inquisitive about other people's affairs.
OTHER WORDS YOU MIGHT USE ARE **curious   nosy   prying**

insect *noun*
VARIOUS INSECTS ARE
**ant   bee   beetle   bluebottle   bumble-bee
butterfly   cockroach   cricket   daddy-long-legs
dragonfly   earwig   fly   glow-worm   gnat
grasshopper   hornet   ladybird   locust   mosquito
moth   nit   wasp**
OTHER CRAWLING CREATURES (WHICH ARE NOT PROPER INSECTS) ARE
centipede   slug   spider   worm

insolent *adjective*
It is insolent to answer back to a teacher.
OTHER WORDS YOU MIGHT USE ARE **cheeky   impertinent   impolite
improper   impudent   rude**
The opposite is polite

inspect *verb*
The man at the garage inspected the damage to the car.
OTHER VERBS YOU MIGHT USE ARE **to check   to examine   to look at**

instant *adjective*
He didn't keep us waiting, but gave us an instant reply.
OTHER WORDS YOU MIGHT USE ARE **immediate   prompt   quick**

instruct *verb*
1 The policeman instructed us to stay where we were.
OTHER VERBS YOU MIGHT USE ARE **to command   to direct   to order**
2 Our teacher instructed us in how to use the PE equipment.
OTHER VERBS ARE **to coach   to teach   to train**

instrument *noun*
The dentist has an interesting instrument for drilling teeth.
OTHER WORDS YOU MIGHT USE ARE   **apparatus   device   gadget
implement   machine tool**
For musical instruments, see **music**

insult *verb*
He insulted me by walking away without speaking.
OTHER VERBS YOU MIGHT USE ARE   **to be rude to   to offend   to snub**

intelligent *adjective*
Our dog is so intelligent that she understands what we say.
OTHER WORDS YOU MIGHT USE ARE   **brainy   bright   clever**
The opposite is stupid

intend *verb*
Jo intends to learn the piano next year.
OTHER VERBS YOU MIGHT USE ARE   **to aim   to plan   to propose**

intense *adjective*
intense heat. intense pain.
OTHER WORDS YOU MIGHT USE ARE   **extreme   great   severe   strong**

intentional *adjective*
The player was sent off the field for an intentional foul.
OTHER WORDS YOU MIGHT USE ARE   **deliberate   intended**
The opposite is accidental

interest *verb*
Dad's stories always interest us.
OTHER VERBS YOU MIGHT USE ARE   **to appeal to   to attract
to fascinate**
The opposite is bore

interested *adjective*
OTHER WORDS YOU MIGHT USE ARE   **attentive   curious   keen**
IF YOU ARE TOO INTERESTED, YOU ARE   **inquisitive   nosy**
The opposite is bored

interfere *verb*
Don't interfere in my business!
OTHER VERBS YOU MIGHT USE ARE   **to intrude   to meddle   to pry**
(*informal*) **to snoop**

interrupt *verb*
It's rude to interrupt when someone is talking.
OTHER VERBS YOU MIGHT USE ARE   (*informal*) **to butt in**   **to interfere**

interval *noun*
1 When we went to the pictures, we had ice cream in the interval.
OTHER WORDS YOU MIGHT USE ARE   **break   intermission**
2 There is an interval between the lightning and the thunder.
OTHER WORDS ARE   **gap   pause   rest   space**

introduce *verb*
Jo introduced me to her friend.
OTHER VERBS YOU MIGHT USE ARE   **to make known   to present**

introduction *noun*
1 an introduction to a book.
OTHER WORDS YOU MIGHT USE ARE   **preface   prologue**
2 an introduction to a ballet.
OTHER WORDS ARE   **overture   prelude**

invade *verb*
to invade a foreign country.
OTHER VERBS YOU MIGHT USE ARE   **to attack   to march into   to occupy
to overrun   to raid**

invent *verb*
Who invented the first computer?
OTHER VERBS YOU MIGHT USE ARE   **to create   to devise   to plan
to put together   to think up**

investigate *verb*
The police spent many weeks investigating the crime.
OTHER VERBS YOU MIGHT USE ARE   **to examine   to explore
to inquire into   to study**

invisible *adjective*
The door into the secret garden was invisible.
OTHER WORDS YOU MIGHT USE ARE   **concealed   hidden   undetectable**
The opposite is visible

invite *verb*
Jo invited me to her party.
ANOTHER VERB IS **to ask**

irritable *adjective*
Dad gets irritable if we chatter while the football is on.
OTHER WORDS YOU MIGHT USE ARE **annoyed   bad-tempered   grumpy**
short-tempered   snappy   touchy
For other words, see **angry**

irritate *verb*
The flies irritated the horse.
OTHER VERBS YOU MIGHT USE ARE **to anger   to annoy   to bother**
to upset   to worry

issue *verb*
The teacher issued one pencil to each child.
OTHER VERBS YOU MIGHT USE ARE **to distribute   to give out**
to pass round

item *noun*
Have you got any items for the jumble sale?
OTHER WORDS YOU MIGHT USE ARE **article   object   thing**

Jj

jab *verb*
He jabbed me with his finger.
OTHER VERBS YOU MIGHT USE ARE **to poke   to prod   to stab**

jagged *adjective*
The broken plank had a jagged edge.
OTHER WORDS YOU MIGHT USE ARE **rough   sharp   uneven**
The opposite is smooth

jail *noun*
see **gaol**

jam *verb*
1 I jammed my things into a box.
   OTHER VERBS YOU MIGHT USE ARE   **to cram**   **to crush**   **to squeeze**
2 Cars jammed the street.
   OTHER VERBS ARE   **to block**   **to fill**
3 Our back door keeps jamming.
   ANOTHER VERB IS **to stick**

jar *noun*
For other things to put things in, see **container**

jealous *adjective*
Jo was a bit jealous when Sam got a lot of money for his birthday.
   OTHER WORDS YOU MIGHT USE ARE   **bitter**   **envious**   **resentful**

jeans *noun*
For things to wear, see **clothes**

jeer *verb*
The crowd jeered at the player who argued with the referee.
   OTHER VERBS YOU MIGHT USE ARE   **to laugh at**   **to mock**   **to sneer at**
   to taunt

jet *noun*
a jet of water.
   OTHER WORDS YOU MIGHT USE ARE   **fountain**   **spray**   **spurt**   **squirt**

jewel *noun*
OTHER WORDS YOU MIGHT USE ARE
gem   **precious stone**

STONES USED IN MAKING JEWELLERY ARE
amber   **diamond**   **emerald**   **jet**   **opal**   **pearl**   **ruby**
sapphire

METALS USED TO MAKE JEWELLERY ARE
gold   **platinum**   **silver**

VARIOUS KINDS OF JEWELLERY ARE
bangle   **beads**   **bracelet**   **brooch**   **chain**   **clasp**
earrings   **locket**   **necklace**   **pendant**   **ring**

job *noun*

1 I have some jobs to do for Mum before I come out to play.
OTHER WORDS YOU MIGHT USE ARE
chore   errand   task

2 Sam's cousin has left school and is looking for a job.
OTHER WORDS ARE
employment   occupation   profession   trade   work
SOME OF THE JOBS PEOPLE DO TO EARN THEIR LIVING ARE
**accountant   actor   air hostess   architect   artist
barber   builder   caretaker   carpenter   chef
chemist   cleaner   clergyman   clerk   cook
decorator   dentist   designer   detective   driver
doctor   dustman   electrician   engineer   entertainer
farmer   fireman   gardener   hairdresser   journalist
lawyer   lecturer   librarian   mechanic   midwife
milkman   model   musician   nurse   optician
photographer   pilot   plumber   policewoman
postman   receptionist   reporter   scientist   secretary
shopkeeper   social worker   teacher   traffic warden
typist   vet   waiter   writer**

join *verb*

1 to join one thing to another.
OTHER VERBS YOU MIGHT USE ARE   **to attach   to connect   to fasten
to fix   to link**
For other verbs, see **fasten**

2 Two motorways join in a mile.
OTHER VERBS ARE   **to come together   to meet   to merge**

joint *noun*

JOINTS IN YOUR BODY ARE
**ankle   elbow   hip   knee   knuckle   shoulder
wrist**

jolt *verb*

The car jolted along the rough road.
OTHER VERBS YOU MIGHT USE ARE   **to bounce   to bump   to jerk
to shake**

journey *noun*
KINDS OF JOURNEY ARE
excursion   expedition   outing   tour   trip

A journey in a ship is a **cruise** or a **sail** or a **voyage**.
A journey in a car is a **drive**.
A journey in a plane is a **flight**.
A journey on a horse or bicycle is a **ride**.
A journey on foot is a
hike   ramble   trek   walk.
A journey with a special purpose is a **mission**.
For other words, see **travel**

judge *verb*
1 The criminal was judged in a court of law.
OTHER VERBS YOU MIGHT USE ARE   **to condemn   to convict   to punish
to sentence**
2 The referee judged that the player was off-side.
OTHER VERBS ARE   **to consider   to decide   to rule**

jumble *noun*
Dad wanted to know why there was a jumble of clothes on the floor.
OTHER WORDS YOU MIGHT USE ARE   **assortment   chaos   clutter
confusion   mess   muddle**

jump *verb*
1 We jumped over the fence.
OTHER VERBS YOU MIGHT USE ARE   **to bound   to hop   to leap   to skip
to vault**
2 The cat jumped on the mouse.
OTHER VERBS ARE   **to spring   to pounce**

just *adjective*
The referee's decision was just.
OTHER WORDS YOU MIGHT USE ARE   **fair   honest   lawful   proper
right   unbiased**
The opposite is unfair

Kk

keen *adjective*

Jo is keen to learn the piano.

    OTHER WORDS YOU MIGHT USE ARE   **anxious**   **eager**   **enthusiastic**

keep *verb*

1 I'll keep some sweets for later.

    OTHER VERBS YOU MIGHT USE ARE   **to save**   **to store**

2 If you can't do it straight away, keep trying!

    OTHER VERBS ARE   **to carry on**   **to continue**   **to persist**

3 Please keep still.

    OTHER VERBS ARE   **to remain**   **to stay**

4 Mum says it's expensive to keep a family.

    OTHER VERBS ARE   **to care for**   **to feed**   **to look after**   **to mind**   **to provide for**   **to support**   **to tend**

kill *verb*

    OTHER VERBS YOU MIGHT USE ARE

    (*informal*) **to finish off**   **to slay**

to kill a famous person

    to assassinate

to kill a criminal

    to execute or **put to death**

to kill a person

    to murder

to kill a lot of people

    to massacre

to kill pests

    to exterminate

to kill an animal that is old or ill

    to put to sleep

to kill an animal for food

    to slaughter

    WAYS TO KILL A PERSON ARE

    to behead   **to choke**   **to crucify**   **to drown**   **to electrocute**   **to gas**   **to hang**   **to knife**   **to poison**   **to shoot**   **to stab**   **to strangle**   **to suffocate**   **to throttle**

kind *adjective*

We are lucky to have kind neighbours.

OTHER WORDS YOU MIGHT USE ARE **considerate** **friendly**
good-natured **helpful** **kind-hearted** **loving** **neighbourly**
sympathetic **thoughtful** **unselfish**

The opposite is unkind

kind *noun*

1 A terrier is a kind of dog.

OTHER WORDS YOU MIGHT USE ARE **breed** **sort** **species** **type**

2 What kind of butter do you buy?

OTHER WORDS ARE **brand** **make** **variety**

kitchen *noun*

THINGS YOU USE IN A KITCHEN TO HEAT OR COOK FOOD ARE
cooker **electric plate** **gas ring** **grill** **hotplate**
kettle **microwave** **oven** **stove** **toaster**

OTHER THINGS YOU USE IN A KITCHEN ARE
baking tin **blender** **bowl** **breadboard** **breadknife**
carving knife **casserole** **chip pan** **crockery** **cutlery**
dishes **dish rack** **dishwasher** **draining board** **jug**
mincer **mixer** **pans** **percolator** **pots** **rolling pin**
salt cellar **saucepan** **scales** **sink** **tea towel**
teapot **tin-opener** **tray** **whisk**

PLACES WHERE YOU KEEP FOOD ARE
freezer **fridge** or **refrigerator** **larder** **pantry**

kneel *verb*

I kneeled down to tie my shoe.

OTHER VERBS YOU MIGHT USE ARE **to bend** **to crouch** **to stoop**

knife *noun*

OTHER WORDS YOU MIGHT USE ARE **carving knife** **dagger** **penknife**

knob *noun*

1 the knob on the door.

ANOTHER WORD IS **handle**

2 a knob of butter.

ANOTHER WORD IS **lump**

knock *verb*
I knocked on the door.
OTHER VERBS YOU MIGHT USE ARE **to rap   to tap**
For other verbs, see **hit**

know *verb*
1 Sam knows the names of all the kings and queens of England.
OTHER VERBS YOU MIGHT USE ARE **to recognize   to remember**
2 Mum knows a bit of French.
ANOTHER VERB IS **to understand**

knowledge *noun*
1 You get a lot of knowledge from an encyclopaedia.
OTHER WORDS YOU MIGHT USE ARE **facts   information**
2 Farmers have a great knowledge of the countryside.
OTHER WORDS ARE **experience   understanding**

Ll

lag *verb*
If we lag behind we'll miss the bus.
OTHER VERBS YOU MIGHT USE ARE **to dawdle**   (*informal*) **to hang about**
to linger   to loiter   to straggle

lake *noun*
For other words, see **water**

lame *adjective*
The lame man used a walking stick.
OTHER WORDS YOU MIGHT USE ARE **crippled   disabled   limping**

land *noun*
1 foreign lands.
OTHER WORDS YOU MIGHT USE ARE **country   nation**
2 land to grow crops on.
OTHER WORDS ARE **earth   ground   soil**

land *verb*
1 The plane landed at the airport.
   OTHER VERBS YOU MIGHT USE ARE **to arrive to come down
   to touch down**
2 The sailors landed on an island.
   OTHER VERBS ARE **to come ashore to disembark**

large *adjective*
   OTHER WORDS YOU MIGHT USE ARE **big broad fat grand great
   long roomy spacious tall wide**
   WORDS FOR VERY LARGE THINGS ARE **colossal enormous giant
   gigantic huge immense infinite massive mighty
   monstrous tremendous vast**
The opposite is small

last *adjective*
Our song was the last item in the concert.
   OTHER WORDS YOU MIGHT USE ARE **concluding final**
The opposite is first

last *verb*
The fine weather lasted all week.
   OTHER VERBS YOU MIGHT USE ARE **to continue to go on to keep on
   to persist to remain to stay**

late *adjective*
The bus is late.
   OTHER WORDS YOU MIGHT USE ARE **delayed overdue**
Opposites are early or punctual

lately *adverb*
   ANOTHER WORD IS **recently**

laugh *verb*
   VARIOUS WAYS WE LAUGH ARE **to chuckle to giggle to grin
   to smile to titter**
   TO LAUGH UNKINDLY AT SOMEONE IS **to jeer to sneer to snigger**
For other verbs, see **mock**

law *noun*
We obey the laws of the country.
   OTHER WORDS YOU MIGHT USE ARE **regulation rule**

lay *verb*

I laid the papers on the desk.

OTHER VERBS YOU MIGHT USE ARE   **to leave   to place   to put
to set down   to spread**

layer *noun*

There was a layer of ice over the playground.

OTHER WORDS YOU MIGHT USE ARE   **coating   film   sheet   skin
thickness**

lazy *adjective*

That cat leads a lazy life!

ANOTHER WORD IS **idle**
The opposite is **busy**

lead *verb*

1 The teacher led the children back to the classroom.

OTHER VERBS YOU MIGHT USE ARE   **to conduct   to guide   to take**

2 The captain led her team with great skill.

OTHER VERBS ARE   **to command   to direct   to manage**

leak *verb*

Water leaked out of the bucket.

OTHER VERBS YOU MIGHT USE ARE   **to drip   to escape   to ooze   to seep
to trickle**

lean *verb*

The sinking ship leaned to one side.

OTHER VERBS YOU MIGHT USE ARE   **to heel over   to list   to slant
to slope   to tilt**

leap *verb*

Sam leaped over the fence.

OTHER VERBS YOU MIGHT USE ARE   **to bound   to jump   to spring
to vault**

learn *verb*

1 We learned a lot about history when we went to the castle.

OTHER VERBS YOU MIGHT USE ARE   **to discover   to find out**

2 We learned the song by heart.

ANOTHER VERB IS **to memorize**

leave *verb*

1 Don't leave your pets when you go on holiday.
   OTHER VERBS YOU MIGHT USE ARE   **to abandon**   **to desert**   **to forsake**
2 The guard blew a whistle to show that the train was ready to leave.
   OTHER VERBS ARE   **to depart**   **to go**   **to set off**
3 Leave the empty milk bottles outside the front door.
   OTHER VERBS ARE   **to deposit**   **to place**   **to put down**   **to set down**

lecture *noun*

A policewoman gave us a lecture on road safety.
   OTHER WORDS YOU MIGHT USE ARE   **lesson**   **speech**   **talk**

leg *noun*

For parts of the body, see **body**

legal *adjective*

Is it legal to park on this road?
   OTHER WORDS YOU MIGHT USE ARE   **allowed**   **lawful**   **permitted**
The opposite is illegal

lend *verb*

Can you lend me a pen?
   ANOTHER VERB IS **to loan**
If you give something to someone to use for a short time, you **lend** it.
If someone gives something to you to use, you **borrow** it.

length *noun*

   OTHER WORDS YOU MIGHT USE ARE   **distance**   **measurement**

let *verb*

1 Sam let Jo ride his bike.
   OTHER VERBS YOU MIGHT USE ARE   **to allow**   **to permit**
2 Aunt Jean lets her caravan to holidaymakers in the summer.
   OTHER VERBS ARE   **to hire**   **to rent**

level *adjective*

1 You need a level field for playing rounders.
   OTHER WORDS YOU MIGHT USE ARE   **even**   **flat**   **horizontal**   **smooth**
2 At half time the scores were level.
   ANOTHER WORD IS **equal**

licence *noun*
You need a licence to go fishing.
ANOTHER WORD IS **permit**

lid *noun*
Put the lid back on the jam.
OTHER WORDS YOU MIGHT USE ARE   **cap   cover   top**

lie *noun*
Don't tell lies!
OTHER WORDS YOU MIGHT USE ARE   **falsehood**   (*informal*) **fib**

lie *verb*
1 Don't believe her - I think she's lying.
OTHER VERBS YOU MIGHT USE ARE   **to bluff**   (*informal*) **to fib**
2 Sam lay on the sofa.
OTHER VERBS ARE   **to lean back   to recline   to sprawl**

life *noun*
Our dog is full of life.
OTHER WORDS YOU MIGHT USE ARE   **energy   liveliness   vitality**

lifelike *adjective*
The wax models were very lifelike.
OTHER WORDS YOU MIGHT USE ARE   **natural   realistic**

lift *verb*
1 Lift the box onto the shelf.
OTHER VERBS YOU MIGHT USE ARE   **to hoist   to raise**
2 Jo lifted baby out of her pram.
ANOTHER VERB IS **to pick up**

light *adjective*
1 a light suitcase.
The opposite is heavy
2 a light room.
OTHER WORDS YOU MIGHT USE ARE   **bright   well-lit**
The opposite is dark
3 light colours.
OTHER WORDS ARE   **faint   pale**
The opposite is strong

light *noun*

THINGS WHICH GIVE LIGHT ARE
**bulb   candle   electric light   floodlight   headlight
lamp   lantern   searchlight   spotlight   streetlight
torch**

LIGHTS USED FOR DECORATION ARE
fairy lights   illuminations

NATURAL LIGHT IS
daylight   moonlight   starlight   sunlight

DIFFERENT WAYS LIGHT SHINES ARE
**blaze   burn   dazzle   flash   flicker   glare   gleam
glimmer   glint   glisten   glitter   glow   shine
spark   sparkle   twinkle**

light *verb*

1 At Christmas we lit the church with candles.
OTHER VERBS YOU MIGHT USE ARE   **to brighten   to illuminate
to lighten**
2 We tried to light the bonfire.
OTHER VERBS ARE   **to ignite   to kindle   to set fire to**

like *verb*

1 We like our neighbours.
OTHER VERBS YOU MIGHT USE ARE   **to approve of   to be fond of
to respect**
For other verbs, see **love**
2 I would like a drink, please.
OTHER VERBS ARE   **to enjoy   to fancy   to want
to wish for**
The opposite is hate

likely *adjective*

1 Rain is likely today.
ANOTHER WORD IS **probable**
2 Sam is a likely person to be captain of the team.
OTHER WORDS ARE   **appropriate   suitable**

limp *adjective*
1 limp covers on a book.
    OTHER WORDS YOU MIGHT USE ARE   **flexible**   **soft**
The opposite is stiff
2 limp lettuce.
    OTHER WORDS ARE   **drooping**   **floppy**
The opposite is crisp

limp *verb*
Jo limped because her shoe hurt.
    ANOTHER VERB IS **to hobble**
For other verbs, see **lame**

line *noun*
1 lines on the road.
    OTHER WORDS YOU MIGHT USE ARE   **dash**   **mark**   **streak**   **stripe**
2 lines on someone's face.
    OTHER WORDS ARE   **crease**   **furrow**   **wrinkle**
3 a railway line.
    OTHER WORDS ARE   **rails**   **route**   **track**
4 We waited in a line.
    OTHER WORDS ARE   **column**   **file**   **queue**   **rank**   **row**

linger *verb*
Don't linger in the playground.
    OTHER VERBS YOU MIGHT USE ARE   **to dawdle**   **to delay**
    (*informal*) **to hang about**   **to loiter**   **to remain**   **to stay**
    to wait about

link *verb*
Sam can link his keyboard to a computer.
    OTHER VERBS YOU MIGHT USE ARE   **to attach**   **to connect**   **to join**

litter *noun*
We get into trouble if we leave litter round the school.
    OTHER WORDS YOU MIGHT USE ARE   **clutter**   **junk**   **rubbish**

little *adjective*
1 Sam's got a little radio that he can put in his pocket.
    OTHER WORDS YOU MIGHT USE ARE   **compact**   **miniature**   **minute**
    small   **tiny**
2 We had a little chat.
    OTHER WORDS ARE   **brief**   **short**

3 She gave us little helpings.
   OTHER WORDS ARE   **mean**   (*informal*) **measly**   **stingy**
4 They had a little argument.
   OTHER WORDS ARE   **minor**   **slight**   **trivial**   **unimportant**
   The opposite is big

live *adjective*
There aren't any live dinosaurs.
   OTHER WORDS YOU MIGHT USE ARE   **existing**   **living**

live *verb*
1 Plants can't live without water.
   OTHER VERBS YOU MIGHT USE ARE   **to exist**   **to remain alive**
   to survive
2 Jo's Granny lives in a flat.
   OTHER VERBS ARE   **to dwell in**   **to inhabit**   **to occupy**

lively *adjective*
Those puppies are lively!
   OTHER WORDS YOU MIGHT USE ARE   **active**   **energetic**   **frisky**
   The opposite is lazy

load *noun*
Can you carry that heavy load?
   OTHER WORDS YOU MIGHT USE ARE   **burden**   **weight**

load *verb*
We loaded the trolley with food.
   OTHER VERBS YOU MIGHT USE ARE   **to fill**   **to pack**

lock *noun*
Mum fitted a lock to the door.
   OTHER WORDS YOU MIGHT USE ARE   **bolt**   **catch**   **latch**   **padlock**

lock *verb*
Did you lock the door?
   OTHER VERBS YOU MIGHT USE ARE   **to fasten**   **to secure**

logical *adjective*
a logical argument.
   OTHER WORDS YOU MIGHT USE ARE   **intelligent**   **reasonable**
   sensible

lonely *adjective*

1   Jo felt lonely when Sam went away.
OTHER WORDS YOU MIGHT USE ARE   **alone   forsaken   friendless   neglected   solitary**

2   We heard a ghost story about a lonely farmhouse.
OTHER WORDS ARE   **isolated   remote   secluded**

long *adjective*

It seemed a long journey.
OTHER WORDS YOU MIGHT USE ARE   **endless   lengthy**
The opposite is short

long *verb*

I longed for a drink.
OTHER VERBS YOU MIGHT USE ARE   **to fancy   to hanker after   to want   to wish for   to yearn for**

look *verb*

1   We looked at the things we had collected on our walk.
OTHER VERBS YOU MIGHT USE ARE   **to examine   to study   to survey   to view**
TO LOOK AT SOMETHING QUICKLY   **to glance   to peep**
TO LOOK FOR A LONG TIME   **to gaze   to stare   to watch**

2   The dog looked friendly.
OTHER VERBS ARE   **to appear   to seem**

3   I helped Mum look for her purse.
OTHER VERBS ARE   **to hunt   to search for   to seek**

loose *adjective*

1   My tooth is loose.
OTHER WORDS YOU MIGHT USE ARE   **shaky   unsteady   wobbly**

2   The animals were all loose.
OTHER WORDS ARE   **at liberty   free**

lorry *noun*

For other words, see **travel**

lose *verb*

1   Sam was upset when he lost his watch.
ANOTHER VERB IS **to mislay**

2   Our team lost on Saturday.
A PHRASE IS **to be defeated**

loud *adjective*
The neighbours complained about the loud music.
OTHER WORDS YOU MIGHT USE ARE   **deafening   noisy   shrill**
The opposite is quiet

lounge *noun*
OTHER WORDS YOU MIGHT USE ARE   **drawing room   living room
sitting room**

love *verb*
OTHER VERBS YOU MIGHT USE ARE   **to adore   to be fond of
to be in love with   to care for   to idolize   to like   to treasure
to worship**

lovely *adjective*
For other words, see **beautiful**

low *adjective*
The opposite is high

loyal *adjective*
Sam is a loyal supporter of his local team.
OTHER WORDS YOU MIGHT USE ARE   **devoted   faithful   reliable
trustworthy**

luck *noun*
Sam found his lost watch by luck.
OTHER WORDS YOU MIGHT USE ARE   **accident   chance
coincidence**

lucky *adjective*
I was lucky to find what I wanted.
ANOTHER WORD IS **fortunate**
The opposite is unlucky

luggage *noun*
The driver put our luggage in the back of the car.
DIFFERENT ITEMS OF LUGGAGE MIGHT BE
bag   box   case   holdall   suitcase   trunk

lump *noun*

1 Uncle gave Jo a lump of chocolate.
OTHER WORDS YOU MIGHT USE ARE **bar   block   chunk   hunk   piece   slab**
2 Dad got a lump on the head where he hit himself.
OTHER WORDS YOU MIGHT USE ARE **bulge   bump   hump   knob   swelling**

luxury *noun*

That cat lives a life of luxury!
OTHER WORDS YOU MIGHT USE ARE **comfort   ease   pleasure   relaxation**

Mm

machine *noun*

The workshop had a machine for doing woodwork.
OTHER WORDS YOU MIGHT USE ARE **apparatus   instrument   tool**
A word you might use for machines in general is **machinery**

mad *adjective*

1 He behaved so strangely that people said he was mad.
OTHER WORDS YOU MIGHT USE ARE *(informal)* **crazy   insane   mentally ill   unbalanced**
2 He's mad to go out in this rain!
For other words, see **silly**

magic *noun*

1 Can witches really do magic?
OTHER WORDS YOU MIGHT USE ARE **charms   enchantments   sorcery   spells   witchcraft**
2 The conjuror did some magic.
A PHRASE YOU MIGHT USE IS **conjuring tricks**

magician *noun*

OTHER WORDS YOU MIGHT USE ARE **conjuror   sorcerer   wizard**

magnificent *adjective*
a magnificent palace.
OTHER WORDS YOU MIGHT USE ARE   **grand   impressive   majestic   noble   splendid   stately**

mail *noun*
For other words, see **post**

main *adjective*
The main ingredient of bread is flour.
OTHER WORDS YOU MIGHT USE ARE   **basic   chief   essential   important   principal**

make *verb*, see next page

make-up *noun*
KINDS OF MAKE-UP ARE
blusher   eye-liner   eye-shadow   face cream   face powder   lipstick   nail varnish

THINGS PEOPLE USE TO MAKE THEMSELVES SMELL NICER ARE
aftershave   deodorant   perfume   scent   talc or **talcum powder**

male *noun*
There are special words for male and female human beings and some animals.

A male human being is a **boy** or **man**.

A male bird is a **cock**.
A male cat is a **tom-cat**.
A male chicken is a **cockerel**.
A male deer is a **buck** or **stag**.
A male duck is a **drake**.
A male goat is a **billy goat**.
A male goose is a **gander**.
A male horse is a **stallion**.
A male pig is a **hog**.
A male rabbit is a **buck**.
A male sheep is a **ram**.
A male swan is a **cob**.

For words for females, see **female**

make *verb*

THIS VERB HAS MANY USES. HERE ARE SOME OF THE WAYS YOU CAN USE IT, AND
SOME OTHER VERBS YOU COULD CHOOSE

1 I made a plan.
to form   to invent   to produce   to think up

2 We made a den in the garden.
to build   to construct   to create   to erect

3 They make cars in that factory.
to assemble   to manufacture

4 Don't make trouble.
to bring about   to cause   to provoke

5 You can't make me do it.
to compel   to force   to oblige   to order

6 The head made a speech.
to deliver   to give

7 It's easy to make a P into a B.
**to alter   to change   to convert   to transform
to turn**

8 How can I make some money?
to earn   to get   to obtain   to receive

9 You'll make a good player if you practise.
to become   to change into   to grow into   to turn into

10 Will our team make the final?
to get to   to reach

11 2 and 2 make 4.
to add up to   to come to

12 Mum made an appointment at the doctor's.
to arrange   to fix

13 I can't make out what happened.
to follow   to hear   to see   to understand

14 She made up an excuse.
to invent   to plan   to think up

man *noun*
OTHER WORDS YOU MIGHT USE ARE

a polite word
gentleman

a married man
husband

a man who is not married
bachelor

a man whose wife has died
widower

a man who has children
father

a young man
boy   youth

manage *verb*
1 The head manages the school.
OTHER VERBS YOU MIGHT USE ARE   **to be in charge of   to control
to look after   to run**
2 Can you manage a big helping?
OTHER VERBS YOU MIGHT USE ARE   **to cope with   to deal with
to handle**
3 Could you manage to help us on Saturday?
ANOTHER VERB IS **to arrange**

manner *noun*
He spoke in a friendly manner.
OTHER WORDS YOU MIGHT USE ARE   **fashion   style   way**

map *noun*
A simple map is a **diagram** or **plan**.
A map used by sailors is a **chart**.
A book of maps is an **atlas**.

mark *noun*
There's a mark on my new dress.

OTHER WORDS YOU MIGHT USE ARE **smear smudge spot stain**

market *noun*
DIFFERENT KINDS OF MARKET ARE
**auction bazaar car boot sale fair
street market**

marsh *noun*
We began to sink into the marsh.

OTHER WORDS YOU MIGHT USE ARE **bog swamp**

marvellous *adjective*
I had a marvellous holiday.

OTHER WORDS YOU MIGHT USE ARE **excellent** (*informal*) **fabulous
splendid wonderful**

mash *verb*
We mashed the baby's dinner until it was soft.

OTHER VERBS YOU MIGHT USE ARE **to crush to pulp to purée
to smash to squash**

mass *noun*
There was a mass of rubbish to clear away.

OTHER WORDS YOU MIGHT USE ARE **heap mound pile quantity
stack**

match *noun*
a boxing match.

OTHER WORDS YOU MIGHT USE ARE **competition contest
game**

material *noun*
1 building materials.

OTHER WORDS YOU MIGHT USE ARE **stuff substances things**
2 material to make curtains.
For other words, see **cloth**

mathematics *noun*

A short word for mathematics is **maths**.
Working with numbers is also called **arithmetic**.

WORDS FOR THINGS YOU DO IN MATHEMATICS ARE

addition or **adding**   **calculation** or **calculating**
counting   **division** or **dividing**   **investigating**
measuring   **multiplication** or **multiplying**
subtraction or **subtracting** or **taking away**   **sums**

VERBS YOU MIGHT USE IN MATHS ARE

to add   **to add up**   **to calculate**   **to count**   **to divide**
to investigate   **to measure**   **to multiply**   **to subtract**
to take away   **to work out**

OTHER WORDS YOU MIGHT USE IN MATHS ARE

angle   **answer**   **area**   **capacity**   **diagonal**
difference   **digit**   **figure**   **fraction**   **graph**
measurement   **minus**   **number**   **pattern**   **plus**
problem   **shape**   **sum**   **symmetry**   **times**   **total**
unit   **volume**

THINGS YOU MIGHT USE TO HELP YOU IN MATHEMATICS ARE

calculator   **compasses**   **computer**   **ruler**   **set square**

For words you might use when you measure things, see **measurement**
For names of different shapes, see **shape**

matter *noun*

1 We have some matters to discuss.
OTHER WORDS YOU MIGHT USE ARE   **business**   **subject**   **topic**
2 What's the matter?
OTHER WORDS ARE   **difficulty**   **problem**   **trouble**

meal *noun*

DIFFERENT MEALS ARE

breakfast   **dinner**   **high tea**   **lunch**   **supper**   **tea**

A very splendid meal is a **banquet** or **feast**.
A meal where you help yourself is a **buffet**.
A small meal is a **snack**.
A meal you eat out of doors is a **picnic**.
A meal you cook out of doors is a **barbecue**.

mean *adjective*
He's mean with his money.
> OTHER WORDS YOU MIGHT USE ARE   **miserly**   (*informal*) **stingy**
The opposite is generous

mean *verb*
1 What does this word mean?
> OTHER VERBS YOU MIGHT USE ARE   **to convey**   **to indicate**   **to say**
> **to stand for**
2 What do you mean to do?
> OTHER VERBS ARE   **to aim**   **to intend**   **to plan**   **to propose**

measurement *noun*
> ANOTHER WORD IS **size**
> OTHER WORDS YOU MIGHT USE ARE

how long something is: **length**
how wide something is: **breadth** or **width**
how tall something is: **height**
> UNITS TO MEASURE LENGTH, BREADTH, OR HEIGHT ARE
> **centimetres   metres   kilometres**
> OLD UNITS ARE
> **inches   feet   yards   miles**

how big a surface is: **area**
> UNITS TO MEASURE AREA ARE
> **square metres   hectares**
> OLD UNITS ARE
> **square feet   square yards   acres**

how much something holds: **volume**
> UNITS TO MEASURE VOLUME ARE
> **cubic centimetres** or **litres**
> OLD UNITS ARE
> **pints** or **gallons**

how heavy something is: **weight**
> UNITS TO MEASURE WEIGHT ARE
> **grams   kilograms   tonnes**
> OLD UNITS ARE
> **ounces   pounds   tons**

meat *noun*

DIFFERENT KINDS OF MEAT ARE

bacon   **beef**   **chicken**   **ham**   **lamb**   **pork**   **turkey**   **veal**   **venison**

YOU CAN BUY MEAT IN THE FORM OF

burgers   **chops**   **joint**   **mince**   **sausage**   **steak**

medicine *noun*

I need medicine for my cough.
For other words, see **health**

medium *adjective*

Sam is medium height for his age.

OTHER WORDS YOU MIGHT USE ARE   **average**   **middling**   **normal**

meet *verb*

1 Two roads meet here.

OTHER VERBS YOU MIGHT USE ARE   **to come together**   **to join**   **to merge**

2 I met my friend in town.

OTHER VERBS ARE   **to encounter**   (*informal*) **to run into**   **to see**

3 All the classes met in the hall.

OTHER VERBS ARE   **to assemble**   **to congregate**   **to gather**

meeting *noun*

DIFFERENT KINDS OF MEETING ARE   **assembly**   **committee**   **conference**   **council**

melt *verb*

The ice melted in the sun.

OTHER VERBS YOU MIGHT USE ARE   **to thaw**   **to unfreeze**

mend *verb*

1 The garage mended the car.

OTHER VERBS YOU MIGHT USE ARE   **to fix**   **to put right**   **to repair**

2 Dad likes mending old furniture.

OTHER VERBS ARE   **to do up**   **to renovate**   **to restore**

3 Sam mended his jeans.

OTHER VERBS ARE   **to darn**   **to patch**   **to sew up**   **to stitch up**

mention *verb*
I mentioned that I was hungry.
OTHER VERBS YOU MIGHT USE ARE **to comment   to remark   to say**

merciful *adjective*
The judge was merciful and let him off with a warning.
OTHER WORDS YOU MIGHT USE ARE **forgiving   kind   sympathetic**
The opposite is cruel

mercy *noun*
The judge showed mercy.
OTHER WORDS YOU MIGHT USE ARE **forgiveness   pity**

merry *adjective*
a merry tune.
OTHER WORDS YOU MIGHT USE ARE **cheerful   happy   jolly   lively**
The opposite is sad

mess *noun*
Clear up this mess!
OTHER WORDS YOU MIGHT USE ARE **chaos   clutter   confusion
jumble   muddle**

message *noun*
I sent a message that I was busy.
OTHER WORDS YOU MIGHT USE ARE **letter   note**

metal *noun*
DIFFERENT METALS ARE
**aluminium   brass   bronze   copper   gold   iron
lead   platinum   silver   steel   tin   uranium   zinc**

method *noun*
Our teacher showed us a good method for doing multiplication.
OTHER WORDS YOU MIGHT USE ARE **procedure   system   technique   way**

middle *noun*
the middle of the earth.
OTHER WORDS YOU MIGHT USE ARE **centre   core   heart**

mild *adjective*
1 mild weather.
OTHER WORDS YOU MIGHT USE ARE **gentle pleasant warm**
2 a mild illness.
ANOTHER WORD IS **slight**
The opposite is severe

mind *noun*
Use your mind!
OTHER WORDS YOU MIGHT USE ARE **brain intelligence understanding**

mind *verb*
1 I'll mind the baby.
OTHER VERBS YOU MIGHT USE ARE **to care for to look after to tend**
2 Do you mind about missing the party?
OTHER VERBS ARE **to care to worry**

mine *noun*
a coal mine.
OTHER WORDS YOU MIGHT USE ARE **pit shaft**
A place where they dig coal from the Earth's surface is an **opencast mine**.
A place where they dig stone is a **quarry**.

mischievous *adjective*
The mischievous puppy stole Dad's slippers.
OTHER WORDS YOU MIGHT USE ARE **badly behaved naughty**

miserable *adjective*
1 Jo's miserable when Sam is away.
OTHER WORDS YOU MIGHT USE ARE **depressed gloomy sad unhappy wretched**
The opposite is happy
2 The refugees live in miserable conditions.
OTHER WORDS ARE **awful bad pitiful poor wretched**

misery *noun*
We can't imagine the misery of the refugees.
OTHER WORDS YOU MIGHT USE ARE **distress grief sadness sorrow suffering unhappiness**

mislead *verb*
She misled us and sent us the wrong way.
OTHER VERBS YOU MIGHT USE ARE **to deceive to fool to trick**

miss *verb*

1   If we leave now we'll miss the rush-hour traffic.
OTHER VERBS YOU MIGHT USE ARE   **to avoid**   **to dodge**   **to steer clear of**
2   I missed the bus.
The opposite is catch
3   Jo missed Sam when he was away.
ANOTHER VERB IS **to pine for**
4   You can miss out the questions you don't understand.
OTHER VERBS ARE   **to leave out**   **to omit**   **to skip**

missing *adjective*

Did you find the missing money?
ANOTHER WORD IS **lost**

mist *noun*

ANOTHER WORD IS **haze**
A thick mist is **fog**.

mistake *noun*

spelling mistakes.
OTHER WORDS YOU MIGHT USE ARE   **blunder**   **error**   (*informal*) **slip**

misty *adjective*

a misty view.
OTHER WORDS YOU MIGHT USE ARE   **blurred**   **dim**   **faint**   **fuzzy**
hazy   **indistinct**   **unclear**
The opposite is clear

mix *verb*

1   Mix the flour, fat, and sugar in a bowl.
OTHER VERBS YOU MIGHT USE ARE   **to blend**   **to combine**   **to mingle**
to stir together
2   Don't mix two packs of cards!
OTHER VERBS ARE   **to confuse**   **to jumble**   **to muddle**

mixture *noun*

I had a mixture of sweets.
OTHER WORDS YOU MIGHT USE ARE   **assortment**   **variety**

moan *verb*

He moaned with pain.
OTHER VERBS YOU MIGHT USE ARE   **to groan**   **to wail**

mock *verb*
It's unkind to mock other people.
OTHER VERBS YOU MIGHT USE ARE   **to laugh at   to make fun of**
to ridicule   to sneer at   to taunt   to tease

moderate *adjective*
Dad drives at moderate speed.
OTHER WORDS YOU MIGHT USE ARE   **medium   middling   normal**
ordinary   reasonable

modern *adjective*
1 Grandad says he doesn't understand modern inventions like computers.
OTHER WORDS YOU MIGHT USE ARE   **new   recent**
The opposite is old
2 Do you like modern clothes?
OTHER WORDS ARE   **fashionable   stylish**   (*informal*) **trendy**
up-to-date
The opposite is old-fashioned

modest *adjective*
1 She was modest about winning the prize.
ANOTHER WORD IS **humble**
The opposite is conceited
2 He was too modest to undress on the beach.
OTHER WORDS YOU MIGHT USE ARE   **bashful   shy**

money *noun*
Money you have in your pocket is **cash** or **change**.
IT MIGHT BE
coins   (*informal*) **coppers   notes   silver**

People can also buy things with a **cheque** or a **credit card**.
A LOT OF MONEY IS
a fortune   wealth

MONEY YOU GET FOR WORK YOU DO IS
earnings   income   pay   salary   wages

Money you get when you retire from work is a **pension**.
Money you save in the bank is your **savings**.
Money people have to pay to the government is **tax**.

monster *noun*
FRIGHTENING CREATURES YOU READ ABOUT IN STORIES ARE

beast	dragon	giant	ogre
troll	vampire	werewolf	

month *noun*
THE MONTHS OF THE YEAR ARE

January	February	March	April
May	June	July	August
September	October	November	December

mood *noun*
Is Dad in a good mood today?
OTHER WORDS YOU MIGHT USE ARE   **humour   temper**

moral *adjective*
a moral person.
OTHER WORDS YOU MIGHT USE ARE   **good   honest   truthful   virtuous**
The opposite is immoral

motive *noun*
What was the motive for the crime?
OTHER WORDS YOU MIGHT USE ARE   **purpose   reason**

motor *noun*
an electric motor.
ANOTHER WORD IS **engine**

mountain *noun*
The top of a mountain is the **summit** or **peak**.
A line of mountains is a **range** or **ridge**.
A mountain which sometimes sends out hot liquid, gases, or ash
is a **volcano**.

move *verb*

THIS VERB HAS MANY USES. HERE ARE SOME OF THE WAYS YOU CAN USE IT, AND SOME OTHER VERBS YOU COULD CHOOSE

1 to move along.
   to come   to fly   to go   to journey   to march
   to pass   to tour   to travel   to walk

2 to move along quickly.
   to canter   to dart   to dash   to fly   to gallop
   to hurry   to race   to run   to rush   to shoot
   to speed   to streak   to tear   (*informal*) to zoom

3 to move along slowly.
   to crawl   to dawdle   to stroll

4 to move along gracefully.
   to dance   to glide   to skate   to skim   to slide
   to slip

5 to move along clumsily.
   to shuffle   to stagger   to stumble   to sway
   to totter   to trip

6 to move along stealthily.
   to crawl   to creep   to slink   to slither

7 to move away from somewhere.
   to depart   to leave   to quit

8 to move back.
   to reverse   to withdraw

9 to move downwards.
   to descend   to drop   to fall   to sink

10 to move upwards.
   to arise   to climb   to mount   to rise

11 to move in somewhere.
   to enter

12 to move round and round.
   to revolve   to roll   to rotate   to spin   to turn
   to twirl   to twist   to whirl

13 to move towards something.
   to advance   to approach

14 to move restlessly.
   to fidget   to shake   to stir   to toss   to tremble
   to twist   to twitch   to wag   to waggle   to wave

15 to move things.
   to budge   to carry   to shift   to transport

mud *noun*
There was some mud on the road.
OTHER WORDS YOU MIGHT USE ARE   **clay   dirt   muck   slime**

muddle *verb*
1 Don't muddle the library books.
OTHER VERBS YOU MIGHT USE ARE   **to jumble   to mix up**
2 You muddle me if you talk fast.
OTHER VERBS ARE   **to bewilder   to confuse**

murder *verb*
For other verbs, see **kill**

music *noun*

DIFFERENT KINDS OF MUSIC ARE
**classical music   disco music   folk music   jazz
musicals   opera   pop music   rap
reggae   rock**

KINDS OF MUSIC FOR SINGING ARE
**ballad   carol   folk song   hymn
lullaby   pop song   shanty   spiritual**

BRASS INSTRUMENTS ARE
**bugle   cornet   horn   trombone
trumpet   tuba**

OTHER INSTRUMENTS YOU PLAY BY BLOWING ARE
**bagpipes   bassoon   clarinet   flute
harmonica or mouthorgan oboe   pan pipes
piccolo   recorder   saxophone**

INSTRUMENTS WITH STRINGS THAT YOU PLAY BY PLUCKING ARE
banjo   guitar   harp   sitar

INSTRUMENTS WITH STRINGS THAT YOU CAN PLAY WITH A BOW ARE
**cello   double bass fiddle   viola
violin**

INSTRUMENTS YOU PLAY BY PRESSING KEYS ARE
**harmonium   harpsichord keyboard   organ
piano**

mysterious *adjective*

1 The doctors didn't know what to do about my mysterious illness.

    OTHER WORDS YOU MIGHT USE ARE   **mystifying**   **puzzling**   **strange**

2 The castle looked mysterious in the moonlight.

    OTHER WORDS ARE   **eerie**   **ghostly**   **magical**   **weird**

mystery *noun*

The detective solved the mystery.

    OTHER WORDS YOU MIGHT USE ARE   **problem**   **puzzle**   **riddle**

PERCUSSION INSTRUMENTS ARE

castanets	**chime bars**	**cymbals**	**drums**
glockenspiel	**gong**	**kettledrum**	**tambourine**
triangle	**tubular bells**	**xylophone**	

PEOPLE WHO MAKE MUSIC ARE

composer	**conductor**	**performer**	**player**
singer			

PEOPLE WHO PLAY INSTRUMENTS ARE

drummer	**fiddler**	**guitarist**	**harpist**
organist	**percussionist**	**pianist**	**piper**
trumpeter	**violinist**		

DIFFERENT SINGING VOICES ARE

alto	**bass**	**soprano**	**tenor**
treble			

People who play or sing on their own are **soloists**.
A singer may also be called a **vocalist**.

GROUPS OF MUSICIANS ARE

band	**choir** or **chorus**		**ensemble**
group	**orchestra**	**quartet**	**quintet**
trio			

Nn

naked *adjective*

> OTHER WORDS YOU MIGHT USE ARE **bare** **nude** **unclothed** **undressed**

name *noun*

> The name that you are given when you are born is your **first name**.
> The name that everyone in your family has is your **surname** or **family name**.
> An invented name which friends give you is a **nickname**.
> A name you use instead of your real name is an **alias**.
> A name an author uses instead of a real name is a **pen name**.
> The name of a book is the **title**.
> The name of a particular make of goods is the **brand**.

narrow *adjective*

> OTHER WORDS YOU MIGHT USE ARE **fine** **slim** **thin**
> The opposite is wide

nasty *adjective*

> 1 nasty weather.
> OTHER WORDS YOU MIGHT USE ARE **bad** **dreadful** **horrible** **unpleasant**
> 2 a nasty mess.
> OTHER WORDS ARE **dirty** **disgusting** **filthy** **foul** **revolting**
> 3 a nasty person.
> OTHER WORDS ARE **rude** **unfriendly** **unkind**
> The opposite is nice

nation *noun*

> People from many nations take part in the Olympic Games.
> OTHER WORDS YOU MIGHT USE ARE **country** **race**

natural *adjective*
It's natural to go to sleep when you are tired.
ANOTHER WORD IS **normal**
The opposite is unnatural

naughty *adjective*
We punished the dog because he had been naughty.
OTHER WORDS YOU MIGHT USE ARE   **bad   disobedient   mischievous
wicked**
The opposite is well-behaved

near *adjective* and *adverb*
Our house is near to the shops.
ANOTHER WORD IS **close**

nearly *adverb*
I've nearly finished.
OTHER WORDS YOU MIGHT USE ARE   **almost   not quite   practically**

neat *adjective*
Jo arranged her books in a neat row.
OTHER WORDS YOU MIGHT USE ARE   **orderly   smart   tidy**
The opposite is untidy

necessary *adjective*
It is necessary to water plants in dry weather.
OTHER WORDS YOU MIGHT USE ARE   **essential   important   vital**
The opposite is unnecessary

neck *noun*
For other parts of the body, see **body**

need *verb*
1 We need some butter to make the sandwiches.
OTHER VERBS YOU MIGHT USE ARE   **to require   to want**
2 The football team needs Sam to play in goal.
OTHER VERBS ARE   **to count on   to depend on   to rely on**

neglect *verb*
You mustn't neglect your pets when you go on holiday.
OTHER VERBS YOU MIGHT USE ARE   **to forget   to ignore   to overlook**
The opposite is look after

nervous *adjective*

Our dog gets nervous when she hears thunder.

OTHER WORDS YOU MIGHT USE ARE   **anxious   edgy   fidgety   jumpy**

The opposite is **calm**

neutral *adjective*

The referee has to be neutral.

OTHER WORDS YOU MIGHT USE ARE   **impartial   unbiased**

new *adjective*

1 new clothes.

OTHER WORDS YOU MIGHT USE ARE   **brand new   unused**

2 new bread.

ANOTHER WORD IS **fresh**

3 a new invention.

OTHER WORDS ARE   **modern   recent   up-to-date**

The opposite is **old**

nice *adjective*

THIS WORD HAS MANY USES. HERE ARE SOME OF THE WAYS YOU CAN USE IT, AND SOME OTHER WORDS YOU COULD CHOOSE

1 nice weather.

beautiful   fine   good   lovely   pleasant

2 nice food.

delicious   enjoyable   tasty

3 a nice person.

friendly   kind   likeable

The opposite is **nasty**

noble *adjective*

1 a noble deed.

OTHER WORDS YOU MIGHT USE ARE   **brave   gallant   heroic   worthy**

2 a noble palace.

OTHER WORDS ARE   **grand   majestic   stately**

noise *noun*

Stop that noise!

OTHER WORDS YOU MIGHT USE ARE   **din   hubbub   (*informal*) racket   row   rumpus   uproar**

For kinds of noise, see **sound**

noisy *adjective*
The neighbours complained that our music was too noisy.
OTHER WORDS YOU MIGHT USE ARE   **deafening   loud   rowdy**
The opposite is silent

nonsense *noun*
Don't talk nonsense!
ANOTHER WORD IS **rubbish**

normal *adjective*
1 It's quite normal for people to sweat in hot weather.
OTHER WORDS YOU MIGHT USE ARE   **common   natural   ordinary   usual**
2 The temperature is normal for this time of year.
ANOTHER WORD IS **average**

nosy *adjective*
The kitten was being nosy and got her head stuck in a tin.
OTHER WORDS YOU MIGHT USE ARE   **curious   inquisitive**

nothing *noun*
OTHER WORDS YOU MIGHT USE ARE   **nought   zero**
Nothing in cricket is a **duck**.
Nothing in football is **nil**.
Nothing in tennis is **love**.

notice *noun*
We put up a notice about our play.
OTHER WORDS YOU MIGHT USE ARE   **advertisement   placard   poster   sign**

notice *verb*
Jo noticed that Mum looked tired.
OTHER VERBS YOU MIGHT USE ARE   **to detect   to observe   to see**

nude *adjective*
OTHER WORDS YOU MIGHT USE ARE   **bare   naked   unclothed   undressed**

nuisance *noun*
That dog is a nuisance!
OTHER WORDS YOU MIGHT USE ARE   **bother   pest   trouble   worry**

number *noun*
We had to add up the numbers.
ANOTHER WORD IS **figure**

nurse *noun*
For people who help us when we are ill, see **health**

nut *noun*
SOME NUTS YOU CAN EAT ARE

almond	brazil	cashew	chestnut
coconut	hazelnut	peanut	walnut

Oo

obedient *adjective*
an obedient dog.
ANOTHER WORD IS **well-behaved**
The opposite is disobedient

obey *verb*
You have to obey the rules.
PHRASES YOU MIGHT USE ARE   **to abide by   to keep to**
The opposite is disobey

object *verb*
We object to bad language.
PHRASES YOU MIGHT USE ARE   **to complain about   to disapprove of
to protest about**

obstinate *adjective*
The donkey was obstinate and refused to move.
OTHER WORDS YOU MIGHT USE ARE   **defiant**   (*informal*) **pig-headed
stubborn   unhelpful**
The opposite is helpful

obtain *verb*
For other verbs, see **get**

obvious *adjective*
Jo thought the answer to the question was obvious.
> OTHER WORDS YOU MIGHT USE ARE **clear** **easy to see**   **plain**

occasional *adjective*
We make occasional visits to the pictures.
> OTHER WORDS YOU MIGHT USE ARE **infrequent**   **rare**
The opposite is regular

occupation *noun*
1 What's your mother's occupation?
> OTHER WORDS YOU MIGHT USE ARE **business**   **employment**   **job**
> **work**
2 Fishing is a quiet occupation.
> OTHER WORDS YOU MIGHT USE ARE **activity**   **hobby**   **pastime**

occupy *verb*
1 Six people occupy our house.
> OTHER VERBS YOU MIGHT USE ARE **to inhabit**   **to live in**
2 The soldiers occupied the town.
> OTHER VERBS ARE   **to capture**   **to conquer**   **to invade**   **to take over**

occur *verb*
A nasty accident occurred today.
> OTHER VERBS YOU MIGHT USE ARE **to happen**   **to take place**

odd *adjective*
1 Jo can't explain her dog's odd behaviour.
> OTHER WORDS YOU MIGHT USE ARE **abnormal**   **curious**   **funny**
> **peculiar**   **queer**   **strange**   **uncommon**   **unusual**   **weird**
The opposite is ordinary
2 Where did this odd sock come from?
> OTHER WORDS YOU MIGHT USE ARE **extra**   **single**   **spare**

offend *verb*
I offended Jo because I didn't go to her party.
> OTHER VERBS YOU MIGHT USE ARE **to annoy**   **to displease**   **to insult**
> **to upset**
The opposite is please

offensive *adjective*
1 There's an offensive smell in the kitchen.
OTHER WORDS YOU MIGHT USE ARE **disgusting   foul   horrible   nasty unpleasant**
2 Don't use offensive language.
OTHER WORDS ARE **improper   indecent   rude**
The opposite is pleasing

offer *verb*
1 I offered some cake to Granny.
ANOTHER VERB IS **to give**
2 Sam offered to wash up.
ANOTHER VERB IS **to volunteer**

often *adverb*
OTHER WORDS YOU MIGHT USE ARE **again and again   frequently regularly   repeatedly**
The opposite is seldom

old *adjective*
1 an old car.
OTHER WORDS YOU MIGHT USE ARE **ancient   old-fashioned**
2 an old man.
OTHER WORDS ARE **aged   elderly**
3 an old magazine.
ANOTHER WORD IS **out-of-date**
4 old bread.
ANOTHER WORD IS **stale**
5 old clothes.
OTHER WORDS ARE **shabby   worn-out**
6 valuable old furniture.
ANOTHER WORD IS **antique**
The opposite is new

omit *verb*
The captain omitted Sam from the team because he was injured.
OTHER VERBS YOU MIGHT USE ARE **to drop   to exclude   to leave out**
The opposite is include

open *adjective*
Leave the door open.
OTHER WORDS YOU MIGHT USE ARE **unfastened   unlocked**
The opposite is shut

open *verb*
Please open the door.
OTHER VERBS YOU MIGHT USE ARE   **to undo   to unfasten   to unlock**
The opposite is close

opening *noun*
1 Jo's tortoise crawled through an opening in the fence.
OTHER WORDS YOU MIGHT USE ARE   **break   crack   gap   hole   space**
2 Sam looks forward to the opening of the football season.
OTHER WORDS ARE   **beginning   start**

opinion *noun*
It's my opinion that the dog stole the sausages.
OTHER WORDS YOU MIGHT USE ARE   **belief   guess   idea   thought   view**

opposite *adjective*
1 the opposite side of the road.
ANOTHER WORD IS **facing**
2 the opposite opinion.
OTHER WORDS YOU MIGHT USE ARE   **contrary   different   opposing**

order *verb*
1 He ordered us to stand still.
OTHER VERBS YOU MIGHT USE ARE   **to command   to direct   to instruct   to tell**
2 We ordered fish and chips.
PHRASES YOU MIGHT USE ARE   **to ask for   to send for**

ordinary *adjective*
1 We spent the holiday doing ordinary things.
OTHER WORDS YOU MIGHT USE ARE   **everyday   normal   typical   unexciting   usual**
2 Most of the birds we saw on our walk were just ordinary ones.
OTHER WORDS ARE   **common   familiar   uninteresting   well-known**
3 I want an ordinary portion of chips.
OTHER WORDS ARE   **regular   standard**
The opposite is special

organize *verb*
Our teacher organized a trip to the zoo.
ANOTHER VERB IS **to arrange**

original *adjective*
Mum said the ideas in Sam's story were very original.
OTHER WORDS YOU MIGHT USE ARE   **fresh   imaginative   new
unusual**

outing *noun*
We went on an outing to the country park.
OTHER WORDS YOU MIGHT USE ARE   **excursion   expedition   trip**

oven *noun*
For things you use to heat or cook food, see **kitchen**

overgrown *adjective*
an overgrown garden.
OTHER WORDS YOU MIGHT USE ARE   **tangled   untidy**

overturn *verb*
The boat overturned.
ANOTHER VERB IS **to capsize**

own *verb*
Do you own a bike?
ANOTHER VERB IS **to possess**
to own up
ANOTHER VERB IS **to confess**

Pp

pack *verb*
We packed everything into the car.
OTHER VERBS YOU MIGHT USE ARE   **to load   to put**

packet *noun*
1 The postman brought an interesting-looking packet.
OTHER WORDS ARE   **package   parcel**
2 I bought a packet of cornflakes.
ANOTHER WORD IS **box**

page *noun*
Jo tore a page out of her notebook.
OTHER WORDS YOU MIGHT USE ARE   **leaf   sheet**

pail *noun*
a pail of water.
ANOTHER WORD IS **bucket**

pain *noun*
OTHER WORDS YOU MIGHT USE ARE   **ache   soreness   sting   twinge**
VERY BAD PAIN IS   **agony   suffering   torture**
For other words, see **hurt**

painful *adjective*
The cut on Jo's knee was painful.
OTHER WORDS YOU MIGHT USE ARE   **aching   hurting   smarting   sore
stinging   throbbing**

paint *noun*
DIFFERENT KINDS OF PAINT ARE
**emulsion   enamel   gloss   oil paint   varnish
watercolour**

pale *adjective*
1 His face went pale when he heard the bad news.
OTHER WORDS YOU MIGHT USE ARE   **colourless   white**
2 Mum decorated the sitting room in pale colours.
OTHER WORDS ARE   **faint   light**

pant *verb*
We were all panting for breath at the end of the race.
OTHER VERBS YOU MIGHT USE ARE   **to gasp   to puff**

paper *noun*
DIFFERENT KINDS OF PAPER ARE
**card   newspaper   notepaper   tissue paper
toilet paper   wallpaper   wrapping paper
writing paper**

parcel *noun*
The postman came with a parcel.
OTHER WORDS ARE **package   packet**

pardon *verb*
The King pardoned the knight who had committed a crime.
OTHER VERBS YOU MIGHT USE ARE **to excuse   to forgive   to let off
to reprieve   to set free   to spare**

park *noun*
DIFFERENT KINDS OF PARK ARE **gardens   recreation ground
safari park   wildlife park**

part *noun*
1 I don't want it all, only a part of it.
OTHER WORDS YOU MIGHT USE ARE **bit   fraction   piece   portion
section**
2 They sell food in a different part of the shop.
ANOTHER WORD IS **department**
3 Granny lives in a nice part of the country.
OTHER WORDS ARE **area   district   region**
4 Which part did you have in the nativity play?
OTHER WORDS ARE **character   role**

particular *adjective*
1 Jo has her own particular way of writing.
OTHER WORDS YOU MIGHT USE ARE **individual   personal**
2 Do you want a particular record, or will any music do?
ANOTHER WORD IS **special**
3 The dog is particular about what he eats.
OTHER WORDS ARE **choosy   fussy**

partner *noun*
1 You can take a partner with you when you go to the party.
OTHER WORDS YOU MIGHT USE ARE **companion   friend**
2 The burglar had a partner.
ANOTHER WORD IS **accomplice**

party *noun*
DIFFERENT KINDS OF PARTY ARE
**ball   barbecue   birthday party   dance   disco
picnic   social   wedding**

pass *verb*

1 We waited for the cars to pass before we crossed the road.

OTHER VERBS YOU MIGHT USE ARE **to go by** **to move along**

2 Jo's knee hurt when she cut it, but the pain soon passed.

OTHER VERBS ARE **to disappear** **to go away** **to vanish**

passage *noun*

1 We went in through the front door and waited in the passage.

OTHER WORDS ARE **corridor** **hall**

2 They say there's a secret passage under the castle.

OTHER WORDS ARE **tunnel** **way**

3 I read my favourite passage from the book.

OTHER WORDS YOU MIGHT USE ARE **extract** **piece** **quotation**

path *noun*

We walked along the path.

DIFFERENT KINDS OF PATH ARE

bridleway **cart track** **footpath** **pavement**
towpath **track** **trail**

patient *adjective*

Although we had to wait a long time, everyone was very patient.

ANOTHER WORD IS **calm**

The opposite is impatient

pattern *noun*

1 I like the patterns on the wallpaper.

OTHER WORDS YOU MIGHT USE ARE **decoration** **design** **shape**

2 Is there a pattern I can copy?

OTHER WORDS ARE **guide** **model**

pause *noun*

There was a pause before the main film.

OTHER WORDS YOU MIGHT USE ARE **break** **delay** **gap** **intermission**
interruption **interval**

pause *verb*

We paused to have a drink.

OTHER VERBS ARE **to rest** **to stop** **to wait**

pay *noun*

OTHER WORDS YOU MIGHT USE ARE
earnings   income   payment

If you are paid by the week, your pay is **wages**.
If you get a regular amount each year, your pay is a **salary**.
The pay for doing one job is a **fee**.

pay *verb*
1 Sam paid £10 for his bike.
   OTHER VERBS YOU MIGHT USE ARE   **to give   to hand over   to spend**
2 When can you pay back the money you owe me?
   OTHER VERBS ARE   **to refund   to repay**

peace *noun*
1 After the war ended there was peace between the two countries.
   ANOTHER WORD YOU MIGHT USE IS **agreement**
   The opposite is war
2 We sat by the lake and enjoyed the peace of the evening.
   OTHER WORDS ARE   **calmness   quiet   stillness**
   Opposites are excitement noise

peaceful *adjective*
It seemed peaceful when the baby went to sleep.
   OTHER WORDS YOU MIGHT USE ARE   **calm   quiet   restful**
The opposite is noisy

pebble *noun*
ANOTHER WORD IS **stone**
A lot of pebbles are called **gravel**
Pebbles on a beach are called **shingle**

peculiar *adjective*
This drink has a peculiar taste.
   OTHER WORDS YOU MIGHT USE ARE   **funny   odd   queer   special
   strange   unusual**

peel *noun*
the peel of an orange.
   OTHER WORDS YOU MIGHT USE ARE   **rind   skin**

pen *noun*
DIFFERENT KINDS OF PEN ARE
ballpoint   Biro   felt tip   fountain pen   quill pen

penalty *noun*
For other words, see **punishment**

people *noun*
For other words, see **person**

perfect *adjective*
1 It's a perfect day for a picnic.
OTHER WORDS YOU MIGHT USE ARE   **excellent   ideal**
2 Jo's new coat was a perfect fit.
ANOTHER WORD IS **exact**

perform *verb*
Everyone in the class performed in the concert.
OTHER VERBS YOU MIGHT USE ARE   **to appear   to take part**
DIFFERENT WAYS TO PERFORM ARE   **to act   to dance**
   to play an instrument   to sing
For other words, see **entertainment**

perfume *noun*
Mum used some nice perfume when she went to the party.
ANOTHER WORD IS **scent**
For other words, see **smell**

period *noun*
For other words, see **time**

perish *verb*
1 Many birds perish in cold weather.
ANOTHER VERB IS **to die**
2 These pears will perish if you don't use them quickly.
OTHER VERBS YOU MIGHT USE ARE   **to decay   to go bad   to rot**

permission *noun*
We had the teacher's permission to go home.
OTHER WORDS YOU MIGHT USE ARE   **approval   consent**

permit *noun*
You need a permit to go fishing.
OTHER WORDS YOU MIGHT USE ARE   **licence   pass   ticket**

permit *verb*
They don't permit smoking on the bus.
OTHER VERBS YOU MIGHT USE ARE   **to agree to   to allow   to approve of**

persist *verb*
If the pain persists you must go to the doctor.
OTHER VERBS YOU MIGHT USE ARE   **to carry on   to continue**

person *noun*, see opposite page

personal *adjective*
1 Jo keeps her personal belongings in a drawer in her bedroom.
ANOTHER WORD IS **private**
2 Don't make personal remarks.
OTHER WORDS ARE   **cheeky   impertinent**

persuade *verb*
We tried to persuade the cat to come down from the tree.
OTHER VERBS YOU MIGHT USE ARE   **to coax   to tempt   to urge**

pester *verb*
Don't pester me when I'm busy!
OTHER VERBS YOU MIGHT USE ARE   **to annoy   to bother   to nag
to torment   to trouble   to worry**

pet *noun*
ANIMALS OFTEN KEPT AS PETS ARE
**budgerigar   canary   cat   dog   ferret   gerbil
goldfish   guinea pig   hamster   mouse   parrot
pigeon   rabbit   rat   tortoise**

phone *verb*
I phoned Granny to ask how she was.
OTHER VERBS YOU MIGHT USE ARE   **to call   to ring   to telephone**

person noun

OTHER WORDS YOU MIGHT USE ARE

character   human being   individual   mortal

a fully grown person
adult   grown-up

a young person
baby   boy   child   girl   infant   toddler

a person who is not a child but is not yet grown up
adolescent   juvenile   teenager

a woman who is married
wife

an unmarried woman
spinster

a woman whose husband has died
widow

the man who plays a woman in a pantomime
dame

a polite word for a woman
lady

a female child
girl

Female members of a family
**aunt   daughter   grandmother   mother   niece
stepdaughter   stepmother**

a man who is married
husband

a man who is not married
bachelor

a man whose wife has died
widower

a polite word for a man
gentleman

informal words for a man
bloke   chap   fellow

a young man
youth

a male child
boy or **lad**

Male members of a family
**father   grandfather   nephew   son   stepfather
stepson   uncle**

photo, photograph *nouns*

DIFFERENT KINDS OF PHOTOGRAPH ARE

enlargement   negative   print   slide or **transparency snapshot**

For other words, see **camera**

pick *verb*

1 You can pick any flavour of ice cream.

OTHER VERBS YOU MIGHT USE ARE   **to choose   to decide on   to select**

2 We picked Sam to be captain.

OTHER VERBS YOU MIGHT USE ARE   **to elect   to vote for**

3 I picked a lot of blackberries.

OTHER VERBS ARE   **to collect   to gather   to harvest**

picture *noun*

DIFFERENT KINDS OF PICTURE ARE

cartoon   collage   drawing   mosaic   mural painting   photograph   print   sketch slide or **transparency**

A picture of countryside is a **landscape**
A picture of a person is a **portrait**
A picture in a book is an **illustration**

piece *noun*

1 Sam had a big piece of cake.

OTHER WORDS YOU MIGHT USE ARE   **chunk   helping   hunk   lump portion   share   slab   slice**

2 Mum told Jo to pick up every single piece of the broken cup.

OTHER WORDS ARE   **bit   chip   fragment**

3 I need a piece of cloth to clean my bike.

OTHER WORDS YOU MIGHT USE ARE   **rag   scrap**

pierce *verb*

The needle pierced my skin.

OTHER VERBS YOU MIGHT USE ARE   **to go through   to penetrate to prick   to puncture**

pig *noun*
A male pig is a **hog**.
A female pig is a **sow**.
A baby pig is a **piglet**.

pile *noun*
Who dumped that pile of rubbish in the yard?
OTHER WORDS YOU MIGHT USE ARE   **heap   mound   stack**

pillar *noun*
The roof was held up on pillars.
OTHER WORDS YOU MIGHT USE ARE   **column   post   support**

pipe *noun*
a pipe to carry water.
OTHER WORDS YOU MIGHT USE ARE   **hose   tube**

pit *noun*
A pit where miners dig for coal is a **mine** or **coal mine**.
For other words, see **hole**

pity *noun*
The soldiers showed no pity for their enemies.
OTHER WORDS YOU MIGHT USE ARE   **kindness   mercy   sympathy**

place *noun*
1 The map showed the place where the treasure was hidden.
OTHER WORDS YOU MIGHT USE ARE   **location   point   position   site   situation   spot**
2 This is a nice place to live.
OTHER WORDS ARE   **area   district   neighbourhood   region**
3 Save me a place next to you.
OTHER WORDS ARE   **chair   seat**

place *verb*
1 Place your rubbish in the bin.
OTHER VERBS YOU MIGHT USE ARE   **to deposit   to leave   to put**
2 Place your work on the table.
OTHER VERBS ARE   **to arrange   to lay   to set out**
3 He placed the ladder against the wall.
OTHER VERBS ARE   **to lean   to rest   to stand**

plain *adjective*
1 She was wearing a plain dress.
   OTHER WORDS YOU MIGHT USE ARE **ordinary** **simple**
   The opposite is decorated
2 She gave a plain signal.
   OTHER WORDS ARE **clear** **definite**
   The opposite is confusing

plan *noun*
1 Sam has a plan for making a den in the garden.
   OTHER WORDS YOU MIGHT USE ARE **idea** **project** **scheme**
2 We drew a plan of the town to show where we all live.
   OTHER WORDS ARE **diagram** **map**

plan *verb*
1 We plan to go to the fair on Saturday.
   OTHER VERBS YOU MIGHT USE ARE **to aim** **to intend**
2 It took weeks to plan our trip.
   OTHER VERBS ARE **to arrange** **to organize** **to prepare for**

plane *noun*
For other words, see **aircraft**

planet *noun*
   THE PLANETS IN THE SOLAR SYSTEM ARE
   Earth **Jupiter** **Mars** **Mercury** **Neptune**
   Pluto **Saturn** **Uranus** **Venus**

plant *noun*
   DIFFERENT KINDS OF PLANT ARE
   bulb **cactus** **climbing plant** **fern** **flower**
   fungus **grass** **moss** **shrub** **tree** **water plant**
   weed

   PLANTS YOU CAN EAT ARE
   cereals **herbs** **vegetables**
   You can eat some kinds of **fungus**.

   For other words, see **flower, tree, vegetable**

play *verb*

1 I play with my friends at the weekend.
   OTHER VERBS YOU MIGHT USE ARE   **to amuse yourself   to have fun**
2 Jo played a tune on the piano.
   ANOTHER VERB IS **to perform**

playful *adjective*

a playful puppy.
   OTHER WORDS YOU MIGHT USE ARE   **frisky   lively**

pleasant *adjective*

THIS WORD HAS MANY USES. HERE ARE SOME OF THE WAYS YOU CAN USE IT, AND SOME OTHER WORDS YOU COULD CHOOSE

1 a pleasant day out.
   enjoyable   nice   pleasing
2 a pleasant person.
   friendly   kind   likeable
3 pleasant weather.
   fine   mild   warm
4 pleasant countryside.
   attractive   peaceful   pretty

The opposite is unpleasant

pleased *adjective*

Was Mum pleased when you gave her the present?
   OTHER WORDS YOU MIGHT USE ARE   **contented   delighted   grateful   satisfied   thankful**
For other words, see **happy**
The opposite is angry

pleasure *noun*

Jo's dog whines with pleasure when you tickle his neck.
   OTHER WORDS YOU MIGHT USE ARE   **contentment   delight   enjoyment   happiness   satisfaction**

plot *verb*

The robbers plotted to steal some jewels.
   OTHER VERBS YOU MIGHT USE ARE   **to conspire   to plan   to scheme**

plunge *verb*
She plunged into the water.
OTHER VERBS YOU MIGHT USE ARE   **to dive   to drop   to jump   to leap**

poem *noun*
OTHER WORDS YOU MIGHT USE ARE   **poetry   rhyme   verse**

point *noun*
1 Don't hurt yourself on the sharp point.
OTHER WORDS YOU MIGHT USE ARE   **spike   tip**
2 We marked the exact point on the map.
OTHER WORDS ARE   **location   place   position   spot**

point *verb*
1 The signpost points the way you have to go.
OTHER VERBS YOU MIGHT USE ARE   **to indicate   to show**
2 Don't point that arrow at me!
OTHER VERBS ARE   **to aim   to direct**

pointed *adjective*
a pointed stick.
ANOTHER WORD IS **sharp**
The opposite is blunt

poisonous *adjective*
Some toadstools are poisonous.
OTHER WORDS YOU MIGHT USE ARE   **deadly   harmful**

poke *verb*
He poked me in the back with a stick.
OTHER VERBS YOU MIGHT USE ARE   **to dig   to jab   to prod**

pole *noun*
We pinned our flag to a pole.
OTHER WORDS YOU MIGHT USE ARE   **post   rod   stick**

police *noun*
DIFFERENT NAMES FOR PEOPLE WHO WORK IN THE POLICE ARE
**constable   detective   inspector   officer
policeman   policewoman   sergeant**

polish *verb*
Jo helped to polish the car.
ANOTHER VERB IS **to shine**
For ways to clean things, see **clean**

polite *adjective*
a polite boy.
OTHER WORDS YOU MIGHT USE ARE   **considerate**   **respectful**
well-mannered
The opposite is rude

pool *noun*
A large pool is a **pond** or **lake**.
A small pool is a **puddle**.
A pool made to swim in is a **swimming pool**.

poor *adjective*
1 The poor family didn't have enough to eat.
OTHER WORDS YOU MIGHT USE ARE   **hard up**   **needy**   **penniless**
poverty-stricken
The opposite is rich
2 Our teacher was angry because we had done poor work.
For other words, see **bad**

poorly *adjective*
Jo stayed at home because she was poorly.
OTHER WORDS YOU MIGHT USE ARE   **ill**   **sick**   **unwell**
The opposite is healthy

popular *adjective*
We sang some popular carols at our concert.
OTHER WORDS YOU MIGHT USE ARE   **famous**   **favourite**   **well-known**

port *noun*
The ship entered port.
For other words, see **harbour**

portion *noun*
Can I have another portion of pie?
OTHER WORDS YOU MIGHT USE ARE   **helping**   **piece**   **share**   **slice**

positive *adjective*
Are you positive you saw a ghost?
> OTHER WORDS YOU MIGHT USE ARE   **certain   convinced   definite   sure**

possess *verb*
Sam only possesses one pair of jeans.
> OTHER VERBS YOU MIGHT USE ARE   **to have   to own**

possessions *noun*
Jo keeps her personal possessions in her bedroom.
> OTHER WORDS YOU MIGHT USE ARE   **belongings   property**

possible *adjective*
The opposite is impossible

post *noun*
1 Dad put up some posts to support the fence.
> OTHER WORDS YOU MIGHT USE ARE   **column   pillar   pole   prop   support**
2 The postman brought the post.
> ANOTHER WORD IS **mail**
> THINGS YOU GET IN THE MAIL ARE   **letter   packet   parcel   postcard**

poster *noun*
We put up a poster to tell people about our concert.
> OTHER WORDS YOU MIGHT USE ARE   **advertisement   notice   placard   sign**

postpone *verb*
They postponed sports day because it was raining.
> A PHRASE IS **to put off**

pottery *noun*
> OTHER WORDS YOU MIGHT USE ARE   **crockery   earthenware**
For other words, see **china**

poultry *noun*
> DIFFERENT KINDS OF POULTRY ARE
> **chicken   cockerel   duck   goose   hen   rooster   turkey**

pour *verb*
1 Water poured through the hole.
OTHER VERBS YOU MIGHT USE ARE   **to flow   to gush   to run   to stream**
2 I poured the cold tea into the sink.
OTHER VERBS ARE   **to empty   to tip**

power *noun*
1 The police have the power to arrest criminals.
OTHER WORDS YOU MIGHT USE ARE   **ability   authority   right**
2 Those big waves have the power to knock you over.
OTHER WORDS ARE   **energy   force   might   strength**

powerful *adjective*
a powerful giant.
OTHER WORDS YOU MIGHT USE ARE   **mighty   strong**
The opposite is weak

practical *adjective*
a practical tool.
OTHER WORDS YOU MIGHT USE ARE   **efficient   handy   useful**
The opposite is useless

practically *adverb*
I've practically finished.
OTHER WORDS YOU MIGHT USE ARE   **almost   nearly**

practise *verb*
If you practise for a concert, you **rehearse**.
If you practise at a sport, you **train** for it.
If you practise for a test, you **revise**.

praise *verb*
Our teacher praised us for working hard today.
OTHER VERBS YOU MIGHT USE ARE   **to compliment   to congratulate**
The opposite is scold

precious *adjective*
precious jewels.
OTHER WORDS YOU MIGHT USE ARE   **costly   dear   expensive   priceless   valuable**
The opposite is worthless

precise *adjective*
What is the precise time?
OTHER WORDS YOU MIGHT USE ARE **accurate**　**correct**　**exact**　**right**

prepare *verb*
Jo asked Sam to help her prepare for her party.
OTHER VERBS YOU MIGHT USE ARE **to get ready**　**to make arrangements**
to organize　**to plan**

present *noun*
Jo got a present from Grandad.
ANOTHER WORD IS **gift**

present *verb*
1　The head presented the prizes on sports day.
OTHER VERBS YOU MIGHT USE ARE **to award**　**to give**　**to hand over**
2　Sam presented the songs to the audience.
ANOTHER VERB IS **to introduce**
3　We presented a nativity play at Christmas.
OTHER VERBS ARE **to act**　**to perform**　**to put on**

preserve *verb*
1　You can preserve food in a freezer.
OTHER VERBS YOU MIGHT USE ARE **to keep**　**to save**
2　The museum put the old book in a glass case to preserve it.
OTHER VERBS ARE **to look after**　**to protect**

press *verb*
1　Press the bell.
ANOTHER VERB IS **to push**
2　Sam pressed his best trousers.
OTHER VERBS YOU MIGHT USE ARE **to flatten**　**to iron**　**to smooth**

pretend *verb*
There are different ways of pretending.
You can **act** or **play** a part in a play.
You can **disguise** yourself as someone else.
You can **imitate** or **impersonate** someone.
You can **deceive** or **trick** someone.

pretty *adjective*
a pretty dress.
OTHER WORDS YOU MIGHT USE ARE   **attractive**   **beautiful**   **lovely**
The opposite is ugly

prevent *verb*
The snow prevented us from going to Granny's.
OTHER VERBS YOU MIGHT USE ARE   **to hinder**   **to stop**

previously *adverb*
OTHER WORDS YOU MIGHT USE ARE   **before**   **earlier**

price *noun*
Before you buy anything, ask what the price is.
OTHER WORDS YOU MIGHT USE ARE   **charge**   **cost**   **fee**   **payment**
The price you pay to ride in a bus or train is the **fare**.

prick *verb*
The doctor pricked my thumb with a needle.
OTHER VERBS YOU MIGHT USE ARE   **to pierce**   **to puncture**

principal *adjective*
This map only shows the principal towns.
OTHER WORDS YOU MIGHT USE ARE   **chief**   **important**   **main**

principles *noun*
Sam taught Jo the principles of chess.
OTHER WORDS YOU MIGHT USE ARE   **laws**   **rules**   **theory**

prison *noun*
ANOTHER WORD IS **gaol** or **jail**
A small room where someone can be locked up is a **cell**.
A prison in a castle is a **dungeon**.

prisoner *noun*
ANOTHER WORD IS **captive**
A person you keep prisoner until you get what you want is a
hostage.

private *adjective*

1 Jo keeps her private things in a drawer in her bedroom.
OTHER WORDS YOU MIGHT USE ARE   **personal   secret**
2 We found a private spot for a picnic.
OTHER WORDS ARE   **hidden   quiet   secluded**
The opposite is public

problem *noun*

1 If you have a problem, tell the teacher.
OTHER WORDS YOU MIGHT USE ARE   **difficulty   worry**
2 The detective had a hard problem to solve.
OTHER WORDS ARE   **mystery   puzzle   question   riddle**

procession *noun*

There was a big procession through the middle of town.
OTHER WORDS YOU MIGHT USE ARE   **march   parade**

prod *verb*

Someone prodded me in the back.
OTHER VERBS YOU MIGHT USE ARE   **to dig   to jab   to poke   to push**

produce *verb*

1 The factory down the road produces television sets.
OTHER VERBS YOU MIGHT USE ARE   **to make   to manufacture**
2 Grandad's garden produces lots of vegetables.
OTHER VERBS ARE   **to grow   to yield**
3 We produce a magazine every term.
OTHER VERBS ARE   **to issue   to publish**
4 The cat produced four kittens.
OTHER VERBS ARE   **to bear   to give birth to**
5 The conjuror produced a rabbit from a hat.
OTHER VERBS YOU MIGHT USE ARE   **to bring out   to present**

progress *noun*

to make progress
OTHER WORDS YOU MIGHT USE ARE   **advance   move forward   proceed**

prohibited *adjective*

Smoking is prohibited on the bus.
OTHER WORDS YOU MIGHT USE ARE   **banned   forbidden   illegal**
The opposite is allowed

promise *verb*
You promised to come to my party.
OTHER VERBS YOU MIGHT USE ARE   **to agree   to give your word
to guarantee   to swear   to vow**

promptly *adverb*
1 Mum replied promptly to Granny's letter.
OTHER WORDS YOU MIGHT USE ARE   **immediately   quickly**
2 The train arrived promptly.
OTHER WORDS ARE   **on time   punctually**

prop *verb*
Jo propped her bike against the wall.
OTHER VERBS YOU MIGHT USE ARE   **to lean   to rest   to stand
to support**

proper *adjective*
1 Put the library books back in their proper places.
OTHER WORDS YOU MIGHT USE ARE   **appropriate   correct   right
suitable   usual**
The opposite is wrong
2 I think it would be proper for you to apologise.
OTHER WORDS ARE   **decent   polite   respectable**
The opposite is rude

protect *verb*
1 The mother bird tried to protect her babies.
OTHER VERBS YOU MIGHT USE ARE   **to defend   to guard   to keep safe
to look after**
2 The hedge protected us from the wind.
OTHER VERBS ARE   **to screen   to shield**

protest *verb*
We protested when they put up the bus fares.
OTHER VERBS YOU MIGHT USE ARE   **to complain   to object**

proud *adjective*
1 He was too proud to admit that he was wrong.
OTHER WORDS YOU MIGHT USE ARE   **boastful   (*informal*) cocky
conceited   (*informal*) stuck up   vain**
The opposite is modest
2 Mum was proud when Jo won a prize.
OTHER WORDS ARE   **happy   pleased**

prove *verb*
They proved that he was guilty.
OTHER VERBS YOU MIGHT USE ARE   **to demonstrate   to show**

provide *verb*
Our teacher provided the paper for us to draw on.
OTHER VERBS YOU MIGHT USE ARE   **to give   to supply**

provoke *verb*
If you provoke the dog, he may bite you.
OTHER VERBS YOU MIGHT USE ARE   **to anger   to annoy   to tease
to torment   to upset   to worry**

pry *verb*
Don't pry in my affairs!
OTHER WORDS YOU MIGHT USE ARE   **to interfere**
(*informal*) **to poke your nose into**

publish *verb*
We publish a magazine every term.
OTHER VERBS YOU MIGHT USE ARE   **to bring out   to issue   to produce**

pudding *noun*
Sam ate so much first course that he didn't have room for pudding.
OTHER WORDS YOU MIGHT USE ARE   (*informal*) **afters   dessert   sweet**

pull *verb*
1 We pulled the heavy box across the floor.
OTHER VERBS YOU MIGHT USE ARE   **to drag   to haul   to tug**
2 The car was pulling a caravan.
ANOTHER VERB IS **to tow**
3 The horse was pulling a cart.
ANOTHER VERB IS **to draw**

punch *verb*
For other ways to hit, see **hit**

punctual *adjective*
The train was punctual.
OTHER WORDS YOU MIGHT USE ARE   **on time   prompt**
The opposite is late

punctuation *noun*

DIFFERENT PUNCTUATION MARKS ARE

apostrophe   '

brackets   ( )

colon   :

comma   ,

dash   –

exclamation mark   !

full stop   .

hyphen   -

question mark   ?

semi-colon   ;

speech marks   "   "

punishment *noun*

DIFFERENT KINDS OF PUNISHMENT ARE

**a beating   detention   execution   a fine
gaol** (or **jail**) or **prison   an imposition   a penalty**

pupil *noun*

OTHER WORDS YOU MIGHT USE ARE   **schoolboy   schoolgirl   student**

pure *adjective*

pure water.

OTHER WORDS YOU MIGHT USE ARE   **clean   clear   natural**
The opposite is dirty

purpose *noun*

He must have a particular purpose to go out in that storm.

OTHER WORDS YOU MIGHT USE ARE   **aim   intention   object   plan
reason**

purse *noun*

Jo put her money in a **purse**.

OTHER THINGS YOU KEEP MONEY IN ARE
handbag   money box   piggy bank   pocket   wallet

pursue *verb*

The police pursued the robbers across the town.

OTHER VERBS YOU MIGHT USE ARE   **to chase   to follow   to hunt**

push *verb*

1 The door will open if you push harder.

OTHER VERBS YOU MIGHT USE ARE   **to press   to shove**

2 I pushed my clothes into a drawer.

OTHER VERBS ARE   **to crush   to force   to squeeze**

put *verb*

1 Put your dirty cups in the sink.

OTHER VERBS YOU MIGHT USE ARE   **to deposit   to leave   to pile   to place   to stack**

2 We put our pictures where everyone could see them.

OTHER VERBS ARE   **to arrange   to lay   to position   to set out**

to put something off

ANOTHER VERB IS **to postpone**

to put up with something

ANOTHER VERB IS **to endure**

puzzle *noun*

Can you solve this puzzle?

OTHER WORDS YOU MIGHT USE ARE   **mystery   problem   question   riddle**

puzzle *verb*

The riddle puzzled me.

OTHER VERBS YOU MIGHT USE ARE   **to bewilder   to confuse   to mystify   to perplex**

Qq

quaint *adjective*
a quaint thatched cottage.
OTHER WORDS YOU MIGHT USE ARE   **old-fashioned   picturesque**

quake *verb*
Jack quaked with fear when he saw the giant.
OTHER VERBS YOU MIGHT USE ARE   **to quiver   to shake   to shudder
to tremble**

quality *noun*
Our butcher only sells meat of the best quality.
OTHER WORDS YOU MIGHT USE ARE   **class   grade   standard
value**

quantity *noun*
In hot weather the shop sells a large quantity of ice cream.
OTHER WORDS YOU MIGHT USE ARE   **amount   volume**

quarrel *verb*
Jo and Sam sometimes quarrel, but they soon make it up.
OTHER VERBS YOU MIGHT USE ARE   **to argue   to disagree   to fall out
to fight   to squabble**

queer *adjective*
1 queer shapes. a queer smell.
OTHER WORDS YOU MIGHT USE ARE   *(informal)* **funny   odd   peculiar
strange   unusual**
2 I feel rather queer.
For other words, see **ill**

queue *noun*
A queue of cars waited at the level-crossing.
OTHER WORDS YOU MIGHT USE ARE   **line   row**

quick *adjective*

1 a quick journey.
OTHER WORDS YOU MIGHT USE ARE **fast**　**rapid**　**speedy**　**swift**
2 quick dance.
ANOTHER WORD IS **lively**
3 a quick reply.
OTHER WORDS ARE **instant**　**prompt**
The opposite is slow
4 The bus came to a quick halt.
OTHER WORDS ARE **hasty**　**sudden**

quiet *adjective*

1 Our teacher told us to be quiet.
ANOTHER WORD IS **silent**
2 I listened to some quiet music.
OTHER WORDS ARE **low**　**soft**
The opposite is noisy

quite *adverb*

1 I'm not quite sure.
OTHER WORDS YOU MIGHT USE ARE **absolutely**　**completely**　**entirely**
totally
2 I'm quite cold.
OTHER WORDS ARE **fairly**　**moderately**　(*informal*) **pretty**　**rather**

quiver *verb*

For other verbs, see **quake**

Rr

radio *noun*

An old-fashioned word is **wireless**.
SOME PROGRAMMES YOU HEAR ON THE RADIO ARE
chat shows　**interviews**　**music**　**news**
phone-in programmes　**plays**　**sport**　**stories**　**talks**
weather forecasts

rail *noun*
There was a rail to stop people falling into the water.
OTHER WORDS YOU MIGHT USE ARE   **bar   railing**

railway *noun*, see next page

rain *noun*
Very heavy rain is a **downpour.**
A short period of rain is a **shower.**
Rain coming down in very small drops is **drizzle.**
For other words, see **weather**

raise *verb*
1 A crane raised the car out of the ditch.
OTHER VERBS YOU MIGHT USE ARE   **to hoist   to lift   to pick up**
2 We raised money for charity.
OTHER VERBS ARE   **to collect   to get   to make**

rapid *adjective*
OTHER WORDS YOU MIGHT USE ARE   **fast   quick   speedy   swift**
The opposite is slow

rare *adjective*
Pandas are rare animals.
OTHER WORDS YOU MIGHT USE ARE   **scarce   uncommon**
The opposite is common

rather *adverb*
I was rather ill yesterday.
OTHER WORDS YOU MIGHT USE ARE   **fairly   moderately**
(*informal*) **pretty   quite**

ration *noun*
You can't have any more because you've had your ration.
OTHER WORDS YOU MIGHT USE ARE   **portion   share**

ravenous *adjective*
We were so ravenous that we ate everything!
OTHER WORDS YOU MIGHT USE ARE   **famished   hungry   starving**

railway *noun*

KINDS OF RAILWAY ARE

**branch line   main line   metro   mountain railway
narrow gauge railway   tramline   underground**

KINDS OF TRAIN ARE

**diesel   electric train   express
freight train** or **goods train   steam train   tram**

PARTS OF A TRAIN ARE

**buffet car   carriage   coach   locomotive
sleeping car   steam engine   wagon**

PARTS OF A RAILWAY LINE MIGHT BE

electric rail   overhead wires   points   sleepers   rails

ALONG THE RAILWAY YOU MIGHT SEE

**cutting   embankment   junction   level crossing
sidings   signals   signal box   station   tunnel**

THINGS YOU SEE AT A STATION ARE

booking office or **ticket office   buffet   platform
timetable   waiting room**

PEOPLE WHO WORK ON THE RAILWAY ARE

**booking clerk   conductor   driver   guard   porter
signalman   ticket collector**

ray *noun*

A ray of light shone through the crack in the door.

OTHER WORDS YOU MIGHT USE ARE   **beam   shaft**

reach *verb*

1 I will hold you if you reach out your hand.

ANOTHER VERB IS **to stretch**

2 We can have something to eat when we reach home.

OTHER VERBS YOU MIGHT USE ARE   **to arrive at   to get to**

ready *adjective*

1 Are you ready to go?

OTHER WORDS YOU MIGHT USE ARE   **prepared   willing**

2 Have you got your money ready?

OTHER WORDS ARE   **available   handy**

real *adjective*
1 Are those real diamonds?
    ANOTHER WORD IS **genuine**
The opposite is artificial
2 You can trust Sam: he's a real friend.
    ANOTHER WORD IS **true**
The opposite is false

realistic *adjective*
The acting was very realistic.
    OTHER WORDS YOU MIGHT USE ARE   **lifelike   natural**

realize *verb*
I suddenly realized that everyone was waiting for me.
    OTHER VERBS YOU MIGHT USE ARE   **to know   to see   to sense   to understand**

rear *noun*
He crashed into the rear of a bus.
    OTHER WORDS YOU MIGHT USE ARE   **back   end**
The opposite is front

rear *verb*
Our cat reared four kittens.
    OTHER VERBS YOU MIGHT USE ARE   **to bring up   to care for   to look after**

reason *noun*
Was there any reason for Sam's funny behaviour?
    OTHER WORDS YOU MIGHT USE ARE   **cause   excuse   explanation**
The reason why someone commits a crime is the **motive**.

reasonable *adjective*
1 Dad paid a reasonable price for his car.
    OTHER WORDS YOU MIGHT USE ARE   **fair   moderate**
2 You can't have a reasonable argument with a tiny baby.
    OTHER WORDS ARE   **intelligent   logical   sensible**

rebel *verb*
The soldiers rebelled because they were so hungry.
    OTHER VERBS YOU MIGHT USE ARE   **to disobey   to revolt**
If sailors rebel on a ship, the word is **mutiny**.

receive *verb*

1 I received ten birthday cards.
   ANOTHER VERB IS **to get**
2 He received £2 for doing odd jobs.
   ANOTHER VERB IS **to earn**

recent *adjective*

Have you got any recent CDs?
   OTHER WORDS YOU MIGHT USE ARE   **new   up-to-date**
The opposite is old

reckless *adjective*

Reckless drivers can kill people.
   OTHER WORDS YOU MIGHT USE ARE   **careless   thoughtless**
The opposite is careful

reckon *verb*

1 Jo reckoned how much the shopping cost.
   OTHER VERBS YOU MIGHT USE ARE   **to add up   to calculate   to count   to work out**
2 I reckon our side will win.
   OTHER VERBS ARE   **to believe   to feel sure   to think**

recognize *verb*

Would you recognize that man if you saw him again?
   OTHER VERBS YOU MIGHT USE ARE   **to identify   to know   to remember**

recommend *verb*

Mum recommends the restaurant down the road.
   OTHER VERBS YOU MIGHT USE ARE   **to approve of   to praise   to speak well of**

record *noun*

1 We kept a record of the birds we saw on holiday.
   OTHER WORDS YOU MIGHT USE ARE
      account   description   diary   log
2 Dad has lots of old pop records.
   KINDS OF GRAMOPHONE RECORD ARE
      album   LP   single
   OTHER KINDS OF RECORD ARE
      cassette   compact disc or CD   tape   video

recover *verb*

1 Mum recovered slowly after her operation.
OTHER VERBS YOU MIGHT USE ARE **to get better** **to heal** **to improve**

2 Did you recover your lost watch?
OTHER VERBS ARE **to find** **to get back** **to retrieve** **to trace**

reduce *verb*

She reduced speed when she saw the police-car.
OTHER VERBS YOU MIGHT USE ARE **to cut** **to decrease** **to lessen**

refer *verb*

1 Did Dad refer to the broken window?
OTHER VERBS YOU MIGHT USE ARE **to comment on** **to mention**

2 I referred to the dictionary to find the spelling.
OTHER VERBS ARE **to consult** **to look up** **to turn to**

refresh *verb*

The drink refreshed us.
OTHER VERBS YOU MIGHT USE ARE **to cool** **to quench the thirst**
to revive

refuse *noun*

Put the refuse in the bin.
OTHER WORDS YOU MIGHT USE ARE **junk** **rubbish** **waste**

refuse *verb*

Why did Jo refuse to go to her friend's party?
ANOTHER VERB IS **to decline**
The opposite is agree

regard *verb*

We regard Sam as the best swimmer in the school.
OTHER VERBS YOU MIGHT USE ARE **to consider** **to think of**

region *noun*

The South Pole is a cold region.
OTHER WORDS YOU MIGHT USE ARE **area** **district** **place** **zone**

regret *verb*

Jo regretted saying nasty things about her friend.
OTHER VERBS YOU MIGHT USE ARE **to be sad about** **to be sorry for**
to repent

regular *adjective*
1 Did the postman come at the regular time today?
    OTHER WORDS YOU MIGHT USE ARE   **customary   normal   usual**
2 The drummer kept a regular rhythm.
    OTHER WORDS ARE   **even   steady**

rehearse *verb*
We rehearsed for the concert all afternoon.
    OTHER VERBS YOU MIGHT USE ARE   **to practise   to prepare**

reject *verb*
Jo rejected the invitation to her friend's party.
    OTHER VERBS YOU MIGHT USE ARE   **to refuse   to turn down**
The opposite is accept

rejoice *verb*
The crowd rejoiced when their team won the cup.
    OTHER VERBS YOU MIGHT USE ARE   **to be happy   to celebrate**

relation *noun*
For other words, see **family**

relax *verb*
I like to relax in a hot bath.
    OTHER VERBS YOU MIGHT USE ARE   **to rest   to unwind**

release *verb*
They released the animals from the cage.
    OTHER VERBS YOU MIGHT USE ARE   **to free   to let loose   to let out**
    to liberate   to set free

reliable *adjective*
You can trust Sam: he's a reliable friend.
    OTHER WORDS YOU MIGHT USE ARE   **faithful   loyal   trustworthy**

relief *noun*
The pills gave me some relief from my headache.
    OTHER WORDS YOU MIGHT USE ARE   **comfort   ease   help**

relieved *adjective*
We were relieved to hear that Jo's accident was not serious.
    OTHER WORDS YOU MIGHT USE ARE   **glad   happy   thankful**

religion *noun*

OTHER WORDS YOU MIGHT USE ARE
belief   creed   faith

SOME RELIGIONS ARE
**Buddhism   Christianity   Hinduism   Judaism   Islam
Sikhism**

PEOPLE WHO FOLLOW A RELIGION ARE
Buddhist   Christian   Hindu   Jewish   Muslim   Sikh

KINDS OF RELIGIOUS SERVICE ARE
baptism or **christening   cremation   funeral
Holy Communion   mass   prayers   wedding
worship**

PARTS OF A MEETING FOR WORSHIP MIGHT BE
anthem   blessing   collection or **offering   confession
devotions   hymn   meditation   prayers   psalm
reading from scripture   sermon**

PLACES WHERE PEOPLE WORSHIP ARE
**cathedral   chapel   church   mosque   pagoda
shrine   synagogue   temple**

RELIGIOUS LEADERS AND TEACHERS ARE
**archbishop   ayatollah   bishop   cardinal   chaplain
clergyman   curate   druid   guru   imam   lama
minister   missionary   parson   pope   priest
prophet   rabbi   rector   vicar**

ADJECTIVES YOU MIGHT USE TO DESCRIBE RELIGIOUS THINGS ARE
blessed   consecrated   divine   holy   sacred

ADJECTIVES YOU MIGHT USE TO DESCRIBE RELIGIOUS PEOPLE ARE
devout   pious

A person who thinks there is no God is an **atheist**.
A person who says you can't know whether there is a God or not
is an **agnostic**.

reluctant *adjective*
I was reluctant to walk home because it was raining.
OTHER WORDS YOU MIGHT USE ARE   **hesitant   unwilling**
The opposite is enthusiastic

rely *verb*
You can rely on Jo to do her best.
> OTHER VERBS YOU MIGHT USE ARE   (*informal*) **to bank on**   **to count on**   **to depend on**   **to trust**

remain *verb*
He told me to remain where I was.
> OTHER VERBS YOU MIGHT USE ARE   **to stay**   **to stop**

remains *noun*
1 We explored the remains of the castle.
> ANOTHER WORD IS **ruins**
2 What shall we do with the remains of this stew?
> OTHER WORDS ARE   (*informal*) **leftovers**   **remainder**   **rest**
3 His remains were buried near the church.
> OTHER WORDS ARE   **body**   **corpse**

remark *verb*
I remarked that it was a nice day.
> OTHER VERBS YOU MIGHT USE ARE   **to comment**   **to mention**   **to say**

remarkable *adjective*
Our team had a remarkable victory.
> OTHER WORDS YOU MIGHT USE ARE   **amazing**   **extraordinary**   **special**   **surprising**   **unusual**

remedy *noun*
Do you know a remedy for a cold?
> OTHER WORDS YOU MIGHT USE ARE   **cure**   **medicine**   **treatment**

remember *verb*
Do you remember our holiday last year?
> OTHER WORDS YOU MIGHT USE ARE   **to recall**   **to recollect**
The opposite is forget

remind *verb*
Jo reminded Mum to buy some sugar.
> A PHRASE YOU MIGHT USE IS **to jog someone's memory**

remove *verb*
1 Please remove this rubbish.
> OTHER VERBS YOU MIGHT USE ARE   **to carry away**   **to get rid of**   **to move**   **to shift**   **to take away**

2 The dentist removed a tooth.
OTHER VERBS ARE **to extract** **to take out**
3 What removes oil from clothes?
ANOTHER VERB IS **to wash off**

repair *verb*
OTHER VERBS YOU MIGHT USE ARE *(informal)* **to fix** **to mend**
to put right
to repair clothes
to darn **to patch** **to sew up**
to repair something old or broken
to do up **to renovate** **to restore**

repeat *verb*
Don't repeat everything I say!
OTHER VERBS YOU MIGHT USE ARE **to go over** **to say again**

reply *verb*
I replied to Granny's letter.
OTHER VERBS YOU MIGHT USE ARE **to answer** **to respond to**

report *verb*
1 We reported that we had finished our work.
OTHER VERBS YOU MIGHT USE ARE **to announce** **to declare** **to state**
2 I reported him to the police.
OTHER VERBS ARE **to complain about** **to inform against**
(informal) **to tell of**

reproduce *verb*
1 Sam can reproduce a lot of bird calls.
OTHER VERBS YOU MIGHT USE ARE **to imitate** **to mimic**
2 We reproduced our work on the copier in the school office.
OTHER VERBS ARE **to copy** **to duplicate** **to photocopy**
3 Rabbits reproduce very quickly.
OTHER VERBS ARE **to breed** **to multiply**

reptile *noun*
DIFFERENT KINDS OF REPTILE ARE
alligator **crocodile** **lizard** **snake** **tortoise** **turtle**

request *verb*
When the work got too hard, we requested help from our teacher.
OTHER VERBS YOU MIGHT USE ARE   **to appeal for   to ask for   to beg for**

require *verb*
We required 3 more runs to win.
OTHER VERBS ARE   **to be short of   to need   to want**

rescue *verb*
Robin Hood rescued the prisoners from the Sheriff's castle.
OTHER VERBS YOU MIGHT USE ARE   **to free   to liberate   to release   to save   to set free**

resemble *verb*
Sam resembles his father.
OTHER VERBS YOU MIGHT USE ARE   **to be similar to   to look like**

reserve *noun*
We have two reserves who can play on Saturday if necessary.
OTHER WORDS ARE   **deputy   stand-in   substitute**

reserve *verb*
1 Jo reserved some sandwiches for people who came late.
OTHER VERBS YOU MIGHT USE ARE   **to keep   to save**
2 We reserved our seats on the train.
ANOTHER WORD IS **to book**

resign *verb*
The manager resigned because the team was doing so badly.
OTHER VERBS YOU MIGHT USE ARE   **to give up   to leave**
   (*informal*) **to quit**

resist *verb*
He made things worse because he resisted the police.
OTHER VERBS YOU MIGHT USE ARE   **to defy   to oppose   to stand up to**

respect *noun*
We should show respect to people who work hard for us.
OTHER WORDS YOU MIGHT USE ARE   **admiration   consideration**
The respect you show towards religious things is **reverence**.

responsible *adjective*
1 Who is responsible for this dog?
   A PHRASE IS **in charge of**
2 Jo was responsible for breaking the window.
   A PHRASE IS **guilty of**
3 We need a responsible person to look after the money.
   OTHER WORDS ARE   **dependable   honest   reliable   trustworthy**

rest *noun*
1 Let's have a rest for a minute.
   OTHER WORDS YOU MIGHT USE ARE   **break   pause**
2 If you have finished, the dog will eat the rest.
   ANOTHER WORD IS **remainder**

rest *verb*
1 Half way up the hill we sat down to rest.
   OTHER VERBS YOU MIGHT USE ARE   **to relax**   (*informal*) **to take it easy**
   When you are resting you might   **doze   lie down   sleep**
      (*informal*) **take a nap**
2 Rest the ladder against the wall.
   OTHER VERBS YOU MIGHT USE ARE   **to lean   to prop   to stand
   to support**

restore *verb*
Uncle David restores old cars.
   OTHER VERBS YOU MIGHT USE ARE   (*informal*) **to do up   to mend
   to renovate   to repair**

result *noun*
The result of getting up late was that I missed the bus.
   OTHER WORDS YOU MIGHT USE ARE   **consequence   effect**

retreat *verb*
The soldiers retreated when they knew that they were losing.
   OTHER VERBS YOU MIGHT USE ARE   **to go back   to move back
   to run away**

return *verb*
1 We returned at tea time.
   OTHER VERBS YOU MIGHT USE ARE   **to come back   to go back**
2 Jo returned the pen I lent her.
   OTHER VERBS ARE   **to give back   to repay**

reveal *verb*

1 We drew back the curtain and revealed the stage.

OTHER VERBS YOU MIGHT USE ARE   **to disclose   to show**

2 Don't ever reveal our secret!

PHRASES ARE   **to let out   to make known**

reverse *verb*

Dad damaged the car when he reversed into a wall.

OTHER VERBS ARE   **to back   to go backwards**

revolt *verb*

The players revolted because they thought the rules were not fair.

OTHER VERBS YOU MIGHT USE ARE   **to disobey   to rebel**

When sailors revolt the word is **mutiny.**

revolting *adjective*

The food was so revolting that nobody would eat it.

OTHER WORDS YOU MIGHT USE ARE   **disgusting   foul   horrible   nasty   unattractive**

The opposite is attractive

rhythm *noun*

Sam likes music with a strong rhythm.

OTHER WORDS YOU MIGHT USE ARE   **beat   pulse**

rich *adjective*

Rich people can buy what they want.

OTHER WORDS YOU MIGHT USE ARE   **prosperous   wealthy   well-off**

The opposite is poor

ride *verb*

For other verbs, see **travel**

ridiculous *adjective*

We laughed at his ridiculous hat.

OTHER WORDS YOU MIGHT USE ARE   **absurd   comic   funny   silly   stupid**

right *adjective*

1 Most people use their right hand to write with.

The opposite is left

2 All Jo's answers were right.

OTHER WORDS YOU MIGHT USE ARE   **accurate   correct**

3 Is that the right time?
OTHER WORDS ARE   **exact**   **precise**   **proper**   **true**
4 It's right to own up when you've been naughty.
OTHER WORDS ARE   **fair**   **honest**   **moral**
5 A thesaurus helps you to find the right word.
OTHER WORDS ARE   **appropriate**   **suitable**
The opposite is wrong

ring *noun*
We all stood in a ring.
ANOTHER WORD IS **circle**

ring *verb*
1 I heard a bell ring.
Loud bells **peal**.
A small bell **tinkles**.
An annoying noisy bell **jangles**.
A clock **chimes**.
2 We ring Granny every Sunday.
OTHER WORDS ARE
to call   **to phone**   **to telephone**

riot *noun*
The police were called to control the riot.
OTHER WORDS YOU MIGHT USE ARE   **disorder**   **disturbance**   **mutiny**
revolt

rip *verb*
Sam ripped his jeans.
OTHER VERBS YOU MIGHT USE ARE   **to split**   **to tear**

rise *verb*
1 I watched the balloon rise into the sky.
OTHER VERBS YOU MIGHT USE ARE   **to ascend**   **to climb**   **to go up**
to lift
The opposite is fall
2 Bus fares are going to rise next week.
ANOTHER VERB IS **to increase**
3 We all rose when the teacher came into the room.
OTHER VERBS ARE   **to get up**   **to stand**

risk *noun*
There's a risk of rain today.
OTHER WORDS YOU MIGHT USE ARE　**chance**　**danger**　**possibility**

rival *noun*
The team we played on Saturday were our old rivals.
OTHER WORDS YOU MIGHT USE ARE　**enemy**　**opponent**

river *noun*
For other words, see **water**

road *noun*
BIG ROADS FOR MOTOR TRAFFIC ARE
bypass　**motorway**　**ring road**

OTHER WORDS YOU MIGHT USE ARE
a road with houses along it
street

a road with trees along it
avenue

a narrow road between buildings
alley

a road where you can only drive one way
one-way street

a road closed at one end
cul-de-sac

a road that goes up to a house
drive

a narrow road in the country
lane

a rough road in the country
track or **cart track**

a path for horses
bridleway

a path along a canal
towpath

robber *noun*
ANOTHER WORD IS **thief**
DIFFERENT KINDS OF ROBBER ARE
**burglar   highwayman   mugger   pick-pocket
shoplifter**
For other words, see **steal**

rock *noun*
ANOTHER WORD IS **stone**
A big piece of rock is a **boulder.**

rock *verb*
1 The boat rocked gently in the breeze.
OTHER VERBS YOU MIGHT USE ARE   **to sway   to swing**
2 The boat rocked violently in the storm.
OTHER VERBS ARE   **to roll   to toss**

rod *noun*
The climbing frame is made of iron rods.
OTHER WORDS YOU MIGHT USE ARE   **bar   pole   rail**

rodent *noun*
THESE ANIMALS ARE RODENTS:
gerbil   hamster   mouse   rat   squirrel

room *noun*
For different rooms, see **house**

rope *noun*
OTHER WORDS YOU CAN USE ARE   **cord   line**

rotten *adjective*
1 rotten wood.
OTHER WORDS YOU MIGHT USE ARE   **decayed   decomposed**
2 rotten food.
OTHER WORDS ARE   **bad   mouldy   smelly**
3 Sam is rotten at tennis!
OTHER WORDS ARE   **bad   hopeless   incompetent   useless**

rough *adjective*

1 We jolted along the rough road.
   OTHER WORDS YOU MIGHT USE ARE   **bumpy   uneven**
The opposite is smooth
2 Sandpaper feels rough.
   OTHER WORDS ARE   **coarse   harsh   scratchy**
The opposite is soft
3 The sea was very rough.
   OTHER WORDS ARE   **stormy   wild**
The opposite is calm
4 I don't like rough games.
   OTHER WORDS ARE   **bad-tempered   boisterous   rowdy   violent**
The opposite is gentle
5 At a rough guess it will cost £100 to mend the car.
   ANOTHER WORD IS **approximate**
The opposite is exact

round *adjective*

Most coins are round.
   ANOTHER WORD IS **circular**
A flat round shape is a **disc.**
A solid round shape is a **ball** or **globe** or **sphere.**

route *noun*

Sam knows a quick route into town.
   ANOTHER WORD IS **way**

row *noun* (rhymes with *cow*)

1 Sam and Jo hardly ever have a row.
   OTHER WORDS YOU MIGHT USE ARE   **disagreement   quarrel   squabble**
2 What was that row in the night?
   OTHER WORDS ARE   **commotion   din   noise   uproar**

row *noun* (rhymes with *toe*)

We stood in a straight row.
   OTHER WORDS YOU MIGHT USE ARE   **file   line   queue**

rubbish *noun*

Throw away that rubbish.
   OTHER WORDS YOU MIGHT USE ARE   (*informal*) **junk   litter   refuse
   scrap   waste**

rude *adjective*

That rude girl shouted at us.

OTHER WORDS YOU MIGHT USE ARE   **bad-mannered   cheeky**
disrespectful   impertinent   impolite   impudent   insulting
offensive

The opposite is polite

ruin *verb*

The storm ruined the flowers in the garden.

OTHER VERBS YOU MIGHT USE ARE   **to destroy   to spoil   to wreck**

rule *noun*

When you play a game, you must obey the rules.

OTHER WORDS YOU MIGHT USE ARE   **law   regulation**

rule *verb*

In the old days, the king used to rule the country.

OTHER VERBS YOU MIGHT USE ARE

to control   to govern   to lead   to manage   to run

DIFFERENT WORDS FOR PEOPLE WHO RULE OVER THEIR SUBJECTS MIGHT BE

dictator   emperor   empress   governor   king
monarch   queen   president   prince   princess
rajah   sovereign   sultan   tyrant   tzar

Some countries are ruled by a **government** with a **prime minister.**

rumour *noun*

It's not fair to spread stories that are only rumour.

ANOTHER WORD IS **gossip**

run *verb*

DIFFERENT WAYS TO RUN ARE

to jog   to race   to scamper   to sprint

For other words, see **rush.**

DIFFERENT WAYS A HORSE RUNS ARE

canter   gallop   trot

runny *adjective*

The jelly hasn't set yet - it's still runny.

OTHER WORDS YOU MIGHT USE ARE **liquid   sloppy   watery**

rush *verb*

Jo was hungry, so she rushed home for something to eat.

OTHER VERBS YOU MIGHT USE ARE **to dash   to hurry   to speed**

For other verbs, see **run**

Ss

sacred *adjective*

The Bible and the Koran are sacred books.

OTHER WORDS YOU MIGHT USE ARE **holy   religious**

sad *adjective*

1 a sad look on someone's face.

OTHER WORDS YOU MIGHT USE ARE **depressed   disappointed   gloomy   heart-broken   melancholy   miserable   mournful   sorrowful   tearful   troubled   unhappy   wretched**

2 sad news.

OTHER WORDS YOU MIGHT USE ARE **depressing   disappointing   distressing   tragic   upsetting**

The opposite is **happy**

safe *adjective*

1 When we got indoors, we felt safe from the storm.

OTHER WORDS YOU MIGHT USE ARE **protected   secure**

2 We were glad to get home safe.

ANOTHER WORD IS **unharmed**

3 Is the dog safe?

OTHER WORDS YOU MIGHT USE ARE **harmless   tame**

sailor *noun*

ANOTHER WORD IS **seaman**

The sailors who sail a ship are the **crew**.

salad *noun*
THINGS YOU EAT IN SALAD ARE
beetroot   celery   cress   cucumber   lettuce
mustard and cress   onion   potato   radish
tomato   watercress

sample *noun*
Jo showed Dad samples of her work.
OTHER WORDS YOU MIGHT USE ARE   **example   specimen**

satisfactory *adjective*
We can go out to play if our work is satisfactory.
OTHER WORDS YOU MIGHT USE ARE   **acceptable   all right   good enough**

satisfy *verb*
He's always grumpy: nothing satisfies him.
OTHER VERBS YOU MIGHT USE ARE   **to content   to make happy
to please**

savage *adjective*
a savage attack.
OTHER WORDS YOU MIGHT USE ARE   **bloodthirsty   brutal   cruel   fierce
heartless   ruthless   vicious   violent**
The opposite is gentle

save *verb*
1 Robin Hood saved the prisoners.
OTHER VERBS YOU MIGHT USE ARE   **to free   to liberate   to release
to rescue   to set free**
2 I saved some sweets for later.
OTHER VERBS ARE   **to keep   to preserve   to put aside**

say *verb*
For other verbs, see **talk**

saying *noun*
'I don't believe it' is a common saying.
OTHER WORDS YOU MIGHT USE ARE   **expression   phrase   remark**
A saying that is supposed to teach a moral, like 'Many hands make light
work', is a **proverb**.

scarce *adjective*
1 Water is scarce in the desert.
A PHRASE IS **in short supply**
The opposite is plentiful
2 Snakes are scarce in England.
OTHER WORDS ARE **rare   uncommon**
The opposite is common

scarcely *adverb*
I could scarcely believe my eyes!
OTHER WORDS YOU MIGHT USE ARE **barely   hardly   only   just**

scare *verb*
The sudden noise scared me.
OTHER VERBS ARE **to alarm   to frighten   to shock   to startle   to terrify   to upset**

scatter *verb*
The baby always scatters her toys round the room.
OTHER VERBS YOU MIGHT USE ARE **to spread   to throw about**

scent *noun*
the scent of roses.
OTHER WORDS YOU MIGHT USE ARE **fragrance   perfume   smell**

school *noun*
DIFFERENT KINDS OF SCHOOL ARE
**boarding school   comprehensive school   first school
infant school   junior school   kindergarten
middle school   nursery school   play group
primary school   secondary school**

For other words, see **educate, teach**

science *noun*
DIFFERENT KINDS OF SCIENCE ARE
**astronomy   biology   botany   chemistry   electronics
engineering   geology   physics   psychology
technology   zoology**

scold *verb*
Jo scolded the dog for eating her chocolate.
OTHER VERBS YOU MIGHT USE ARE   **to reprimand**   (*informal*) **to tell off**
(*informal*) **to tick off**

scramble *verb*
I scrambled over the rocks.
OTHER VERBS YOU MIGHT USE ARE   **to clamber   to climb   to crawl**

scrap *noun*
1 We put scraps of food out for the birds.
OTHER WORDS YOU MIGHT USE ARE   **bit   crumb   piece**
2 Dad took some scrap to the tip.
OTHER WORDS YOU MIGHT USE ARE   (*informal*) **junk   rubbish   waste**

scrape *verb*
1 I scraped my knee on the stones.
OTHER VERBS YOU MIGHT USE ARE   **to graze   to scratch**
2 Jo scraped the mud off her shoe.
OTHER VERBS ARE   **to clean   to rub   to scrub**

scratch *verb*
Dad scratched the car on the gate.
OTHER VERBS YOU MIGHT USE ARE   **to damage   to graze   to scrape**

scream *verb*
Everyone screamed when the ride went faster and faster.
OTHER VERBS ARE   **to cry out   to howl   to screech   to shriek
to squeal   to yell**

sculpture *noun*
OTHER WORDS ARE   **carvings   statues**

sea *noun*
ANOTHER WORD IS **ocean**

seal *verb*
Remember to seal the envelope.
OTHER VERBS YOU MIGHT USE ARE   **to close   to fasten   to stick down**

search *verb*
I was searching for my watch.
OTHER VERBS YOU MIGHT USE ARE   **to hunt for   to look for**

seaside *noun*
We had a trip to the seaside.
OTHER WORDS YOU MIGHT USE ARE
beach　coast
Another word for beach is **shore**.

THINGS YOU MIGHT SEE AT THE SEASIDE ARE
**breakwater　cliffs　pier　promenade　rocks
rock pools　sand　sand dunes　shingle　waves**

THINGS YOU MIGHT FIND ARE
pebbles　seaweed　shellfish　shells

season *noun*
THE SEASONS OF THE YEAR ARE
spring　summer　autumn · winter

seat *noun*
DIFFERENT THINGS YOU SIT ON ARE
**armchair　bench　chair　deckchair　pew
pouffe　rocking chair　settee　sofa　stool**

The seat a king or queen sits on for official occasions is a **throne**.

secret *adjective*
1 a secret diary.
OTHER WORDS YOU MIGHT USE ARE　**intimate　personal　private**
2 a secret place.
OTHER WORDS ARE　**concealed　hidden　unknown**
The opposite is public

secure *adjective*
Make sure the ladder is secure before you climb it.
OTHER WORDS YOU MIGHT USE ARE　**firm　fixed　safe　steady**
The opposite is loose

see *verb*
1 Did you see anyone you know?
OTHER VERBS YOU MIGHT USE ARE   **to make out**   **to notice**
to recognize   **to spot**
To see someone or something very briefly is to **glimpse** it.
2 We saw a good film.
OTHER VERBS ARE   **to look at**   **to view**   **to watch**
3 If you see an accident, tell the police.
ANOTHER VERB IS **to witness**

seem *verb*
Granny seems better today.
OTHER VERBS YOU MIGHT USE ARE   **to appear**   **to look**

seize *verb*
1 I seized the end of the rope.
OTHER VERBS YOU MIGHT USE ARE   (*informal*) **to grab**   **to hold**
to snatch
2 The police seized the thief.
OTHER VERBS ARE   **to arrest**   **to capture**   **to catch**

seldom *adverb*
It seldom snows in May.
ANOTHER WORD IS **rarely**
The opposite is often

select *verb*
1 You can select some sweets from the tin.
OTHER VERBS YOU MIGHT USE ARE   **to choose**   **to pick**
2 We selected Jo to be captain.
OTHER VERBS ARE   **to appoint**   **to decide on**   **to vote for**

selfish *adjective*
It's selfish to keep the best sweets for yourself.
OTHER WORDS YOU MIGHT USE ARE   **greedy**   **mean**   **thoughtless**
The opposite is generous

send *verb*
We sent a parcel to Grandad.
OTHER VERBS YOU MIGHT USE ARE   **to dispatch**   **to post**

sense *noun*

1 If you've got any sense, you won't go out in the rain.
   OTHER WORDS YOU MIGHT USE ARE
   intelligence   wisdom
2 We use our five senses to recognize things.
   OUR FIVE SENSES ARE
   hearing   sight   smell   taste   touch

sensible *adjective*

Sensible people stay in when it rains.
   OTHER WORDS YOU MIGHT USE ARE   **reasonable   thoughtful   wise**
The opposite is silly

sensitive *adjective*

Jo has a sensitive skin.
   OTHER WORDS YOU MIGHT USE ARE   **delicate   soft   tender**

separate *adjective*

1 They kept the sick children separate from the rest of us.
   OTHER WORDS ARE   **apart   divided   isolated   segregated**
2 The infants are in a separate building from the juniors.
   OTHER WORDS ARE   **detached   different   distinct**

series *noun*

We had a series of accidents.
   OTHER WORDS ARE   **row   sequence   string   succession**

serious *adjective*

1 Sam takes a serious interest in his work.
   OTHER WORDS YOU MIGHT USE ARE   **careful   sincere   thoughtful**
2 She had a serious look on her face.
   OTHER WORDS ARE   **grave   sad   solemn**
3 Several people were hurt in the serious accident.
   OTHER WORDS ARE   **awful   bad   dreadful   severe   terrible**

service *noun*

   KINDS OF RELIGIOUS SERVICE ARE
   baptism or **christening   funeral   Holy Communion
   mass   prayers   wedding service   worship**
For other words, see **religion**

set *verb*

1 Has the glue set yet?
    ANOTHER VERB IS **to harden**
2 We set out our work for the parents to see.
    OTHER VERBS YOU MIGHT USE ARE　**to arrange**　**to lay out**　**to put out**
3 We set off at breakfast time.
    OTHER VERBS ARE　**to depart**　**to start**

settle *verb*

Have you settled on what to do?
    OTHER VERBS YOU MIGHT USE ARE　**to agree**　**to decide**　**to fix**

severe *adjective*

1 a severe teacher.
    OTHER WORDS YOU MIGHT USE ARE　**stern**　**strict**
2 a severe illness.
    OTHER WORDS ARE　**bad**　**serious**
The opposite is mild

sew *verb*

ANOTHER WORD IS **to stitch**
To sew up a hole is **to darn**.
To sew with loose stitches is **to tack**.

sewing

OTHER WORDS ARE　**embroidery**　**needlework**

shabby *adjective*

shabby clothes.
    OTHER WORDS YOU MIGHT USE ARE　**faded**　**old**　**ragged**
    (*informal*) **scruffy**　**worn**
The opposite is smart

shade *noun*

1 We sat in the shade of a tree.
    ANOTHER WORD IS **shadow**
2 My coat is a pretty shade of red.
    OTHER WORDS YOU MIGHT USE ARE　**colour**　**hue**　**tinge**

shady *adjective*

We sat down in a shady place.
    OTHER WORDS YOU MIGHT USE ARE　**shaded**　**shadowy**

shaggy *adjective*
The dog had a shaggy coat.
OTHER WORDS YOU MIGHT USE ARE **hairy   rough   woolly**

shake *verb*
1 I shook with fear.
OTHER VERBS YOU MIGHT USE ARE **to quake   to quiver   to shiver   to shudder   to tremble**
2 The house shook in the earthquake.
OTHER VERBS ARE **to rock   to sway   to vibrate   to wobble**

shallow *adjective*
The opposite is deep

shame *noun*
We'll never forget the shame of losing 14-0!
OTHER WORDS YOU MIGHT USE ARE **disgrace   embarrassment**

shape *noun*
OTHER WORDS YOU MIGHT USE ARE
form   outline

DIFFERENT SHAPES ARE
circle   heptagon   hexagon   oblong   octagon   oval   pentagon   rectangle   semi-circle   spiral   square   triangle

DIFFERENT SOLID SHAPES ARE
cone   cube   cuboid   cylinder   hemisphere   prism   pyramid   sphere   spiral

share *noun*
1 We all had a share of the money.
OTHER WORDS YOU MIGHT USE ARE **fraction   part**
2 Mum made sure that everyone had a fair share of the pudding.
OTHER WORDS ARE **helping   portion   ration**

share *verb*
We shared the food between us.
OTHER VERBS YOU MIGHT USE ARE **to deal out   to distribute   to divide   to split**

sharp *adjective*

1 a sharp stick.
   ANOTHER WORD IS **pointed**
2 a sharp knife.
   OTHER WORDS YOU MIGHT USE ARE   **keen   razor-sharp**
The opposite is blunt
3 a sharp bend in the road.
   ANOTHER WORD IS **sudden**
4 a sharp girl.
   OTHER WORDS ARE   **bright   clever   intelligent   quick   smart**
The opposite is dull

shed *verb*

A lorry shed its load on the motorway.
   OTHER VERBS ARE   **to drop   to scatter**

sheet *noun*

1 a sheet on a bed.
For things you have on a bed, see **bed**
2 a sheet of paper.
   OTHER WORDS YOU MIGHT USE ARE   **leaf   page**

shelter *noun*

The animals looked for shelter from the storm.
   OTHER WORDS ARE   **cover   protection   refuge   safety**

shelter *verb*

The hedge sheltered us from the wind.
   OTHER VERBS YOU MIGHT USE ARE   **to guard   to hide   to protect
   to shield**

shift *verb*

For other verbs, see **move**

shine *verb*

Things shine in different ways.
   THEY CAN:
   **blaze   burn   dazzle   flash   flicker   glare   gleam
   glimmer   glint   glisten   glitter   glow   shine
   sparkle   twinkle**

shiny *adjective*
a shiny new coin.
OTHER WORDS YOU MIGHT USE ARE **bright** **gleaming** **glossy**
polished **shining**
The opposite is dull

shiver *verb*
I was shivering with cold.
OTHER VERBS YOU MIGHT USE ARE **to quiver** **to shake** **to shudder**
to tremble

shock *verb*
1 The explosion shocked everyone.
OTHER VERBS YOU MIGHT USE ARE **to alarm** **to frighten** **to startle**
to stun **to surprise**
2 The swearing shocked us.
OTHER VERBS ARE **to disgust** **to offend** **to upset**

shoe *noun*
THINGS YOU WEAR ON YOUR FEET ARE
boots **clogs** **plimsolls** **sandals** **slippers** **trainers**
wellingtons

shoot *verb*
He shot at the target.
OTHER VERBS YOU MIGHT USE ARE **to aim** **to fire**

shop *noun*
ANOTHER WORD IS **store**
BIG SHOPS THAT SELL ALL KINDS OF GOODS ARE
department store **hypermarket** **supermarket**

DIFFERENT KINDS OF SHOP ARE

baker	**bank**	**barber**	**book shop**
butcher	**chemist**	**clothes shop**	**dairy**
delicatessen	**DIY shop**	**fishmonger**	**florist**
greengrocer	**grocer**	**hairdresser**	**ironmonger**
jeweller	**launderette**	**newsagent**	**off-licence**
post office	**shoe shop**		

short *adjective*
1 a short poem.
ANOTHER WORD IS **brief**
The opposite is long
2 a short person.
OTHER WORDS ARE   **little   small**
The opposite is tall

shout *verb*
Sam shouted so loud that the people next door heard him.
OTHER VERBS YOU MIGHT USE ARE   **to call   to cry out   to roar   to scream   to shriek   to yell**

show *noun*
an art show.
OTHER WORDS ARE   **display   exhibition**

show *verb*
1 We showed our work to the visitors.
OTHER VERBS YOU MIGHT USE ARE   **to display   to exhibit   to present**
2 She showed me how to do it.
OTHER VERBS ARE   **to explain   to teach   to tell**
3 We drew pictures to show how people used to dress in Victorian times.
OTHER VERBS ARE   **to illustrate   to portray   to represent**

shrill *adjective*
a shrill whistle.
OTHER WORDS YOU MIGHT USE ARE   **high   piercing   sharp**

shrivel *verb*
The plants shrivelled in the heat.
OTHER VERBS YOU MIGHT USE ARE   **to dry up   to shrink   to wither**

shudder *verb*
I shuddered when I thought of the monster.
OTHER VERBS YOU MIGHT USE ARE   **to quake   to quiver   to shake   to tremble**

shut *verb*
Shut the door.
OTHER VERBS ARE   **to close   to fasten   to lock   to seal**
To shut a door loudly is to **slam** it.
The opposite is open

shy *adjective*

He was too shy to say that he knew the answer.

OTHER WORDS YOU MIGHT USE ARE **bashful** **modest** **nervous** **timid**

The opposite is bold

sick *adjective*

Jo was away from school because she was sick.

OTHER WORDS YOU MIGHT USE ARE **ill** (*informal*) **poorly** **unwell**

to be sick

OTHER WORDS ARE (*informal*) **throw up** **vomit**

For other words, see **health**

side *noun*

1 A cube has six sides.

OTHER WORDS ARE **face** **surface**

2 I stood at the side of the road.

ANOTHER WORD IS **edge**

A grassy side of a road is a **verge**

sight *noun*

1 The optician says that Sam has good sight.

OTHER WORDS YOU MIGHT USE ARE **eyesight** **vision**

2 The hills are a lovely sight.

OTHER WORDS ARE **scene** **spectacle**

sign *noun*

1 He gave a sign that it was my turn.

OTHER WORDS YOU MIGHT USE ARE **hint** **reminder** **signal**

2 The doctor said that spots might be a sign of measles.

OTHER WORDS ARE **indication** **symptom**

silent *adjective*

1 During the night the house is completely silent.

OTHER WORDS YOU MIGHT USE ARE **quiet** **soundless**

The opposite is noisy

2 Sam was silent when he heard the bad news.

OTHER WORDS ARE **dumb** **speechless**

silky *adjective*

The cat has a silky coat.

OTHER WORDS YOU MIGHT USE ARE **sleek** **smooth** **soft**

The opposite is rough

silly *adjective*
It's silly to go out in the rain.
OTHER WORDS ARE   (*informal*) **daft   foolish   ridiculous   senseless   stupid**
The opposite is sensible

similar *adjective*
The two girls had similar dresses.
ANOTHER WORD IS **matching**
The opposite is different

simple *adjective*
1 a simple problem.
OTHER WORDS YOU MIGHT USE ARE   **clear   easy   straightforward**
The opposite is complicated
2 a simple dress.
ANOTHER WORD IS **plain**

sincere *adjective*
He was sincere when he said he was glad to see us.
OTHER WORDS YOU MIGHT USE ARE   **genuine   honest   truthful**
The opposite is dishonest

singer *noun*
ANOTHER WORD IS **vocalist**
A group of singers is a **choir** or a **chorus**.
Someone who sings on their own is a **soloist**.
SINGERS WITH DIFFERENT KINDS OF VOICE ARE
alto   bass   contralto   soprano   tenor   treble
For other words to do with music, see **music**

single *adjective*
There wasn't a single sweet left!
ANOTHER WORD IS **solitary**

site *noun*
We found a nice site to put up the tent.
OTHER WORDS YOU MIGHT USE ARE   **plot   position   situation   spot**

situation *noun*

1 My house is in a nice situation.
OTHER WORDS YOU MIGHT USE ARE **place** **position** **spot**
2 I was in an awkward situation when I lost my money.
ANOTHER WORD IS **position**

size *noun*

For other words, see **measurement**

skate *verb*

He skated gracefully over the ice.
OTHER VERBS YOU MIGHT USE ARE **to glide** **to skim** **to slide**

skeleton *noun*

For other parts of the body, see **body**

skid *verb*

The car skidded on the ice.
OTHER VERBS YOU CAN USE ARE **to slide** **to slip**

skilful *adjective*

a skilful player.
OTHER WORDS YOU MIGHT USE ARE **clever** **expert** **talented**

skill *noun*

Sam admired the player's skill.
OTHER WORDS YOU MIGHT USE ARE **ability** **cleverness** **talent**

skin *noun*

WORDS FOR ANIMALS' SKIN ARE **fur** **hide**
Words for the skin of an orange are **peel** or **rind**.

skip *verb*

The lambs skipped about the field.
OTHER VERBS ARE **to dance** **to frisk** **to hop** **to jump** **to leap**
to prance **to spring**

slanting *adjective*

a slanting line.
OTHER WORDS ARE **sloping** **tilting**

slay *verb*

For other verbs, see **kill**

sledge *noun*
OTHER WORDS ARE   sleigh   toboggan

sleep *verb*
DIFFERENT WAYS TO GO TO SLEEP ARE
to doze   (*informal*) **to drop off   to nod off   to slumber
to snooze**   (*informal*) **to take a nap**

When animals sleep for a long time in the winter, they **hibernate.**

sleepy *adjective*
I was sleepy so I went to bed.
OTHER WORDS YOU MIGHT USE ARE   **drowsy   tired   weary**

slender *adjective*
She has a slender figure.
ANOTHER WORD IS **graceful**
For other words, see **slim**

slide *verb*
We slid on the ice.
OTHER VERBS YOU MIGHT USE ARE   **to glide   to skate   to skid   to slip**

slight *adjective*
a slight accident.
OTHER WORDS YOU MIGHT USE ARE   **minor   small   unimportant**
The opposite is serious

slim *adjective*
He could get through the hole in the fence because he was so slim.
OTHER WORDS YOU MIGHT USE ARE   **lean   slender   slight   thin**
The opposite is fat

slip *verb*
Sam slipped and fell over.
OTHER VERBS YOU MIGHT USE ARE   **to skid   to slide**

slippery *adjective*
Take care: the floor is slippery.
OTHER WORDS ARE   **greasy   icy   oily   slimy   slithery   smooth**

slope *noun*

It's hard to run up a steep slope.

OTHER WORDS ARE   **bank   gradient   hill   ramp   rise**

slope *verb*

The beach slopes down to the sea.

ANOTHER VERB IS **to slant**

slot *noun*

I put a coin in the slot.

OTHER WORDS YOU MIGHT USE ARE   **groove   opening   slit**

slow *adjective*

1 There was a slow change in the weather.

ANOTHER WORD IS **gradual**

2 I'm sorry I'm late, but my watch is slow.

The opposite is fast

sly *adjective*

They say the fox is a sly animal.

OTHER WORDS ARE   **crafty   cunning**   (*informal*) **sneaky   wily**

smack *verb*

For other verbs, see **hit**

small *adjective*

1 The book was small enough to put in my pocket.

OTHER WORDS YOU MIGHT USE ARE   **compact   little   minute   tiny**

2 Sam made a small model of the castle.

ANOTHER WORD IS **miniature**

3 She gave us small helpings.

OTHER WORDS ARE   **mean**   (*informal*) **measly   stingy**

4 We had a small problem.

OTHER WORDS ARE   **minor   slight   unimportant**

The opposite is big

smart *adjective*

1 He looked smart in his new clothes.

OTHER WORDS YOU MIGHT USE ARE   **neat   posh   tidy   well-dressed**

The opposite is untidy

2 That's a smart dog if he understands what you say.

OTHER WORDS YOU MIGHT USE ARE   **bright   clever   intelligent**

The opposite is stupid

smart *verb*
The wasp sting made Sam's hand smart.
OTHER VERBS YOU MIGHT USE ARE   **to hurt**   **to sting**   **to throb**

smear *verb*
I smeared ointment on the sore place.
OTHER VERBS YOU MIGHT USE ARE   **to rub**   **to spread**   **to wipe**

smell *noun*
ANOTHER WORD IS **odour**
WORDS FOR A NICE SMELL ARE   **aroma**   **fragrance**   **perfume**   **scent**
A word for a nasty smell is **stink**.
A word for a slight smell is **whiff**.

smile *verb*
For other verbs, see **laugh**

smoke *noun*
the smoke from an engine.
OTHER WORDS YOU MIGHT USE ARE   **exhaust**   **fumes**

smooth *adjective*
1 a smooth surface.
OTHER WORDS YOU MIGHT USE ARE   **even**   **flat**   **level**
The opposite is rough
2 a smooth sea.
ANOTHER WORD IS **calm**
The opposite is stormy

smudge *noun*
I smudged the wet paint.
OTHER WORDS YOU MIGHT USE ARE   **smear**   **streak**

snatch *verb*
The dog snatched the sandwich out of my hand.
OTHER VERBS YOU MIGHT USE ARE   **to grab**   **to seize**   **to take**

sneak *verb*
She sneaked up behind me and made me jump.
OTHER VERBS YOU MIGHT USE ARE   **to creep**   **to steal**

soft *adjective*
1 The baby cuddled a soft toy.
> OTHER WORDS TO DESCRIBE SOFT THINGS ARE   **flexible   floppy   limp   spongy   springy   squashy**
The opposite is hard
2 Jo's dress is made of soft material.
> OTHER WORDS YOU MIGHT USE ARE   **silky   smooth   velvety**
The opposite is rough
3 They played soft music when we went into church.
> OTHER WORDS YOU MIGHT USE ARE   **gentle   low   quiet   restful**
The opposite is loud

soil *noun*
Sam planted his seeds in the soil.
> OTHER WORDS YOU MIGHT USE ARE   **earth   ground**

soldier *noun*
> ANOTHER WORD IS **serviceman** or **servicewoman**
Soldiers who go on horseback are the **cavalry**.
Soldiers who go on foot are the **infantry**.
A soldier trained for specially daring raids is a **commando**.
A soldier trained to fight on land or at sea is a **marine**.
A soldier who goes into battle by parachute is a **paratrooper**.
> WORDS FOR A LOT OF SOLDIERS ARE
> **army   troops**
For other fighters, see **fight**

solemn *adjective*
They looked solemn when they heard the news.
> OTHER WORDS YOU MIGHT USE ARE   **grave   serious   thoughtful**

solid *adjective*
1 Cricket balls are solid.
The opposite is hollow
2 We were glad to get out of the mud onto solid ground.
> OTHER WORDS YOU MIGHT USE ARE   **firm   hard**
The opposite is soft

solution *noun*
Did you get the solution to the puzzle?
> OTHER WORDS YOU MIGHT USE ARE   **answer   explanation**

solve *verb*
Jo solved the puzzle in a couple of minutes.
OTHER VERBS YOU MIGHT USE ARE   **to answer**   **to explain**   **to work out**

song *noun*
DIFFERENT KINDS OF MUSIC FOR SINGING ARE
**ballad   carol   folksong   hymn   lullaby
pop song   shanty**
For other words to do with music, see **music**

soothe *verb*
Quiet music soothes your nerves.
OTHER VERBS YOU MIGHT USE ARE   **to calm**   **to comfort**   **to relax**
The opposite is disturb

sore *adjective*
Jo had a sore place on her knee.
OTHER WORDS YOU MIGHT USE ARE   **aching   inflamed   painful   raw
red   tender**

sorrow *noun*
Jo was full of sorrow when his dog died.
OTHER WORDS YOU MIGHT USE ARE   **grief   misery   sadness
unhappiness**

sorry *adjective*
1 He was sorry when he saw the damage he had done.
OTHER WORDS ARE   **apologetic   ashamed   regretful   repentant**
2 Jo was sorry for the sick boy.
OTHER WORDS ARE   **sad   sympathetic**

sort *noun*
1 Which sort of cake do you like?
OTHER WORDS YOU MIGHT USE ARE   **brand   kind   type   variety**
2 What sort of dog is that?
OTHER WORDS ARE   **breed   species**

sort *verb*
Sam sorted the library books.
OTHER VERBS YOU MIGHT USE ARE   **to arrange**   **to classify**   **to organize**

sound *adjective*
1 Jo's dog is in a sound condition.
OTHER WORDS YOU MIGHT USE ARE **healthy   strong**
2 The teacher said we had done sound work.
OTHER WORDS YOU MIGHT USE ARE **correct   good   reasonable**

sound *noun* and *verb*, see opposite page

sour *adjective*
a sour taste.
OTHER WORDS YOU MIGHT USE ARE **acid   sharp   tangy , tart**
The opposite is sweet

source *noun*
the source of a river.
OTHER WORDS ARE **beginning   origin   starting point**

space *noun*
1 Give me a bit of space.
ANOTHER WORD IS **room**
2 Write your answer in the space.
ANOTHER WORD IS **blank**
3 What goes in that empty space?
OTHER WORDS YOU MIGHT USE ARE **gap   hole   opening**

spacecraft *noun*
DIFFERENT KINDS OF SPACECRAFT ARE **rocket   spaceship   space shuttle**

spare *adjective*
Take some spare socks in case you get your feet wet.
OTHER WORDS YOU MIGHT USE ARE **additional   extra**

spare *verb*
The cruel soldier would not spare his enemy.
OTHER VERBS YOU MIGHT USE ARE **to be merciful to   to forgive
to let off   to pardon   to reprieve   to save**

sparkle *verb*
The firework sparkled in the dark.
OTHER VERBS YOU MIGHT USE ARE **to flash   to spark**

speak *verb*
For other verbs, see **talk**

sound *noun* and *verb*

DIFFERENT SOUNDS WE CAN MAKE ARE

bawl	boo	clap	cry
groan	hiccup	hiss	jeer
lisp	moan	scream	shout
shriek	sigh	sniff	snore
sob	wail	whistle	yell

For other sounds we make, see **talk**

DIFFERENT SOUNDS ANIMALS MAKE ARE

bark	bellow	bleat	bray
croak	growl	grunt	howl
jabber	low	miaow	moo
neigh	purr	roar	screech
snarl	snort	squeak	squeal
whine	whinny	yap	

SOUNDS DIFFERENT BIRDS MAKE ARE

cackle	chirp	cluck	coo
crow	hoot	quack	screech
squawk	twitter	warble	

SOUNDS INSECTS MAKE ARE

buzz	drone	hum	murmur

DIFFERENT SOUNDS THINGS MAKE ARE

bang	blare	bleep	boom
chime	clang	clank	clash
clatter	click	clink	crack
crackle	crash	creak	jangle
jingle	peal	ping	plop
pop	rattle	ring	rumble
rustle	sizzle	slam	snap
splutter	swish	throb	thud
thunder	tick	tinkle	twang
whiz			

For other words, see **music, noise**

spear *noun*
A spear used by knights in old times was a **lance**.
A spear used to kill whales is a **harpoon**.
A spear you throw as a sport is a **javelin**.

special *adjective*
1 Your birthday is a special day.
   ANOTHER WORD IS **important**
2 Petrol has a special smell.
   OTHER WORDS ARE **different**   **distinct**
3 Jo has tea in her special mug.
   OTHER WORDS YOU MIGHT USE ARE **individual** **particular** **personal**

specimen *noun*
Show me a specimen of your work.
   OTHER WORDS YOU MIGHT USE ARE **example** **illustration** **sample**

speck *noun*
a speck of dust.
   OTHER WORDS ARE **bit** **dot** **grain** **spot**

speckled *adjective*
a speckled pattern.
   OTHER WORDS ARE **dotted** **mottled** **spotty**

spectacular *adjective*
a spectacular fireworks display.
   OTHER WORDS YOU MIGHT USE ARE **big** **exciting** **impressive**

speech *noun*
We listened to the speech.
   OTHER WORDS YOU MIGHT USE ARE **lecture** **talk**

speed *noun*
We walked at an ordinary speed.
   OTHER WORDS YOU MIGHT USE ARE **pace** **rate**

spell *noun*
'a magic spell.
   OTHER WORDS YOU MIGHT USE ARE **charm** **enchantment**

spend *verb*
1 How much money did you spend?
OTHER VERBS YOU MIGHT USE ARE   **to pay**   **to use**
2 We spent a nice day by the sea.
ANOTHER VERB IS **to pass**

spike *noun*
There were spikes along the top of the railings.
OTHER WORDS YOU MIGHT USE ARE   **point**   **prong**

spill *verb*
Who spilt the milk on the carpet?
OTHER VERBS YOU MIGHT USE ARE   **to drop**   **to slop**   **to tip**   **to upset**

spin *verb*
The top spun round and round.
OTHER VERBS ARE   **to revolve**   **to turn**   **to twirl**   **to whirl**

spirit *noun*
Another word for your spirit is your **soul**.
SPIRITS YOU READ ABOUT IN STORIES ARE
**demon   devil   fairy   genie   ghost   gremlin
imp   phantom   poltergeist**   (*informal*) **spook**

spiteful *adjective*
Jo doesn't like people who make spiteful remarks.
OTHER WORDS YOU MIGHT USE ARE   (*informal*) **catty   hurtful   nasty
unkind**
The opposite is kind

splash *verb*
The car splashed water over us.
OTHER VERBS YOU MIGHT USE ARE   **to shower**   **to slop**   **to spatter**

splendid *adjective*
1 The soldiers wore splendid uniforms.
OTHER WORDS YOU MIGHT USE ARE   **brilliant   gorgeous   grand
impressive   magnificent**
2 We had a splendid holiday.
For other words, see **good**

split *verb*

1 He split the log with an axe.
   OTHER VERBS YOU MIGHT USE ARE   **to chop**   **to crack**   **to cut**
   to slice
2 We split into two teams.
   OTHER VERBS ARE   **to divide**   **to separate**

spoil *verb*

The stain has spoilt my new dress.
   OTHER VERBS YOU MIGHT USE ARE   **to damage**   (*informal*) **to mess up**
   to ruin   **to wreck**

sport *noun*

DIFFERENT SPORTS ARE

athletics	baseball	basketball	boxing
climbing	cricket	darts	fishing
football	golf	gymnastics	hockey
ice hockey	rounders	rugby	running
sailing	showjumping	skating	skiing
snooker	soccer	squash	surfing
surf-riding	swimming	table tennis	tennis
volleyball	water-skiing	windsurfing	wrestling
yachting			

spot *noun*

1 You've got a dirty spot on your new trousers.
   OTHER WORDS YOU MIGHT USE ARE
   blot   dot   mark   speck   stain
2 I've got spots on my face.
   DIFFERENT KINDS OF SPOTS ARE
   boil   freckle   mole   pimple
   A spot on your eyelid is a **sty**.
   A large number of spots is a **rash**.

3 Here's a nice spot for a picnic.
   OTHER WORDS ARE
   place   position   situation

spray *verb*
The bus sprayed us with water when it went through the puddle.
OTHER VERBS YOU MIGHT USE ARE   **to scatter**   **to shower**
to spatter   **to splash**   **to sprinkle**

spread *verb*
We spread the map on the table.
OTHER VERBS YOU MIGHT USE ARE   **to lay out**   **to open out**   **to unfold**

spring *verb*
1 The cat crouched, ready to spring on the mouse.
OTHER VERBS YOU MIGHT USE ARE   **to jump**   **to leap**   **to pounce**
2 Weeds sprang up all over the garden.
OTHER VERBS ARE   **to grow**   **to shoot**

sprout *verb*
The seeds began to sprout.
OTHER VERBS YOU MIGHT USE ARE   **to grow**   **to shoot up**   **to spring up**

squabble *verb*
Those boys are always squabbling.
OTHER VERBS YOU MIGHT USE ARE   **to argue**   **to fight**   **to quarrel**

squeeze *verb*
1 I squeezed an orange to make some juice.
OTHER VERBS YOU MIGHT USE ARE   **to crush**   **to press**
2 They squeezed us into a little room.
OTHER VERBS ARE   **to crowd**   **to push**   **to shove**   **to squash**

squirt *verb*
Water squirted out of the hole.
OTHER VERBS YOU MIGHT USE ARE   **to pour**   **to spout**   **to spurt**
to stream

stack *noun*
a stack of books.
OTHER WORDS ARE   **heap**   **mound**   **pile**

stage *noun*
1 We stood on the stage to sing.
ANOTHER WORD IS **platform**
2 Baby is at the crawling stage.
OTHER WORDS ARE   **period**   **phase**

stain *noun*
What's that stain on your shirt?
OTHER WORDS ARE   **blot**   **mark**   **smudge**   **spot**

stairs *noun*
OTHER WORDS YOU MIGHT USE ARE   **staircase**   **steps**

stale *adjective*
1 stale bread.
OTHER WORDS YOU MIGHT USE ARE   **dry**   **old**
2 stale news.
ANOTHER WORD IS **out-of-date**
The opposite is fresh

stalk *noun*
a flower on a stalk.
ANOTHER WORD IS **stem**

stand *verb*
1 We all stood when the visitors arrived.
OTHER VERBS YOU MIGHT USE ARE   **to get up**   **to rise**
2 I stood my books on the shelf.
OTHER VERBS ARE   **to arrange**   **to place**   **to position**

standard *noun*
Our teacher expects a high standard of work.
OTHER WORDS YOU MIGHT USE ARE   **level**   **quality**

stare *verb*
For other verbs, see **look**

start *verb*
1 What time does the film start?
OTHER VERBS YOU MIGHT USE ARE   **to begin**   **to commence**
2 Our teacher has started a chess club.
OTHER VERBS ARE   **to create**   **to introduce**   **to set up**
3 They started on their journey at dawn.
OTHER VERBS ARE   **to depart**   **to embark**   **to set off**   **to set out**

startle *verb*
The explosion startled us.
OTHER VERBS YOU MIGHT USE ARE   **to alarm**   **to frighten**   **to shock**
   to surprise   **to upset**

starving *adjective*
For other words, see **hungry**

state *verb*
Dad stated that he had no money.
OTHER VERBS YOU MIGHT USE ARE   **to announce   to declare   to report
to say**

statement *noun*
The police issued a statement about the burglary.
OTHER WORDS YOU MIGHT USE ARE   **announcement   communication**

statue *noun*
We saw some statues in the museum.
OTHER WORDS YOU MIGHT USE ARE   **carving   figure   sculpture**

stay *verb*
1 Stay here until I come back.
OTHER VERBS YOU MIGHT USE ARE   **to remain   to stop   to wait**
2 Stay on the path.
OTHER VERBS ARE   **to carry on   to continue   to keep on**
3 Jo went to stay with Granny.
ANOTHER WORD IS **to visit**

steady *adjective*
1 Make sure the ladder is steady.
OTHER WORDS YOU MIGHT USE ARE   **firm   secure   solid**
2 The music had a steady rhythm.
OTHER WORDS ARE   **constant   continuous   even   regular**

steal *verb*
OTHER VERBS YOU MIGHT USE ARE
(*informal*) **to pinch   to take**

Someone who steals things is a **robber** or a **thief**.
Someone who steals things from someone's house is a **burglar**.
Someone who steals things in a riot is a **looter**.
Someone who steals things from a shop is a **shoplifter**.
Someone who steals by attacking people in the street is
a **mugger**.
Someone who steals things out of your pocket is a **pickpocket**.
Someone who used to steal things from travellers was
a **highwayman**.

step *noun*

1 We all moved forwards one step.
OTHER WORDS YOU MIGHT USE ARE   **pace**   **stride**

2 I climbed up the steps.
ANOTHER WORD IS **stair**

stern *adjective*

She had a stern look on her face.
OTHER WORDS YOU MIGHT USE ARE   **angry**   **grim**   **severe**   **strict**

stick *noun*

DIFFERENT KINDS OF STICK ARE:
a long straight stick
  pole   **rod**

a stick that is part of a plant
  branch   **stalk**   **twig**

a stick used in a relay race or by the conductor of a band
  baton

a stick used to support plants
  bamboo   **cane**

a stick used as a weapon
  club   **truncheon**

a stick used to help someone walk
  crutch   **walking stick**

a magician's stick
  wand

stick *verb*

1 The door has stuck.
ANOTHER VERB IS **to jam**

2 This glue will stick plastic.
OTHER VERBS YOU MIGHT USE ARE   **to fasten**   **to fix**   **to glue**

3 She stuck a pin in me!
OTHER VERBS ARE   **to jab**   **to stab**

stiff *adjective*

1 stiff cardboard.
OTHER WORDS YOU MIGHT USE ARE   **hard**   **rigid**

2 stiff paste.
ANOTHER WORD IS **thick**

still *adjective*
It was a very still evening.
OTHER WORDS ARE   **calm**   **peaceful**   **quiet**

stir *verb*
1 Sam stirred the cake mixture.
OTHER VERBS YOU MIGHT USE ARE   **to beat**   **to mix**   **to whisk**
2 Mum called Jo and said it was time to stir.
OTHER VERBS ARE   **to get going**   **to get up**   **to move**

stitch *noun*
For other words, see **sew**

stomach *noun*
AN INFORMAL WORD IS **tummy**
A word some people think is impolite is **belly**.

stone *noun*
DIFFERENT KINDS OF STONE ARE   **boulder**   **cobble**   **gravel**   **jewel**
pebble   **rock**

stoop *verb*
I stooped down to pull up my sock.
OTHER VERBS YOU MIGHT USE ARE   **to bend**   **to bow**   **to crouch**
to kneel

stop *verb*
1 The policeman stopped the traffic.
OTHER VERBS YOU MIGHT USE ARE   **to check**   **to halt**   **to hold up**
2 The bus stopped.
OTHER VERBS ARE   **to draw up**   **to halt**   **to pull up**
3 The noise suddenly stopped.
OTHER VERBS ARE   **to cease**   **to end**   **to finish**
4 You can stop for tea.
ANOTHER VERB IS **to stay**

store *verb*
We store food in the fridge.
OTHER VERBS YOU MIGHT USE ARE   **to keep**   **to put away**   **to save**

storm *noun*
DIFFERENT KINDS OF STORM:
a violent storm
tempest

a snow storm
blizzard

a storm with a lot of wind
gale   hurricane   tornado   whirlwind

a storm with a lot of rain
deluge   downpour   rainstorm

a storm with thunder and lightning
thunderstorm

For other words, see **weather**

story *noun*
OTHER WORDS YOU MIGHT USE ARE
narrative   tale

DIFFERENT KINDS OF STORY ARE
**adventure story   comedy   fable   fairy tale   fantasy
folk tale   legend   love story   myth   novel   parable
romance**

stout *adjective*
a stout person.
OTHER WORDS YOU MIGHT USE ARE   **fat   overweight   plump**
(*informal*) **tubby**
The opposite is thin

straight *adjective*
a straight line. a straight road.
ANOTHER WORD IS **direct**
The opposite is crooked

strain *verb*

1 He strained to escape from the monster's grip.
OTHER VERBS YOU MIGHT USE ARE   **to make an effort   to struggle   to try hard**
2 Jo strained a muscle when she was running.
OTHER VERBS ARE   **to damage   to hurt   to injure**
3 Don't strain yourself!
OTHER VERBS ARE   **to exhaust   to tire out   to wear out**

strange *adjective*

1 When I woke up I was in a strange place.
OTHER WORDS YOU MIGHT USE ARE   **different   foreign   new   unfamiliar   unknown**
The opposite is familiar
2 A strange thing happened.
OTHER WORDS ARE   **curious   extraordinary   funny   mysterious   odd   peculiar   puzzling   queer   surprising   unusual**
The opposite is ordinary

stranger *noun*

Please show me the way, because I am a stranger here.
A stranger might be a **foreigner** or a **visitor**.

stray *verb*

Whatever you do, don't stray in the forest.
OTHER VERBS YOU MIGHT USE ARE   **to get lost   to roam about   to wander**

streak *noun*

The plane left a white streak in the sky.
OTHER WORDS YOU MIGHT USE ARE   **line   stripe**

stream *noun*

We paddled across a stream.
ANOTHER WORD IS **brook**
A big stream is a **river**.
For other words, see **water**

strength *noun*

Have you got the strength to lift this box?
OTHER WORDS ARE   **force   might   power**

strength**en** *verb*

Dad put in some posts to strengthen the fence.

OTHER VERBS YOU MIGHT USE ARE   **to reinforce   to support**

The opposite is weaken

stretch *verb*

You can stretch elastic.

OTHER VERBS YOU MIGHT USE ARE   **to lengthen   to pull out**

strict *adjective*

a strict teacher.

OTHER WORDS YOU MIGHT USE ARE   **firm   severe   stern**

string *noun*

OTHER THINGS YOU MIGHT USE TO TIE THINGS UP ARE

cord   lace   line   ribbon   rope   wire

strip *verb*

We stripped off our clothes to go swimming.

OTHER VERBS YOU MIGHT USE ARE   **to peel off   to remove   to take off**

stripe *noun*

Sam's football shirt has red and white stripes.

OTHER WORDS ARE   **band   line   strip**

strong *adjective*

1 a strong person.

OTHER WORDS YOU MIGHT USE ARE   **healthy   muscular   sturdy   tough   wiry**

2 a strong rope. strong walking shoes.

OTHER WORDS ARE   **sound   stout   thick**

The opposite is weak

struggle *verb*

1 The thief struggled to get away.

OTHER VERBS YOU MIGHT USE ARE   **to fight   to wrestle**

2 We struggled to put the tent up.

OTHER VERBS ARE   **to exert yourself   to make an effort   to strive   to try**

stubborn *adjective*
The stubborn animal refused to move.
> OTHER WORDS YOU MIGHT USE ARE   **defiant   disobedient   obstinate**

study *verb*
1 Mum is studying for an exam.
> OTHER VERBS YOU MIGHT USE ARE   **to learn   to revise**   (*informal*) **to swot**
2 The police studied the evidence.
> OTHER VERBS ARE   **to analyse   to consider   to examine   to investigate   to think about**

stuff *noun*
1 What's this stuff in the jar?
> ANOTHER WORD IS **substance**
2 What's that stuff in the attic?
> OTHER WORDS ARE   **articles   odds and ends   things**
3 I put my stuff in a box.
> OTHER WORDS ARE   **belongings   possessions**

stuffy *adjective*
a stuffy room.
> OTHER WORDS YOU MIGHT USE ARE   **close   muggy   stifling   warm**

stumble *verb*
I stumbled over a big stone.
> OTHER VERBS YOU MIGHT USE ARE   **to blunder   to stagger   to trip**

stun *verb*
1 The hit on the head stunned her.
> OTHER VERBS YOU MIGHT USE ARE   **to daze   to knock out**
2 The unexpected news stunned us.
> OTHER VERBS ARE   **to amaze   to astonish   to shock   to surprise**

stupid *adjective*
1 a stupid idea.
> OTHER WORDS YOU MIGHT USE ARE   **crazy   foolish   idiotic   silly**
2 a stupid person.
> OTHER WORDS ARE   **dense   dim   dull   slow**   (*informal*) **thick**
The opposite is clever

style *noun*
Jo likes the new style of dancing.
> OTHER WORDS YOU MIGHT USE ARE   **fashion   way**

subject *noun*

Sam chose an interesting subject for his project.

> OTHER WORDS YOU MIGHT USE ARE   **theme**   **topic**

submit *verb*

1 The wrestler submitted to his opponent.
> OTHER VERBS YOU MIGHT USE ARE   **to give in**   **to surrender**
> **to yield**

2 We must submit our work today.
> OTHER VERBS ARE   **to give in**   **to hand in**   **to present**

substance *noun*

What's this sticky substance?

> OTHER WORDS YOU MIGHT USE ARE   **material**   **stuff**

subtract *verb*

Our teacher subtracts marks for untidy work.

> OTHER VERBS YOU MIGHT USE ARE   **to deduct**   **to take away**

succeed *verb*

1 Jo succeeded in winning the race.
> OTHER VERBS YOU MIGHT USE ARE   **to be successful**   **to do well**

2 Did your plan succeed?
> ANOTHER VERB IS **to work**

sudden *adjective*

The car came to a sudden halt.

> OTHER WORDS YOU MIGHT USE ARE   **abrupt**   **hasty**   **quick**
> **unexpected**

The opposite is gradual

suffer *verb*

I hate to see animals suffer pain.

> OTHER VERBS YOU MIGHT USE ARE   **to bear**   **to endure**   **to go through**
> **to put up with**   **to stand**

suffering *noun*

For other words, see **pain**

sufficient *adjective*

Have you got sufficient money for your journey?

> OTHER WORDS YOU MIGHT USE ARE   **adequate**   **enough**

suggest *verb*
What do you suggest we should do?
> OTHER VERBS YOU MIGHT USE ARE **to advise** **to propose**
> **to recommend**

suitable *adjective*
Is this dress suitable for a wedding?
> OTHER WORDS YOU MIGHT USE ARE **appropriate** **proper** **right**

sulky *adjective*
After Mum told him off he was sulky for hours.
> OTHER WORDS ARE **bad-tempered** **cross** **gloomy** **moody**
> **sullen**
The opposite is cheerful

sunny *adjective*
sunny weather.
> OTHER WORDS YOU MIGHT USE ARE **bright** **clear** **cloudless** **fine**

supply *noun*
There's a supply of paper in the cupboard.
> OTHER WORDS YOU MIGHT USE ARE **reserve** **stock**

supply *verb*
We took our own sandwiches, and our teacher supplied the drinks.
> OTHER VERBS YOU MIGHT USE ARE **to contribute** **to give** **to provide**

support *verb*
1 Those pillars support the roof.
> OTHER VERBS YOU MIGHT USE ARE **to bear** **to hold up** **to prop up**
2 Our friends supported us when we were in trouble.
> OTHER VERBS ARE **to aid** **to assist** **to encourage** **to help**
> **to stand up for**

supporter *noun*
Sam is a supporter of the local team.
> OTHER WORDS ARE **fan** **follower**

suppose *verb*
Let's suppose that Jo's the queen.
> OTHER VERBS YOU MIGHT USE ARE **to assume** **to believe** **to imagine**
> **to pretend**

sure *adjective*
  1 I'm sure he will come.
    OTHER WORDS YOU MIGHT USE ARE **certain** **confident** **convinced** **definite** **positive**
  2 He's sure to come.
    ANOTHER WORD IS **bound**

surprise *verb*
  The unexpected news surprised us.
    OTHER VERBS YOU MIGHT USE ARE **to amaze** **to astonish** **to shock** **to startle** **to stun**

surrender *verb*
  After a long fight, the army surrendered.
    OTHER VERBS YOU MIGHT USE ARE **to give in** **to submit** **to yield**

survey *noun*
  We did a survey to find out who comes to school by car.
    OTHER WORDS YOU MIGHT USE ARE **investigation** **study**

survive *verb*
  Some plants don't survive through the winter.
    OTHER VERBS YOU MIGHT USE ARE **to keep going** **to last** **to live**

suspect *verb*
  Mum suspects that I broke her mug.
    OTHER VERBS ARE **to guess** **to have a feeling** **to think**

swamp *noun*
  The lorry got stuck in the swamp.
    OTHER WORDS ARE **bog** **marsh**

swarm *noun*
  For other words, see **group**

swear *verb*
  1 Do you swear that you'll tell the truth?
    OTHER VERBS YOU MIGHT USE ARE **to give your word** **to promise** **to vow**
  2 He swore when he hit his finger.
    ANOTHER VERB IS **to curse**

sweep *verb*
> I swept the floor.
>> ANOTHER VERB IS **to brush**
>
> For ways to clean things, see **clean**

sweet *adjective*
> For other words to describe how things taste, see **taste**
> The opposite is sour

swell *verb*
> You can see the tyre swell while you pump it up.
>> OTHER VERBS ARE   **to blow up**   **to bulge**   **to get bigger**   **to grow**   **to puff up**

swelling *noun*
> I got a nasty swelling where the wasp stung me.
>> OTHER WORDS YOU MIGHT USE ARE   **bulge**   **bump**   **lump**

swift *adjective*
> a swift journey.
>> OTHER WORDS YOU MIGHT USE ARE   **fast**   **quick**   **rapid**   **speedy**
>
> The opposite is slow

swill *verb*
> Swill the plates under the tap.
>> OTHER VERBS YOU MIGHT USE ARE   **to rinse**   **to wash**

swindle *verb*
> He swindled us and made us pay too much.
>> OTHER VERBS YOU MIGHT USE ARE   **to cheat**   **to deceive**   **to fool**   **to trick**

swing *verb*
> The branches swung to and fro in the wind.
>> ANOTHER VERB IS **to sway**

switch *verb*
> I switched places with my friend.
>> OTHER VERBS YOU MIGHT USE ARE   **to change**   **to exchange**   **to swap**

swoop *verb*
> The owl swooped down on its prey.
>> OTHER VERBS ARE   **to dive**   **to pounce**

sympathy *noun*

He didn't have much sympathy when I was ill!

OTHER WORDS YOU MIGHT USE ARE **consideration** **feeling** **mercy**
pity

symptom *noun*

Spots might be a symptom of measles.

OTHER WORDS ARE **indication** **sign**

Tt

take *verb*

1 Take my hand.

OTHER VERBS YOU MIGHT USE ARE **to clasp** **to get hold of** **to grasp**
to hold **to seize**

2 The bus takes you into town.

OTHER VERBS ARE **to bring** **to carry** **to transport**

3 The army took many prisoners.

OTHER VERBS ARE **to capture** **to catch** **to seize**

4 The burglar took the jewels.

OTHER VERBS ARE **to remove** **to steal**

5 The dentist took out one of my teeth.

OTHER VERBS ARE **to extract** **to remove**

talent *noun*

Sam has great talent in football.

OTHER WORDS YOU MIGHT USE ARE **ability** **skill**

talented *adjective*

Jo is a talented musician.

OTHER WORDS YOU MIGHT USE ARE **clever** **expert** **gifted** **skilful**

talk *noun*

1 I had a nice talk with Granny.

OTHER WORDS YOU MIGHT USE ARE **chat** **conversation** **discussion**

2 The head gave us a long talk.

OTHER WORDS ARE **address** **lecture** **speech**

talk *verb*
OTHER VERBS YOU MIGHT USE ARE
to communicate   to express yourself   to say something
to speak

THERE ARE DIFFERENT WAYS OF TALKING. YOU CAN

call out	chat	chatter	exclaim
gossip	have a conversation		lisp
mumble	murmur	mutter	prattle
recite a poem	scream	screech	shout
shriek	snap at someone		snarl
splutter	stammer	stutter	whisper
yell			

tall *adjective*
a tall tower.
ANOTHER WORD IS **high**
The opposite is low or short

tame *adjective*
These animals are very tame.
OTHER WORDS YOU MIGHT USE ARE   **gentle   meek   obedient
safe**
The opposite is dangerous or wild

tangled *adjective*
tangled string.
OTHER WORDS YOU MIGHT USE ARE   **knotted   muddled   twisted**

tank *noun*
A tank to keep fish in is an **aquarium**.

tap *verb*
She tapped on the door.
OTHER VERBS YOU MIGHT USE ARE   **to knock   to rap**

task *noun*
OTHER WORDS YOU MIGHT USE ARE   **job   work**

taste *noun*

1 Do you like the taste of this?
ANOTHER WORD IS **flavour**
2 Can I have a taste of your ice cream?
OTHER WORDS YOU MIGHT USE ARE
bit   lick   mouthful   nibble   piece

WORDS TO DESCRIBE THINGS THAT TASTE NICE ARE
appetizing   delicious   luscious   tasty

WORDS TO DESCRIBE THINGS THAT TASTE NASTY ARE
bad   (*informal*) **off   stale   uneatable**

OTHER WORDS TO DESCRIBE HOW THINGS TASTE ARE
**acid   bitter   creamy   fruity   hot   meaty   peppery
salty   savoury   sharp   sour   spicy   sugary   sweet
tangy**

taste *verb*

Taste a bit of this!
OTHER VERBS YOU MIGHT USE ARE   **to nibble   to sample   to sip   to try**

teach *verb*

OTHER WORDS YOU MIGHT USE ARE
to teach someone in school
educate
to teach someone to do a job
instruct   train
to teach someone to be good at a sport
coach

teacher *noun*

DIFFERENT KINDS OF TEACHER ARE   **lecturer   professor   schoolteacher
tutor**
a person who teaches us to play games properly   **coach   trainer**
a person who teaches you how to do a particular thing **instructor**

team *noun*

a football team.
ANOTHER WORD IS **side**

tear *verb*
Sam tore his jeans.
OTHER VERBS ARE   **to rip**   **to slit**   **to split**

tease *verb*
If you tease the cat she'll scratch.
OTHER VERBS YOU MIGHT USE ARE   **to annoy**   **to laugh at**   **to make fun of**   **to pester**   **to torment**

telephone *verb*
I telephoned Grandad to ask him to come to tea.
OTHER VERBS YOU MIGHT USE ARE   **to call**   **to dial**   **to phone**   **to ring**

television *noun*
DIFFERENT KINDS OF TV PROGRAMME ARE
cartoons   chat shows   comedy   commercials   films   interviews   music   nature programmes   news   plays   quiz shows   serials   sport

tell *verb*
1 He told me he'd be home for tea.
OTHER VERBS YOU MIGHT USE ARE   **to inform**   **to promise**
2 Our teacher told the story.
OTHER VERBS ARE   **to narrate**   **to relate**
3 I told the police what happened.
OTHER VERBS ARE   **to describe to someone**   **to explain to someone**
4 Mum told us to stop shouting.
OTHER VERBS ARE   **to command**   **to instruct**   **to order**
to tell someone off
OTHER VERBS YOU MIGHT USE ARE   **to reprimand**   **to scold**
(*informal*) **to tick off**

temper *noun*
1 Is Dad in a good temper?
ANOTHER WORD IS **mood**
2 Baby yells when she's in a temper.
OTHER WORDS YOU MIGHT USE ARE   **rage**   **tantrum**
to lose your temper
A PHRASE IS **get angry**

tend *verb*

1 Grandad tends to fall asleep in the evening.
A PHRASE YOU MIGHT USE IS **to be liable to**
2 Nurses tend sick people.
OTHER VERBS YOU MIGHT USE ARE   **to care for**   **to look after**   **to mind**

tender *adjective*

1 I gave the baby a tender smile.
OTHER WORDS YOU MIGHT USE ARE   **affectionate**   **fond**   **gentle**   **kind**
   loving
The opposite is cruel
2 The baby has tender skin.
OTHER WORDS ARE   **delicate**   **soft**
The opposite is tough
3 I had a tender place where I hit my head.
OTHER WORDS ARE   **sensitive**   **sore**

terrible *adjective*

There was a terrible storm.
OTHER WORDS YOU MIGHT USE ARE   **alarming**   **awful**   **bad**   **dreadful**
   frightening   **horrible**   (*informal*) **scary**   **terrific**

terrific *adjective*

1 I had a terrific idea.
For other words, see **good**
2 There was a terrific storm.
For other words, see **terrible**

terrify *verb*

The dog terrified the baby.
OTHER VERBS YOU MIGHT USE ARE   **to alarm**   **to frighten**   **to scare**
   to upset

terror *noun*

People ran away from the fire in terror.
OTHER WORDS YOU MIGHT USE ARE   **alarm**   **fear**   **fright**   **panic**

test *noun*

1 a spelling test. a driving test.
ANOTHER WORD IS **exam** or **examination**
2 a scientific test.
OTHER WORDS YOU MIGHT USE ARE   **experiment**   **research**   **trial**

thankful *adjective*

I was thankful it wasn't raining.

OTHER WORDS YOU MIGHT USE ARE   **grateful   pleased**

thaw *verb*

The snow thawed when the sun came out.

OTHER VERBS YOU MIGHT USE ARE   **to melt   to unfreeze**

The opposite is freeze

theatre *noun*

We went to the theatre for a Christmas treat.

OTHER WORDS YOU MIGHT USE ARE   **performance   show**

THINGS YOU SEE IN A THEATRE ARE

**ballet   comedy   drama   musical   opera
pantomime   play**

For other words, see **entertainment**

thick *adjective*

1 a thick line.

OTHER WORDS YOU MIGHT USE ARE   **broad   wide**

2 a thick slice of cake.

AN INFORMAL WORD IS **chunky**

The opposite is thin

3 thick gravy.

The opposite is runny

thief *noun*

For different kinds of thief, see **steal**

thin *adjective*

1 a thin line.

OTHER WORDS YOU MIGHT USE ARE   **fine   narrow**

The opposite is thick

2 a thin person.

KIND WORDS YOU MIGHT USE ARE   **lean   slender   slim**

AN UNKIND WORD IS **skinny**

The opposite is fat

3 thin gravy.

OTHER WORDS ARE   **runny   watery**

The opposite is thick

thing *noun*

1 What are these things in the cupboard?
OTHER WORDS YOU MIGHT USE ARE   **article**   **item**   **object**
2 I've got several things on my mind.
OTHER WORDS ARE   **idea**   **thought**   **worry**
3 I saw a funny thing today.
ANOTHER WORD IS **happening**

think *verb*

1 If you think, you won't make a mistake.
OTHER VERBS YOU MIGHT USE ARE   **to attend**   **to concentrate**
2 We thought about what to do.
OTHER VERBS ARE   **to consider**   **to reflect**
3 I think you are right.
OTHER VERBS ARE   **to believe**   **to feel**   **to guess**   **to suppose**

thorough *adjective*

1 a thorough job.
OTHER WORDS YOU MIGHT USE ARE   **careful**   **proper**
2 a thorough mess.
OTHER WORDS ARE   **absolute**   **complete**   **utter**

thoughtful *adjective*

1 You look thoughtful today.
OTHER WORDS YOU MIGHT USE ARE   **serious**   **solemn**
2 It's thoughtful of you to wash up.
OTHER WORDS ARE   **considerate**   **friendly**   **helpful**   **unselfish**

threaten *verb*

For other verbs, see **frighten**

thrilling *adjective*

The band played thrilling music.
OTHER WORDS ARE   **exciting**   **rousing**   **stirring**

throw *verb*

She threw a stone and broke the glass.
OTHER VERBS YOU MIGHT USE ARE   **to bowl**   **to cast**   (*informal*) **to chuck**
to fling   **to hurl**   **to lob**   **to pitch**   **to sling**   **to toss**

tidy *adjective*

Mum asked Jo to make her room tidy.
OTHER WORDS YOU MIGHT USE ARE   **neat**   **orderly**   **smart**   **trim**

tie *verb*

1 Can you tie this string?
   ANOTHER VERB IS **to knot**
2 I tied a bandage round my leg.
   OTHER VERBS YOU MIGHT USE ARE   **to bind**   **to fasten**   **to fix**   **to wind**
3 They tied up the boat.
   OTHER VERBS ARE   **to anchor**   **to moor**
4 The farmer tied up the bull.
   ANOTHER VERB IS **to tether**

tight *adjective*

1 Make sure the lid is tight.
   OTHER WORDS YOU MIGHT USE ARE   **firm**   **fixed**   **secure**
2 These shoes are a bit tight.
   OTHER WORDS ARE   **close-fitting**   **small**
The opposite is loose

tilt *verb*

The boat tilted to one side.
   OTHER VERBS ARE   **to lean**   **to slant**   **to slope**   **to tip**

time *noun*, see next page

timid *adjective*

He was too timid to ask for more.
   OTHER WORDS ARE   **cowardly**   **fearful**   **nervous**   **shy**
The opposite is brave

tiny *adjective*

Some insects are tiny.
   OTHER WORDS ARE   **little**   **microscopic**   **minute**   **small**
The opposite is big

tip *noun*

1 the tip of a pencil.
   OTHER WORDS ARE   **end**   **point**
2 the tip of an iceberg.
   OTHER WORDS ARE   **head**   **top**

tip *verb*

A big wave tipped the boat over.
   OTHER VERBS YOU MIGHT USE ARE   **to capsize**   **to overturn**   **to turn over**
      to upset

time *noun*

1 Is this a good time to ring Granny?
OTHER WORDS YOU MIGHT USE ARE
moment   opportunity

2 Shakespeare lived in the time of Elizabeth I.
OTHER WORDS ARE
age   era   period

UNITS USED TO MEASURE TIME ARE
**centuries   days   fortnights   hours   minutes
months   seconds   weeks   years**

DIFFERENT TIMES OF THE DAY ARE
**afternoon   bedtime   dawn   dusk   evening
midday   midnight   morning   night   noon
sunrise   sunset   twilight**

THE SEASONS OF THE YEAR ARE
spring   summer   autumn   winter

SPECIAL TIMES OF THE YEAR ARE
**an anniversary   your birthday   Christmas   Diwali
Easter   Hallowe'en   Hogmanay   Midsummer
New Year   Passover   Ramadan   St Valentine's Day
Yom Kippur**

THINGS WE USE TO MEASURE TIME ARE
**calendar   clock   digital watch   hourglass   sundial
watch**

tired *adjective*

1 We were tired after our walk.
OTHER WORDS YOU MIGHT USE ARE   **exhausted   weary   worn out**

2 Go to bed: you look tired.
OTHER WORDS ARE   **drowsy   sleepy**

tiring *adjective*

tiring work.
OTHER WORDS YOU MIGHT USE ARE   **exhausting   hard**
The opposite is easy

toilet *noun*

OTHER WORDS YOU MIGHT USE ARE   **lavatory   (*informal*) loo   WC**

token *noun*
I've got a token for a free drink.
OTHER WORDS ARE **counter   coupon   voucher**

tomb *noun*
OTHER WORDS ARE **grave   gravestone   memorial   monument tombstone**

tone *noun*
Her voice had a gentle tone.
OTHER WORDS YOU MIGHT USE ARE **expression   note   sound**

tool *noun*
Dad has tools for every job.
OTHER WORDS YOU MIGHT USE ARE
device   gadget   implement   instrument

TOOLS USED FOR WOODWORK ARE
chisel   clamp   drill   hammer   pincers   plane saw   vice

TOOLS YOU MIGHT USE ON THE CAR ARE
jack   lever   oil can   pliers   screwdriver   spanner

TOOLS USED IN THE GARDEN ARE
broom   fork   hoe   lawn-mower   rake   shears spade   trowel   watering can

OTHER TOOLS PEOPLE USE ARE
axe   chopper   crowbar   file   ladder   pick   shovel sledgehammer   wrench

top *noun*
1 the top of a hill.
OTHER WORDS YOU MIGHT USE ARE **head   peak   summit   tip**
The opposite is bottom
2 the top of a jar.
OTHER WORDS ARE **cap   cover   lid**

topic *noun*
We all wrote about different topics.
OTHER WORDS YOU MIGHT USE ARE **subject   theme**

torment *verb*

1 I hate it when people torment animals.
OTHER VERBS YOU MIGHT USE ARE   **to annoy   to distress   to tease**
2 Sam saw a big boy tormenting some little ones.
OTHER VERBS ARE   **to bully   to victimize**

torture *verb*

It's horrible to think of people torturing each other.
OTHER VERBS ARE   **to be cruel to   to hurt**

total *adjective*

Because it rained, the picnic was a total disaster.
OTHER WORDS YOU MIGHT USE ARE   **absolute   complete**

total *noun*

Count the money and tell me the total.
OTHER WORDS ARE   **amount   answer   sum**

touch *verb*

OTHER VERBS YOU MIGHT USE ARE
to contact   to feel   to handle

DIFFERENT WAYS TO TOUCH PEOPLE OR ANIMALS ARE
**to caress   to cuddle   to embrace   to fondle   to kiss
to pat   to rub   to stroke   to tickle**

DIFFERENT WAYS TO TOUCH THINGS ARE
**to fiddle with   to fidget with   to finger   to handle
to hold**

tough *adjective*

You need tough shoes to walk in the hills.
OTHER WORDS YOU MIGHT USE ARE   **hard-wearing   stout   strong
sturdy**

tour *verb*

We toured the castle before we had our picnic.
OTHER VERBS ARE   **to go round   to visit**

tow *verb*

The car was towing a caravan.
OTHER VERBS YOU MIGHT USE ARE   **to haul   to pull**

town *noun*

A big town is a **city**.
A small town is a **village**.
The areas at the edge of a town are the **outskirts** or **suburbs**.

THINGS YOU OFTEN FIND IN A TOWN ARE

**bank   bus station   café   car park   church   cinema
college   factory   flats   hotel   leisure centre
library   museum   offices   park   police station
post office   railway station   school   shopping centre
supermarket   theatre   town hall**

For other words, see **shop**

IN THE OUTSKIRTS OF A TOWN YOU MIGHT FIND

housing estate   industrial estate   retail park

track *verb*

The hounds tracked the fox across the fields.

OTHER VERBS YOU MIGHT USE ARE   **to chase   to follow   to hunt
to pursue   to trail**

traffic *noun*

TRAFFIC YOU SEE ON THE ROADS INCLUDES

**bicycles   buses   cars   coaches   lorries
motorbikes** or **motorcycles   taxis   vans**

For other words, see **travel**

tragedy *noun*

The plane crash was a terrible tragedy.

OTHER WORDS YOU MIGHT USE ARE   **calamity   catastrophe   disaster
misfortune**

trail *noun*

For other words, see **path**

trail *verb*

1 The police trailed him for miles.
For other verbs, see **track**
2 Jo's scarf is so long that it trails in the mud.

ANOTHER VERB IS **to drag**

train *noun*

We went to London on the train.
For other words, see **railway**

train *verb*

1 Jo's Dad trains the school team.
OTHER VERBS YOU MIGHT USE ARE **to coach** **to instruct** **to teach**
2 The team trains every Thursday.
OTHER VERBS ARE **to exercise** **to practise**

trainer *noun*

1 Sam's feet are too big for his old trainers.
For other things you wear on your feet, see **shoe**
2 Our team has a new trainer.
ANOTHER WORD IS **coach**

transfer *verb*

1 A bus transferred us from the airport to the hotel.
OTHER VERBS YOU MIGHT USE ARE **to carry** **to take** **to transport**
2 The goalkeeper was transferred to another team.
OTHER VERBS ARE **to move** **to switch**

transform *verb*

The fairy transformed the pumpkin into a coach.
OTHER VERBS YOU MIGHT USE ARE **to change** **to turn**

transport *noun*

For different kinds of transport, see **travel**

trap *verb*

We trapped the mouse in a box.
OTHER VERBS YOU MIGHT USE ARE **to capture** **to catch** **to corner**

travel *verb*, see opposite page

treacherous *adjective*

Take care: that dog's treacherous.
OTHER WORDS YOU MIGHT USE ARE **dangerous** **untrustworthy**
The opposite is loyal

tread *verb*

Don't tread on the flowers.
· OTHER VERBS YOU MIGHT USE ARE **to step** **to trample** **to walk**

travel *verb*

DIFFERENT WAYS TO TRAVEL ARE

cruise   cycle   drive   fly   hitch-hike   ride   sail
walk

DIFFERENT KINDS OF JOURNEY ARE

cruise   drive   expedition   flight   hike   outing
pilgrimage   ramble   ride   safari   tour   trek   trip
voyage   walk

A person who travels is a **traveller.**

OTHER WORDS FOR PEOPLE WHO TRAVEL ARE

a person who drives a car: **motorist**
a person who travels while someone else drives: **passenger**
a person who goes on foot
    hiker   pedestrian   rambler   walker
a person who travels to work every day: **commuter**
a traveller to a holy place: **pilgrim**
a person who travels on holiday
    holidaymaker   tourist
a person who travels in a boat
    sailor   yachtsman   yachtswoman
a person who travels to find somewhere new: **explorer**
people who travel about because that's how they like to live
    gypsies   nomads   tramps   travellers

Something you travel in is a **vehicle.**

DIFFERENT VEHICLES THAT PEOPLE TRAVEL IN ON THE ROADS ARE

bus   car   coach   jeep   minibus
motorbike or motorcycle   taxi   tram

OTHER FORMS OF TRANSPORT FOR PASSENGERS ARE

aeroplane   bicycle   ferry   railway   underground

WAYS PEOPLE USED TO TRAVEL ARE

carriage   horse   stagecoach

VEHICLES THAT CARRY GOODS ARE

articulated lorry   cart   lorry   pick-up truck   truck
van   wagon

OTHER KINDS OF TRANSPORT FOR GOODS ARE

aircraft   goods train   ship

VEHICLES MADE TO DO SPECIAL JOBS ARE

ambulance   bulldozer   caravan   digger   dustcart
fire engine   horsebox   milk float   police car
steamroller   tanker   tractor

For other words, see **aircraft, boat, car, railway**

treat *verb*
1 Treat your pets well.
OTHER VERBS YOU MIGHT USE ARE   **to care for**   **to look after**
2 How shall we treat this problem?
OTHER VERBS ARE   **to attend to**   **to deal with**   **to tackle**

tree *noun*
DIFFERENT KINDS OF TREE ARE
**ash   beech   birch   cedar   chestnut   elm   fir
holly   larch   lime   maple   oak   palm tree   pine
plane   poplar   sycamore   willow   yew**

tremble *verb*
I trembled with fear.
OTHER VERBS YOU MIGHT USE ARE   **to quake**   **to quiver**   **to shake**
to shiver   **to shudder**

tremendous *adjective*
1 We heard a tremendous explosion.
OTHER WORDS ARE   **alarming   awful   fearful   frightful   terrible
terrific**
2 Granny gave us tremendous helpings of dinner.
OTHER WORDS ARE   **big   enormous   huge   large**

trick *noun*
1 That was a nasty trick!
OTHER WORDS YOU MIGHT USE ARE   **cheat   deception   fraud   hoax**
2 The dolphins did some amazing tricks.
ANOTHER WORD IS **stunt**

trick *verb*
He tricked us into buying rubbish.
OTHER VERBS YOU MIGHT USE ARE   **to cheat**   **to fool**   **to hoax**
to mislead   **to swindle**

trickle *verb*
Water trickled out of the crack.
OTHER VERBS YOU MIGHT USE ARE   **to dribble**   **to drip**   **to leak**
to ooze   **to run**   **to seep**

trip *noun*
a trip to the seaside.
> OTHER WORDS YOU MIGHT USE ARE   **excursion   expedition   outing   visit**
For other words, see **travel**

trouble *noun*
1   Mum had a lot of trouble lately.
> OTHER WORDS YOU MIGHT USE ARE **distress   grief   hardship   misery   misfortune   problems   sadness   worry**
2   There was some trouble in the playground at dinner time.
> OTHER WORDS ARE **bother   commotion   disorder   fighting   fuss   row**
3   Sam takes trouble with his work.
> OTHER WORDS ARE **care   effort**

trouble *verb*
Do wasps trouble you?
> OTHER VERBS YOU MIGHT USE ARE   **to annoy   to bother   to upset   to worry**

trousers *noun*
For other words, see **clothes**

true *adjective*
1   Is that story true?
> OTHER WORDS YOU MIGHT USE ARE   **correct   factual   genuine   real**
2   Jo is a true friend.
> OTHER WORDS ARE **faithful   loyal   reliable   trustworthy**

trust *verb*
You can trust Jo to do her best.
> PHRASES YOU MIGHT USE ARE   (*informal*) **to bank on   to be sure of   to count on   to depend on   to have faith in   to rely on**

try *verb*
1   Sam tried to swim ten lengths.
> OTHER VERBS ARE **to aim   to attempt   to endeavour   to exert yourself   to make an effort   to strive**
2   Can I try the cake?
> ANOTHER VERB IS **to sample**
3   Try the brakes before you ride your bike.
> OTHER VERBS ARE **to experiment with   to test**

tube *noun*

ANOTHER WORD IS **pipe**

A tube to take water from the tap to where you want it is a **hose**.

tune *noun*

Jo played a well-known tune.

ANOTHER WORD IS **melody**

tunnel *noun*

A tunnel that a rabbit makes is a **burrow**.

A tunnel under a road is a **subway** or **underpass**.

turn *noun*

It's your turn to play next.

OTHER WORDS ARE   **chance   go   opportunity**

turn *verb*

1 The wheel began to turn.

OTHER VERBS YOU MIGHT USE ARE   **to revolve   to rotate   to spin   to twirl   to whirl**

For other verbs, see **twist**

2 Tadpoles turn into frogs.

OTHER VERBS ARE   **to become   to change into**

3 We turned the attic into a playroom.

OTHER VERBS ARE   **to convert   to transform**

twinkle *verb*

The lights twinkled in the distance.

OTHER VERBS ARE   **to flicker   to shine   to sparkle**

For other verbs, see **light**

twist *verb*

1 The road twisted up the hill.

OTHER VERBS YOU MIGHT USE ARE   **to bend   to curve   to zig-zag**

2 I twisted the wires round each other.

OTHER VERBS ARE   **to coil   to curl   to loop   to turn   to wind**

type *noun*

1 What type of music do you like?

OTHER WORDS YOU MIGHT USE ARE   **kind   sort**

2 What type of dog is that?

OTHER WORDS ARE   **breed   species   variety**

typical *adjective*
In England, showers are typical April weather.
OTHER WORDS YOU MIGHT USE ARE   **common   normal   ordinary
usual**
The opposite is unusual

Uu

ugly *adjective*
We screamed when we saw the ugly monster.
OTHER WORDS YOU MIGHT USE ARE   **foul   frightful   hideous
monstrous   repulsive   unattractive**
The opposite is beautiful

uncommon *adjective*
Eagles are uncommon in this country.
OTHER WORDS YOU MIGHT USE ARE   **infrequent   rare
unusual**
The opposite is common

unconscious *adjective*
If you are unconscious, you may be **knocked out** or you may have
fainted.
The opposite is conscious

understand *verb*
Do you understand what I mean?
OTHER VERBS YOU MIGHT USE ARE   **to follow   to grasp   to know
to realize   to see**

undo *verb*
Jo undid the parcel.
OTHER VERBS YOU MIGHT USE ARE   **to unfasten   to untie**

unemployed *adjective*
PHRASES ARE   **on the dole   out of work**

uneven *adjective*
1 We jolted along the uneven road.
   OTHER WORDS YOU MIGHT USE ARE **bumpy** **rough**
The opposite is smooth
2 The music had an uneven beat.
   ANOTHER WORD IS **irregular**
The opposite is regular

unfair *adjective*
1 It's unfair if she gets more than me.
   OTHER WORDS YOU MIGHT USE ARE **unjust** **unreasonable** **wrong**
2 We complained that the referee was unfair.
   OTHER WORDS YOU MIGHT USE ARE **biased** **prejudiced**
The opposite is fair

unfriendly *adjective*
Mum was upset by our neighbour's unfriendly remarks.
   OTHER WORDS YOU MIGHT USE ARE **aggressive** **angry** **disagreeable** **hostile** **nasty** **offensive** **rude**
For other words, see **unkind**
The opposite is friendly

unhappy *adjective*
He was unhappy after his dog died.
   OTHER WORDS ARE **depressed** **gloomy** **glum** **heart-broken** **miserable** **sorrowful** **tearful** **troubled** **wretched**
The opposite is happy

unite *verb*
We united to sing the last song.
   OTHER VERBS YOU MIGHT USE ARE **to combine** **to join together**

unkind *noun*
Jo hates to see people being unkind to animals.
   OTHER WORDS ARE **cruel** **heartless** **spiteful** **thoughtless**
For other words, see **unfriendly**
The opposite is kind

unlikely *adjective*
I don't believe his unlikely story.
   OTHER WORDS YOU MIGHT USE ARE **far-fetched** **improbable** **incredible** **unconvincing**
The opposite is likely

unlucky *adjective*
We were unlucky to miss the bus.
> ANOTHER WORD IS **unfortunate**

The opposite is lucky

unpleasant *adjective*
1 The accident was an unpleasant experience.
> OTHER WORDS YOU MIGHT USE ARE   **awful   dreadful   frightening   painful   terrible   upsetting**

2 I hate touching unpleasant things.
> OTHER WORDS ARE   **disgusting   horrible   nasty   objectionable**

3 The noisy neighbours were very unpleasant.
> OTHER WORDS ARE   **rude   unfriendly**

The opposite is pleasant

untidy *adjective*
1 Our teacher hates untidy work.
> OTHER WORDS YOU MIGHT USE ARE   **careless   disorganized   scruffy**

2 Everything was in an untidy pile on the floor.
> OTHER WORDS ARE   **confused   disorderly   jumbled   muddled**

The opposite is tidy

unusual *adjective*
It's unusual to have snow in May.
> OTHER WORDS YOU MIGHT USE ARE   **extraordinary   odd   peculiar   strange   surprising   uncommon**

The opposite is common

upset *verb*
1 The thunder upset the dog.
> OTHER VERBS YOU MIGHT USE ARE   **to alarm   to bother   to distress   to frighten   to trouble   to worry**

2 Sam upset the milk.
> OTHER VERBS ARE   **to knock over   to overturn   to spill**

urge *noun*
I had an urge to giggle.
> OTHER WORDS ARE   **desire   wish**

urge *verb*
Mum urged us to be quick.
> OTHER VERBS YOU MIGHT USE ARE   **to appeal to   to beg   to encourage   to entreat   to plead with**

use *verb*
1 They used the most up-to-date machines to dig the tunnel.
   ANOTHER VERB IS **to employ**
2 Have we used all the milk?
   OTHER VERBS YOU MIGHT USE ARE   **to consume**   **to finish**

useful *adjective*
1 Dad's penknife is a useful tool.
   OTHER WORDS YOU MIGHT USE ARE   **convenient**   **handy**   **practical**
2 Sam is a useful member of the team.
   OTHER WORDS ARE   **helpful**   **valuable**
The opposite is useless

useless *adjective*
1 A car is useless without petrol.
   ANOTHER WORD IS **unusable**
2 He was a useless goalkeeper.
   OTHER WORDS ARE   **incompetent**   **worthless**
The opposite is useful

usual *adjective*
1 Ten o'clock is my usual bedtime.
   OTHER WORDS YOU MIGHT USE ARE   **normal**   **ordinary**   **regular**
2 It's usual to put milk in tea.
   OTHER WORDS ARE   **common**   **expected**   **typical**
The opposite is unusual

Vv

vague *adjective*
1 He made some vague comments, but nothing definite.
   OTHER WORDS YOU MIGHT USE ARE   **broad**   **general**
2 He was a vague sort of person.
   OTHER WORDS ARE   **absent-minded**   **forgetful**   **scatterbrained**
The opposite is definite

vain *adjective*
He's so vain that he's always looking in the mirror.
OTHER WORDS ARE **boastful   conceited   proud**
The opposite is modest

valuable *adjective*
1 valuable jewels.
OTHER WORDS YOU MIGHT USE ARE   **expensive   precious   priceless**
The opposite is worthless
2 He gave me some valuable advice.
OTHER WORDS ARE **helpful   useful   worthwhile**
The opposite is useless

vanish *verb*
The robber vanished into the crowd.
ANOTHER VERB IS **to disappear**

variety *noun*
1 There's a variety of things to eat.
OTHER WORDS YOU MIGHT USE ARE   **assortment   mixture**
2 Mum grows many varieties of flowers.
OTHER WORDS ARE **kind   sort   type**

various *adjective*
We made various sandwiches.
OTHER WORDS YOU MIGHT USE ARE   **assorted   different   mixed**

vary *verb*
The date of Easter varies each year.
OTHER VERBS YOU MIGHT USE ARE   **to alter   to change**

vegetable *noun*
VEGETABLES PEOPLE EAT INCLUDE
**asparagus   beans   Brussels sprouts   cabbage   carrot
cauliflower   greens   leek   marrow   nuts   onion
parsnip   pea   potato   pumpkin   spinach   swede
turnip**

vehicle *noun*
For other words, see **travel**

version *noun*

1 Jo's version of the accident is different from Sam's.
   OTHER WORDS YOU MIGHT USE ARE   **account   description   story**
2 Mum makes a vegetarian version of shepherd's pie.
   OTHER WORDS ARE   **kind   sort   type**

vertical *adjective*

The opposite is horizontal

vessel *noun*

For other words, see **boat**

vibrate *verb*

When the engine started we felt the boat vibrate.
   OTHER VERBS YOU MIGHT USE ARE   **to quiver   to shake   to shudder
   to throb**

victory *noun*

We celebrated our team's victory.
   OTHER WORDS YOU MIGHT USE ARE   **success   triumph   win**
The opposite is defeat

view *verb*

We viewed the the stars through a telescope.
   OTHER VERBS YOU MIGHT USE ARE   **to look at   to watch**

vigorous *adjective*

1 Jo took her dog out for some vigorous exercise.
   OTHER WORDS YOU MIGHT USE ARE   **active   energetic**
2 You need to use fertilizer if you want to grow vigorous plants.
   OTHER WORDS ARE   **healthy   strong**

villain *noun*

I guessed he was the villain at the very beginning of the film.
   OTHER WORDS ARE   *(informal)* **baddy   rascal   scoundrel**
The opposite is hero

violent *adjective*

1 a violent attack.
   OTHER WORDS ARE   **cruel   ferocious   fierce   savage**
2 a violent storm.
   OTHER WORDS ARE   **rough   severe   strong**
The opposite is gentle

visible *adjective*
Is the ink stain still visible?
OTHER WORDS ARE   **clear   noticeable   obvious   plain**
The opposite is invisible

visit *verb*
Granny visited us on Sunday.
OTHER VERBS YOU MIGHT USE ARE   **to call**   (*informal*) **to drop in**

visitor *noun*
Are you expecting a visitor?
OTHER WORDS ARE   **caller   guest**

vivid *adjective*
1 vivid colours.
OTHER WORDS YOU MIGHT USE ARE   **bright   brilliant   colourful**
2 a vivid imagination.
ANOTHER WORD IS **lively**
3 a vivid dream.
OTHER WORDS ARE   **clear   lifelike**
The opposite is dull

voice *noun*
For different ways you can use your voice, see **talk**

volume *noun*
1 The tank holds a large volume of oil.
OTHER WORDS ARE   **amount   mass   quantity**
2 How many volumes are there in the library?
ANOTHER WORD IS **book**

volunteer *verb*
Sam volunteered to wash up.
ANOTHER VERB IS **to offer**

vote *verb*
Who did you vote for?
OTHER VERBS YOU MIGHT USE ARE   **to choose   to pick   to select**

vow *verb*
He vowed never to do it again.
OTHER VERBS YOU MIGHT USE ARE   **to give your word   to guarantee   to promise   to swear**

voyage *noun*
For other words, see **travel**

vulgar *adjective*
We don't like vulgar language.
OTHER WORDS YOU MIGHT USE ARE **bad-mannered   coarse   impolite
improper   indecent   rude**
The opposite is polite

wait *verb*
1 Wait there!
OTHER VERBS YOU MIGHT USE ARE **to halt   to keep still   to remain
to rest   to stay   to stop**
2 Don't wait: get on with it!
OTHER VERBS ARE **to delay   to hesitate   to pause**

wake *verb*
I asked Mum to wake me early.
OTHER VERBS YOU MIGHT USE ARE **to call   to rouse**

walk *verb*
DIFFERENT WAYS TO WALK ARE

to creep	**to hobble**	**to limp**	**to march**
to plod	**to prowl**	**to shuffle**	**to stagger**
to stride	**to strut**	**to stumble**	**to totter**
to trot	**to trudge**		

to go for a gentle walk: **to stroll**
to go for a long country walk
   to hike   to ramble   to trek

When a baby tries to walk it **crawls**.

DIFFERENT WORDS FOR A WALKER ARE
a person who walks in the street: **pedestrian**
a person who goes for a walk in the country
   hiker   rambler

wander *verb*
The sheep wander about the hills.
OTHER VERBS YOU MIGHT USE ARE   **to ramble**   **to roam**   **to stray**

want *verb*
You can't always have what you want.
OTHER VERBS YOU MIGHT USE ARE   **to desire**   **to fancy**   **to long for**
to wish for   **to yearn for**

war *noun*
THINGS THAT HAPPEN IN WAR ARE:
**ambush   attack   battle   fighting   invasion
retreat   siege   surrender**

For other words, see **weapon**

warm *adjective*
If something is very warm it is **hot**.
If something is slightly warm it is **luke-warm** or **tepid**.
WORDS TO DESCRIBE WARM WEATHER ARE   **close   humid   sultry**

warn *verb*
The policeman warned him not to do it again.
ANOTHER VERB IS **to caution**

wash *verb*
DIFFERENT WAYS TO WASH THINGS ARE
**to bath   to mop   to rinse   to scrub   to shampoo
to sponge down   to swill   to wipe**

waste *noun*
Put the waste in the bin.
OTHER WORDS YOU MIGHT USE ARE   **junk   litter   refuse   rubbish**

watch *verb*
1 I watched the ducks on the lake.
OTHER VERBS ARE   **to gaze at   to look at   to observe   to stare at**
2 Will you watch my things while I go for a swim?
OTHER VERBS YOU MIGHT USE ARE   **to guard   to look after   to mind**

water *noun*

KINDS OF WATER YOU CAN DRINK ARE

mineral water   **spring water**   **tap water**

OTHER KINDS OF WATER ARE

big stretches of water
lake   **ocean**   **reservoir**   **sea**

small areas of water
pond   **puddle**

water that spreads over land that is usually dry
flood

water which goes along a channel
brook   **canal**   **ditch**   **river**   **stream**   **waterway**

water which rushes over rocks
cascade   **cataract**   **rapids**   **waterfall**

places where water comes out of the ground
spring   **well**

water which spurts out of a hole
fountain   **jet**   **spray**

A place where water seems to spin round and round is
a **whirlpool**.

wave *noun*

Big waves are **breakers** or **surf**.
Small waves are **ripples**.

wave *verb*

The flags waved in the breeze.

OTHER VERBS YOU MIGHT USE ARE   **to flap**   **to flutter**   **to shake**

way *noun*

1 Sam thinks his way of building a den is the best.

OTHER WORDS YOU MIGHT USE ARE   **method**   **technique**

2 She does her hair in a pretty way.

OTHER WORDS ARE   **fashion**   **manner**   **style**

3 What is the best way home?

ANOTHER WORD IS **route**

weak *adjective*

1 a weak person.

OTHER WORDS YOU MIGHT USE ARE **delicate   feeble   frail**

For other words, see **ill**

2 a weak branch.

OTHER WORDS YOU MIGHT USE ARE **brittle   flimsy   fragile   thin**

3 weak tea.

OTHER WORDS YOU MIGHT USE ARE **tasteless   watery**

The opposite is strong

wealthy *adjective*

a wealthy millionaire.

OTHER WORDS YOU MIGHT USE ARE **prosperous   rich   well-off**

The opposite is poor

weapon *noun*

WEAPONS WHICH FIRE THINGS ARE

**airgun   bow and arrow   cannon   catapult   crossbow
machinegun   musket   pistol   revolver   rifle
shotgun**

WEAPONS WHICH BLOW UP ARE

**bomb   grenade   mine   missile   nuclear weapons
time bomb   torpedo**

WEAPONS WHICH CUT WITH A SHARP EDGE ARE

cutlass   dagger   sabre   sword

WEAPONS WITH A SHARP POINT ARE

bayonet   harpoon   javelin   lance   spear

weary *adjective*

I was weary after the long walk.

OTHER WORDS YOU MIGHT USE ARE **exhausted   tired   worn out**

weather *noun*, see next page

weep *verb*

He wept when his dog died.

OTHER VERBS YOU MIGHT USE ARE **to cry   to shed tears   to sob**

weather *noun*

WORDS TO DO WITH DIFFERENT KINDS OF WEATHER ARE

cloud	drought	fog	frost	hail
heatwave	ice	lightning	mist	rain
rainbow	snow	storm	sunshine	thaw
thunder	wind			

WORDS FOR DIFFERENT KINDS OF RAIN

a short fall of rain
  shower
very heavy rain
  downpour
very fine light rain
  drizzle
mixed rain and snow
  sleet

DIFFERENT KINDS OF WIND

a very strong wind
  gale
a gentle wind
  breeze
a sudden puff of wind
  gust

DIFFERENT KINDS OF STORM

a violent storm
  tempest
a snow storm
  blizzard
a storm with a lot of wind
  gale   hurricane   tornado   whirlwind
a storm with a lot of rain
  deluge   rainstorm
a storm with thunder and lightning
  thunderstorm

WORDS YOU MIGHT USE TO DESCRIBE THE WEATHER ARE

blustery	bright	clear	cloudless	cloudy
cold	drizzly	dull	fair	fine
foggy	freezing	frosty	hazy	hot
icy	misty	rainy	showery	snowy
stormy	sultry	sunny	thundery	wet
windy	wintry			

weird *adjective*
1 What a weird thing to do!
   OTHER WORDS YOU MIGHT USE ARE   **curious   funny   odd   peculiar   queer   strange**
2 There was a weird atmosphere in the castle.
   OTHER WORDS ARE   (*informal*) **creepy   ghostly**   (*informal*) **scary**

welcome *verb*
We welcomed the guests at the door.
   OTHER VERBS YOU MIGHT USE ARE   **to greet   to receive**

well *adjective*
I hope you are well.
   OTHER WORDS ARE   **fit   healthy**
The opposite is **ill**

well-known *adjective*
a well-known pop star.
   OTHER WORDS YOU MIGHT USE ARE   **familiar   famous**

wet *adjective*
1 I got wet in the storm.
   OTHER WORDS YOU MIGHT USE ARE   **drenched   soaked**
2 The field is too wet to play on.
   OTHER WORDS ARE   **muddy   soggy   waterlogged**
3 It was a wet day.
   OTHER WORDS ARE   **drizzly   rainy   showery**
If something is slightly wet it is **damp** or **moist**.
The opposite is **dry**

whip *verb*
For other verbs, see **hit**

whirl *verb*
The wheel whirled round.
   OTHER VERBS YOU MIGHT USE ARE   **to revolve   to rotate   to spin   to turn   to twirl**

whiskers *noun*
   OTHER WORDS ARE   **hairs   bristles**

whisper *verb*
For other verbs, see **talk**

whole *adjective*
1 We ate the whole cake.
   OTHER WORDS YOU MIGHT USE ARE   **complete**   **entire**
2 Yasmin dropped the cake but it stayed whole.
   OTHER WORDS ARE   **intact**   **undamaged**

wicked *adjective*
It's wicked to take food from starving people.
   OTHER WORDS YOU MIGHT USE ARE   **bad**   **evil**   **immoral**   **sinful**
   wrong
The opposite is good

wide *adjective*
1 The stream was too wide to jump.
   ANOTHER WORD IS **broad**
2 There's a wide gap between the two scores.
   ANOTHER WORD IS **large**

wild *adjective*
1 wild animals.
   OTHER WORDS YOU MIGHT USE ARE   **free**   **natural**   **untamed**
The opposite is tame
2 wild weather.
   OTHER WORDS ARE   **rough**   **stormy**   **violent**   **windy**
The opposite is calm
3 wild behaviour.
   OTHER WORDS ARE   **boisterous**   **disorderly**   **excited**   **noisy**
   rowdy   **unruly**
The opposite is orderly

willing *adjective*
1 Sam is willing to help us.
   OTHER WORDS YOU MIGHT USE ARE   **happy**   **prepared**   **ready**
2 Jo is a willing worker, too.
   OTHER WORDS ARE   **cooperative**   **helpful**   **obliging**
The opposite is reluctant

win *verb*
1 Jo won first prize.
   OTHER VERBS YOU MIGHT USE ARE   **to earn**   **to gain**   **to receive**
2 The better team won.
   OTHER VERBS ARE   **to come first**   **to succeed**   **to triumph**
The opposite is lose

wind (rhymes with *tinned*) *noun*
  KINDS OF WIND ARE
a very strong wind
  gale
a gentle wind
  breeze
a sudden puff of wind
  gust

A **whirlwind** blows round and round and can do a lot of damage.

For other words, see **weather**
A kind of wind you feel if someone leaves a door open indoors is a **draught**.

wind (rhymes with *find*) *verb*
I wound the string into a ball.
  OTHER VERBS YOU MIGHT USE ARE   **to coil   to curl   to loop   to turn to twist**

windy wintry *adjectives*
For other words, see **weather**

wipe *verb*
  DIFFERENT WAYS TO WIPE THINGS ARE   **to dry   to dust   to mop to polish   to rub   to scour   to sponge   to wash**

wire *noun*
an electric wire.
  OTHER WORDS YOU MIGHT USE ARE   **cable   flex   lead**

wise *adjective*
If you're wise you won't go out in the rain.
  OTHER WORDS YOU MIGHT USE ARE   **intelligent   reasonable   sensible thoughtful**
The opposite is silly

wish *verb*
For other verbs, see **want**

wither *verb*
The plants withered in the dry weather.
OTHER VERBS YOU MIGHT USE ARE   **to dry up   to shrink
to shrivel   to wilt**

wobble *verb*
1 Jo wobbled a bit when she first rode a bike.
OTHER VERBS YOU MIGHT USE ARE   **to be unsteady   to sway
to waver**
2 The jelly wobbles when you move the plate.
OTHER VERBS ARE   **to shake   to tremble**

woman *noun*

OTHER WORDS YOU MIGHT USE ARE
a polite word
lady
a married woman
wife
a woman who is not married
spinster
a woman whose husband has died
widow
a woman who has children
mother
a young woman
girl

The man who plays a woman in a pantomime is the **dame**.

wonder *verb*
I wonder if it will be fine tomorrow.
ANOTHER VERB IS **to ask yourself**

wonderful *adjective*
We had a wonderful time.
OTHER WORDS YOU MIGHT USE ARE   **amazing   excellent**
(*informal*) **fabulous   marvellous   special**
The opposite is dreadful

wood *noun*

1 Dad bought some wood to make a table.
ANOTHER WORD IS **timber**
KINDS OF TIMBER ARE
   beams   boards   planks   posts
2 We went for a walk in the wood.
ANOTHER WORD IS **woodland**
A large wood is a **forest**.
A small wood is a **copse** or **grove** or **thicket**.
A place where fruit trees are growing is an **orchard**.

word *noun*, see next page

work *noun*

1 Keeping a garden tidy takes a lot of work.
   OTHER WORDS YOU MIGHT USE ARE   **effort   exertion   labour   toil**
2 What kind of work does Dad do?
   OTHER WORDS ARE   **job   occupation   profession   trade**
3 Our teacher set us work to do.
   OTHER WORDS ARE   **assignment   project   task**

work *verb*

1 We worked hard all morning.
   OTHER VERBS YOU MIGHT USE ARE   **to labour**   (*informal*) **to slave away
   to toil**
2 Does your watch work?
   ANOTHER VERB IS **to go**
3 Can you work this machine?
   ANOTHER VERB IS **to operate**

worry *verb*

1 Don't worry; everything will be all right.
   PHRASES YOU MIGHT USE ARE   **to be anxious   to be concerned
   to be troubled   to feel uneasy**
2 Don't worry the cat when she's sleeping.
   OTHER VERBS ARE   **to annoy   to bother   to disturb   to pester
   to trouble   to upset**

worship *verb*

Jo worships her Grandad.
   OTHER VERBS YOU MIGHT USE ARE   **to adore   to love**

word *noun*

Different words do different jobs and so they belong to different groups called parts of speech.

THE EIGHT PARTS OF SPEECH ARE
adjective   adverb   conjunction
interjection or **exclamation   noun   preposition**
pronoun   verb

Words which are the names of people, things, or ideas are nouns.
For example: *girl*, *animal*, and *happiness* are all nouns.

A word which you use instead of a noun is a pronoun.
For example: *I*, *you*, *she*, and *it* are pronouns.

A word which describes a noun is an adjective.
In the phrase '*an old green car*' *old* and *green* are adjectives.

A word which goes in front of a noun to make a phrase is a preposition.
In the phrases '*near my house*' and '*under the table*' *near* and *under* are prepositions.

Words which show what someone does or what happens are verbs.
In the sentences '*Jo ran home*' and '*The rain stopped*' *ran* and *stopped* are verbs.

A word which tells you how, when, or where something happens is an adverb.
For example: in the sentences '*Jo ran home quickly*' and '*Put it here*' *quickly* and *here* are adverbs.

Words like *and* or *but* which we use to join words or ideas are conjunctions.

A word like *Hello!* or *Well!* is an interjection or exclamation

worthless *adjective*
worthless rubbish.
ANOTHER WORD IS **useless**
The opposite is valuable

wound *verb*
Was anyone wounded in the accident?
OTHER VERBS YOU MIGHT USE ARE   **to harm   to hurt   to injure**
THERE ARE DIFFERENT WAYS YOU CAN BE WOUNDED
An animal can **bite** you.
A knock or fall can **bruise** you.
Something very hot **burns** you.
A knife will **cut** you.
You can **break** or **fracture** a bone.
You can **graze** your skin on something rough.
A gun can **shoot** you.
You can **sprain** a joint by twisting it.
A dagger can **stab** you.
Some insects can **sting** you.

wrap *verb*
I wrapped the parcel in paper.
OTHER VERBS YOU MIGHT USE ARE   **to cover   to enclose**

wreck *verb*
The accident wrecked the car.
OTHER VERBS YOU MIGHT USE ARE   **to break up   to destroy   to ruin
to shatter   to smash**

write *verb*, see next page

wrong *adjective*
1 I gave a wrong answer.
OTHER WORDS YOU MIGHT USE ARE   **false   inaccurate   incorrect
mistaken   untrue**
2 It is wrong to steal.
OTHER WORDS ARE   **dishonest   illegal   immoral**
3 Cruelty to animals is wrong.
OTHER WORDS ARE   **evil   wicked**
The opposite is right

write *verb*

THERE ARE DIFFERENT WAYS TO WRITE THINGS

Musicians **compose** music.
When you are bored, you **doodle**.
You **jot** down rough notes.
People **print** books and newspapers.
When you are in a hurry you **scrawl** or **scribble**.
You can **type** things or use a wordprocessor.

DIFFERENT KINDS OF WRITING

articles for a magazine or paper   **diary**   **essays**   **films**
letters   **novels**   **plays**   **poems**   **stories**
programmes for radio and TV

Another word for a writer is **author**.

DIFFERENT KINDS OF WRITER ARE

a writer of novels
 novelist
a writer for a newspaper
 journalist
a person who writes poetry
 poet
a person who writes for radio or TV
 scriptwriter
a person who writes plays
 dramatist or **playwright**

Someone who writes music is a **composer**.

Xx Yy

xylophone *noun*

For other musical instruments, see **instrument**

yell *verb*

He yelled angrily at me.

OTHER VERBS YOU MIGHT USE ARE   **to call**   **to shout**

young *adjective*

SOMETIMES THERE ARE SPECIAL WORDS FOR YOUNG THINGS

A young tree is a **sapling**.
A young plant is a **seedling**.

A young bird is a **fledgling** or **nestling**.
A young duck is a **duckling**.
A young goose is a **gosling**.
A young hen is a **chick** or **pullet**.
A young swan is a **cygnet**.

A young bear is a **cub**.
A young cat is a **kitten**.
A young cow or whale is a **calf**.
A young deer is a **fawn**.
A young dog is a **puppy**.
A young goat is a **kid**.
A young horse is a **foal**.
A young pig is a **piglet**.
A young sheep is a **lamb**.

A young person
baby   boy   child   girl   infant   toddler

A person who is not a child but is not yet grown up
adolescent   juvenile   teenager

Zz

zero

OTHER WORDS YOU MIGHT USE ARE   **nil   nothing   nought**

zigzag *noun*

a zigzag line.
OTHER WORDS YOU MIGHT USE ARE   **bendy   crooked**